ECUADOR: CONSTITUTIONS AND CAUDILLOS

ECUADOR: CONSTITUTIONS AND CAUDILLOS

BY
GEORGE I. BLANKSTEN

UNIVERSITY OF CALIFORNIA PRESS
BERKELEY AND LOS ANGELES
1951

UNIVERSITY OF CALIFORNIA PUBLICATIONS IN POLITICAL SCIENCE
EDITORS (LOS ANGELES): W. W. CROUCH, R. N. FITZGIBBON, R. G. NEUMANN

Volume 3, No. 1, pp. xiv + 1–196, 1 map

Submitted by editors December 7, 1949
Issued March 23, 1951
Price, cloth, $3.00; paper, $2.00

UNIVERSITY OF CALIFORNIA PRESS
BERKELEY AND LOS ANGELES
CALIFORNIA

◆

CAMBRIDGE UNIVERSITY PRESS
LONDON, ENGLAND

"Ecuador is a very difficult country to govern."
JOSÉ MARÍA VELASCO IBARRA

FOREWORD

IT IS CONTENDED, quite properly, that "comparative government" ought to *compare* features and problems of government. A necessary prerequisite, however, is possession of knowledge about individual governments and political systems so as to make comparisons meaningful. Even before the days of Bagehot and Bryce, of Lowell and Wilson, we had a sufficient fund of information about the governmental systems of Britain and the United States to make comparisons of those two major governments useful and popular. Gradually, some of the blind spots, especially those affecting the principal governments of continental Europe and, to a lesser extent, certain of the British dominions, began to be filled in. But, until recent decades, the politics and governments of the Far, Near, and Middle East and other large areas of the world remained, in essence, almost as much of a dark continent as the government of United States counties had earlier been said to be.

One of those lacunae was, by and large, Latin America. By the end of the first quarter of the present century, almost the only serious and substantial studies of individual Latin American governmental systems in print were the three volumes published by the Carnegie Institution of Washington, written by Messrs. Rowe, James, and Stuart, and dealing respectively with Argentina, Brazil, and Peru. These volumes were the first ones in a projected series, the plan for which was later abandoned; only one other volume in that series was published. During the second decade of the century the number of books published about Mexico was legion, but with a few notable exceptions they were journalists' accounts of the turbulent politics of that turbulent decade and were not objective studies of a political system as such. The articles that have been published in magazines and newspapers about politics elsewhere in Latin America have usually been about the more newsworthy—which sometimes has seemed synonymous with "sensational"—aspects of Latin American politics.

The Latin Americans themselves have been peculiarly slow to examine carefully the anatomy and physiology of their political systems. The reason may lie in considerable part in the fact that many Latin American intellectuals tend to approach the subjects of their attention with the view of an artist rather than that of a scientist. A particular government is of interest not so much because of the details of its inner structure and operation as because of the external and complete picture which it makes. In the organization of their university curricula, the Latin

Americans do not establish departments (or "faculties") of "political science" or "government." It is true that we encounter the terms *ciencias políticas* and *ciencias económicas* (though *ciencias sociales* is more common). But the use of the plural is significant: it betokens a concern with interrelationships which is rather strikingly in contrast with the increasing compartmentalization of studies in the United States.

Each of the approaches doubtless has its advantages. It remains generally true, however, that, at least for purposes of the study in this country of comparative government, we must know much more, very much more, about some of the blind spots. Professor Blanksten, in this study of Ecuador, admirably fills in these gaps with respect to the "Republic of the Equator."

It is gratifying that the author should have chosen as the subject of his analysis one of the less well-known states of Latin America. The smaller states or the more "backward" (that adjective is ungracious but sometimes not avoidable) have with one or two exceptions been little studied. But it is fully as important that we know why political Ecuador is as it is as that we have the same comprehension of Argentina or Brazil or Mexico. What is important is not the relative weight that the particular state carries internationally but rather the sort of contribution it can make to our knowledge and understanding of comparative government as a whole. Ecuador definitely makes a contribution of significance.

Professor Blanksten surveys the political scene in Ecuador penetratingly and sympathetically. He does not stop with merely a compendium of governmental and administrative data but inquires searchingly into the more obscure political forces and problems as well. His understanding of the country's political problems came not only from library study in the United States but also from extensive research in Ecuador. Nor was that research limited to Quito. It extended to other centers in the Sierra, to Guayaquil and other parts of the Coast, and even to the Oriente. The Galápagos (as the fourth more or less formal division of the country) can well be left to Dr. William Beebe and his confreres.

Easy generalization about Latin America is a sin any student of the area should avoid religiously. But to the slight extent that it would seem permissible, this study of Ecuador may be regarded as a case study of states similarly developed. First and most important, however, it gives us much the best study, of any length and in any language, of Ecuador's constitutional and political problems. For that we are in Professor Blanksten's debt.

RUSSELL H. FITZGIBBON

University of California, Los Angeles
March, 1950

PREFACE

"WHY DID YOU choose Ecuador?" The question invariably has been thrust at me by friends and associates throughout my work on this volume. It is my hope that the following pages will make a twofold contribution to our understanding of problems common to much of the Latin American area.

In the first place, this book offers an interpretation of political instability in an American republic with a large Indian population. The interpretation is addressed specifically to Ecuador, but I suspect that work on that country might be of some use in inquiring into similar problems in a number of other American nations. Ecuadorans say that theirs is the "classic" country in which to study Latin American revolutions. The chronic political problems of Ecuador—revolution, *caudillismo,* ineffective written constitutions—plague many another Hispano-American state. Moreover, political instability in these countries is little understood in the United States. I do not claim that the reader will find in this book the whole answer to this problem, either in Latin America as a whole or in Ecuador particularly; but I believe it is justified if it adds a measure of insight to our search for an appreciation of some of the difficulties of a number of the other American republics.

Second, the development of a Latin American literature in political science has long been hampered by the paucity of basic information on the individual countries. Research in each of these republics must precede the emergence of a solid general literature on the political problems of this area. I hope that this volume may add something to our knowledge of Ecuador and thereby serve as a step, however small, in the accumulation of basic data necessary to the evolution of a workable literature on the area as a whole.

My especial interest in Ecuador stems from a four-year sojourn in Washington, D.C., beginning in 1942, when I was associated with the Office of the Coördinator of Inter-American Affairs and later with the Department of State. However, no country—and certainly not Ecuador—can be studied adequately from afar, and in March, 1948, I journeyed to the tiny "Republic of the Equator." During my six-month stay in Ecuador, I visited all three continental regions of the country and lived with the people and their problems. Documentary materials are abundant in the republic, and I used them liberally; but this book is not pieced together from documents. I shared the life of the Sierra Indian in some of his villages; I attended sessions of congress and of a number of the courts; I lived in picturesque and formal Quito and in lazy, easygoing Guayaquil; and I bounced in a jeep through a part of the fabulous Oriente. I believe I know the Ecuadoran people, and I feel a warm friendship for them. I hope that this sentiment has not mitigated the objectivity—the "irrational passion for dispassionate rationality"—which I have endeavored to preserve in the following pages.

I was aided by a number of Ecuadorans while I was in their country, and it is difficult to single out a few of them for mention here. I am particularly grateful to Aníbal and Barbara Buitrón—she is a North American—for their warm hospitality and invaluable aid on Indian questions, and to Dr. Pío Jaramillo Alvarado, the venerable dean of Ecuador's students of Indian life, for his assistance in understanding a number of social problems. Dr. Homero Viteri Lafronte and his son, Jorge Viteri de la Huerta; former Presidents Carlos Alberto Arroyo del Río and Federico Páez; and Mayor Rafael Guerrero Valenzuela of Guayaquil gave unstintingly of their time in aiding with political data. Dr. José Vicente Trujillo and Fernando Barredo Hidalgo were exceedingly helpful in the development of information and viewpoints on the judicial function; and I profited greatly from Dr. Carlos A. Rolando's knowledge of the field of administrative history. To José Coronel Robles, my "man Friday" at Guayaquil, I am exceedingly thankful.

I owe a debt of gratitude to Dr. Russell H. Fitzgibbon of the University of California, Los Angeles, for innumerable forms of aid, not the least of which was a most helpful critical reading of the manuscript; and to Drs. Foster H. Sherwood and Robert G. Neumann, also of the University of California, Los Angeles, who likewise made valuable suggestions. Also, sections of the text were criticized by Drs. Charles S. Hyneman and Paul P. Van Riper, both of Northwestern University. I wish, further, to acknowledge the help of the Honorable John F. Simmons, the United States Ambassador at Quito, and the assistance of the Division of International Exchange of Persons, United States Department of State, which made possible my stay in Ecuador from March to September of 1948. None of these people, of course, is guilty of complicity in any errors of fact or judgment which may have crept into the book; the responsibility for them is my own.

G. I. B.

Evanston, Illinois
March, 1950

CONTENTS

CHAPTER	PAGE
I. Survey of the Republic of the Equator	1

Physical and Political Geography—Emergence of the Ecuadoran State—Development of the Republic—Era of General Flores, 1830–1845—Period, 1845–1859—Era of García Moreno, 1859–1875—Period, 1875–1895—Radical Liberal Era, 1895–1944—Period since 1944.

II. The Ecuadoran Pattern 14

The Sierra—The Coast—The Oriente—The Galápagos Islands—Regionalism in Ecuador.

III. Political Instability in Ecuador 32

In the Wake of Monarchy—The Caudillo—Constitutions and Revolutions—A Case Study in Caudillismo: José María Velasco Ibarra—The Constitutions of 1945 and 1946—The Month of Four Presidents.

IV. Parties and Elections 58

Ecuadoran Party Politics—Political Parties—The Conservative Party—The Radical Liberal Party—"Third" Parties—"Ad Hoc" Parties—Elections—The Election of 1948.

V. The National Administration 83

The Presidential System in Ecuador—The Council of State—The Presidency—The Vice-Presidency—Ministries and Cabinet.

VI. The National Legislature 100

The Legislative Function—The Senate—The Chamber of Deputies—Powers and Operation of Congress.

VII. The National Judiciary 120

Structure of the Judicial System—Supreme Court—Superior Courts—Provincial Courts—Cantonal Courts—Some Ecuadoran Judicial Practices—Case of Cardozo v. Suárez—Interpretation of the Laws.

VIII. Provincial and Local Government 141

Ecuador as a Unitary State—Provinces, Cantons, and Parishes—The Ecuadoran Municipality—Quito and Guayaquil.

IX. The Ecuadoran System: A Recapitulation 169

Monarchy in Republican Dress—Political Ills and Remedies.

Bibliography 179

Index 189

TABLES

	PAGE
1. Estimates of the Population of Ecuador, 1942–1947	3
2. Ecuadoran Chief Executives, 1830–1948	10
3. The Sierra Provinces: Selected Data for the Election of June 6, 1948	20
4. The Coastal Provinces: Selected Data for the Election of June 6, 1948	24
5. Official Results of the Election of June 6, 1948	81
6. Vice-Presidents of Ecuador, 1830–1948	93
7. Party Composition of Ecuadoran Congress on August 10, 1948	113
8. The Provinces of Ecuador: Selected Data	148
9. Official Results of the Guayaquil Municipal Election of November 2, 1947	167

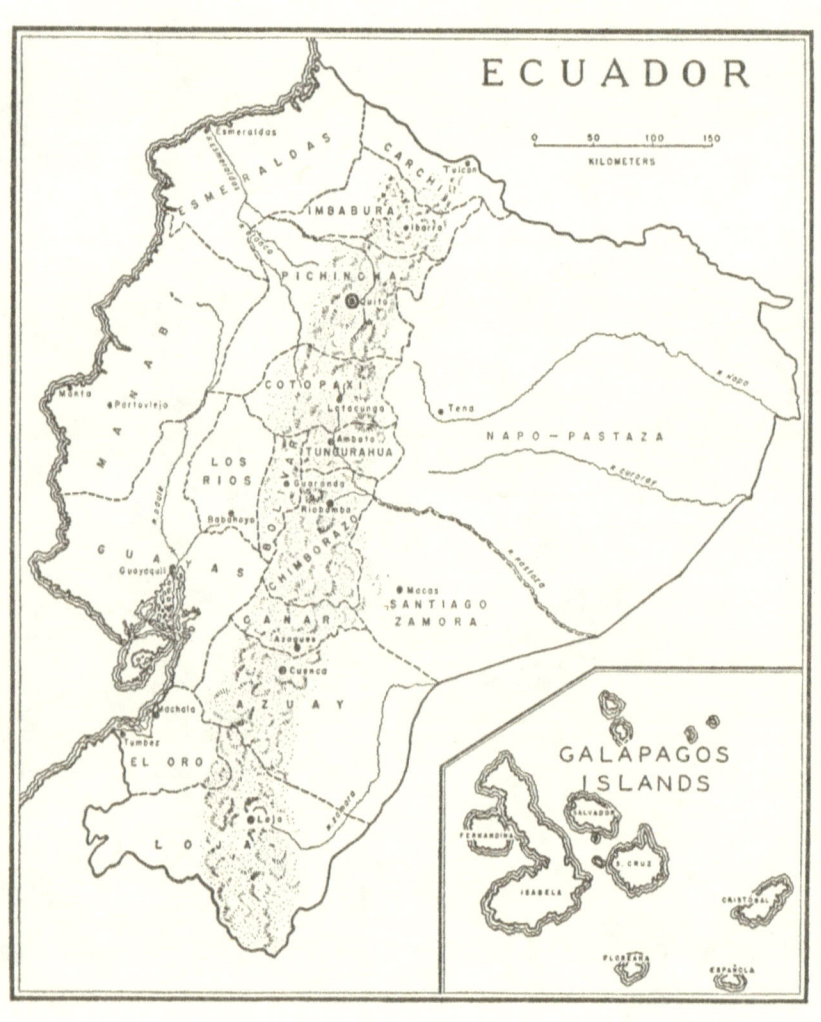

CHAPTER I
SURVEY OF THE REPUBLIC OF THE EQUATOR

A GLANCE at a political map of the west coast of South America might well convey the impression that the tiny republic of Ecuador had been wedged in between Colombia to the north and Peru to the south. North Americans have been accustomed to accepting the name "Ecuador," for after all, the state does lie athwart the equator; but a strong sector of Ecuadoran opinion holds that the naming of the country was unfortunate. It is argued that "Ecuador" spreads confusion abroad by contributing to tendencies in some quarters not only to associate unbearable equatorial heat with the republic (this association is especially false with respect to the Andean highlands), but even to confound the state with the equator.

Moreover, many of the more historically minded Ecuadorans point out that the choice of their republic's name was made in defiance of the usage of a thousand years. The area had been known for some ten centuries as Quito—the kingdom of Quito in pre-Hispanic times, and the Presidencia of Quito and the Audiencia of Quito during the Spanish colonial period. It has been suggested that this ancient designation, which now refers only to the country's capital city, be revived on a national scale; but this proposal sharply divides Ecuadorans along regional lines, being bitterly opposed in the coastal provinces.

PHYSICAL AND POLITICAL GEOGRAPHY

The Andes, towering at several points to a height of more than 15,000 feet above sea level,[1] divide the continental territory of the republic into three regions. In the inter-Andean highlands between the roughly parallel eastern and western cordilleras of the Andes, running from north to south through Ecuador, lies the lofty region known as the Sierra. The second region, the Coast, is west of the Sierra, being bounded on the north by Colombia, on the east by the western cordillera, on the south by Peru, and on the west by the Pacific Ocean. The third region, sparsely populated, lies in the Amazon jungle area east of the Andes, and is known as the Oriente. The rest of the nation's territory is a group

---
[1] Mount Chimborazo, "the King of the Ecuadoran Andes," reaches a height of 20,702 feet above sea level. Other notable peaks include Cotopaxi, 19,345 feet; Cayambe, 19,023 feet; Antisana, 18,490 feet; Altar, 17,725 feet; Sangay, 17,459 feet; Iliniza, 17,405 feet; Tungurahua, 16,684 feet; and Carahuairazo, 16,515 feet.

of some sixty Pacific islands, the Galápagos, which straddle the equator between five hundred and seven hundred miles off the Ecuadoran coast.

Compared with the other nine states of South America, Ecuador is economically underdeveloped and small in area and population. Only one of these other countries, Paraguay, normally has a smaller export trade than Ecuador; fewer motor vehicles are used only in Bolivia and Uruguay; and only Paraguay possesses a smaller total mileage of railroad tracks and highways in use. Ecuador's budget for 1949 came to only a little more than $23,000,000. United States investments are smaller in this republic than in any other South American state.

In Ecuador's history there have been repeated downward revisions of estimates of the country's area. It was thought at Quito during the latter days of the Spanish colonial period that the Audiencia of Quito contained an area of 394,398 square miles. When, some generations later, Ecuador established its independence as a national state, its government claimed that the newborn republic covered an area of 268,584 square miles. This figure, however, included areas which Brazil, Colombia, and Peru also claimed; and following a frontier treaty with Brazil in 1904, the Ecuadoran figure was reduced to 242,067 square miles. A boundary agreement entered into by Colombia and Ecuador in 1916 reduced the latter state's claim to an area of 179,588 square miles.

However, the Peruvians still regarded this claim as excessive, since it assumed Ecuadoran sovereignty over territory, largely in the jungle region east of the Andes, long in dispute between the two republics. Rival Peruvian and Ecuadoran claims at length culminated in mid-1941 in a tragic border war. A protocol signed by representatives of the two states at Rio de Janeiro in 1942 established the basis for a new frontier, the demarcation of which was uncompleted at the end of 1949. It seemed at that time not unreasonable to estimate that the new boundary would leave to Ecuador an area of approximately 100,600 square miles. This figure, if not seriously wide of the mark, would add to the dismay of those Ecuadorans who have protested that their country has almost disappeared from the map. It would mean that only 1.48 per cent of the area of South America lay within the boundaries of the Republic of Ecuador, and that only one state on the continent, Uruguay, possessed a smaller area.

No population census of Ecuador has ever been taken, although many have been ordered. In May, 1948, the Ecuadoran government tentatively approved projected expenditures for a national census to be taken in

TABLE 1
ESTIMATES OF THE POPULATION OF ECUADOR, 1942–1947

Regions and provinces	1942 estimate[a]		1946 estimate[b]		1947 estimate[c]	
	Population	Per cent of Ecuador	Population	Per cent of Ecuador	Population	Per cent of Ecuador
Totals	*3,089,078*	*100.00*	*3,241,328*	*100.00*	*3,383,655*	*100.00*
Sierra	*1,886,748*	*61.08*	*1,990,278*	*61.37*	*2,066,160*	*61.06*
Carchi	77,755	2.51	80,803	2.49	84,702	2.68
Imbabura	146,360	4.73	151,593	4.67	156,045	4.61
Pichincha	305,175	9.88	328,138	10.12	341,353	10.08
Cotopaxi	199,190	6.45	205,261	6.33	211,436	6.24
Tungurahua	207,138	6.70	213,363	6.58	219,299	6.48
Chimborazo	261,963	8.48	282,081	8.70	292,492	8.64
Bolívar	102,825	3.32	113,137	3.49	118,680	3.50
Cañar	122,809	3.98	127,379	3.92	131,524	3.88
Azuay	258,447	8.37	269,485	8.31	278,987	8.24
Loja	205,086	6.64	219,083	6.75	231,622	6.84
Coast	*1,007,018*	*32.60*	*1,070,758*	*33.03*	*1,136,533*	*33.58*
Esmeraldas	57,496	1.87	60,873	1.87	64,639	1.91
Manabí	321,041	10.40	342,931	10.58	367,263	10.85
Los Ríos	131,276	4.26	137,457	4.24	144,294	4.26
Guayas	415,734	13.47	443,372	13.67	469,315	13.87
El Oro	81,471	2.63	86,125	2.64	91,024	2.69
Oriente	*189,005*	*6.11*	*179,553*	*5.53*	*180,386*	*5.33*
Galápagos	*2,192*	*0.08*	*779*	*0.02*	*737*	*0.02*
Floating	4,115	0.13	[d]	[d]	653	0.01

[a] Based on official estimates published in Dirección Nacional de Estadística, *Ecuador en Cifras* (Quito, 1944), p. 56.
[b] From data appearing in Robert F. Cremieux, *Geografía Económica del Ecuador* (Guayaquil, 1946), Vol. I, 70–71.
[c] Based on figures published in *Registro Oficial*, No. 38, November 8, 1947 (Quito).
[d] The Cremieux estimates have made no allowance for floating population.

conjunction with the over-all Census of the Americas planned for 1950. This census, if successfully completed, would be the first to be taken in Ecuador. In the absence of definitive population figures, only guesses and estimates are available as guides to the probable number of Ecuador's inhabitants. It was officially estimated in 1942 that the country's population came to 3,089,078; an apparently reasonable estimate in 1946 placed the nation's population at 3,241,328; and the Ecuadoran government estimated in 1947 that 3,383,655 persons lived within the country's frontiers. Should Ecuador's first national population census demonstrate that these estimates were not major departures from the truth, it would appear that 3.68 per cent of the population of South America is Ecuadoran, and that only two countries on the continent (Uruguay and Paraguay) have populations smaller than Ecuador's.

EMERGENCE OF THE ECUADORAN STATE

Little is known of the origin of the Quitu Indians, apparently the first inhabitants of the area to which they gave their name. Their civilization, however, apparently reached its peak early in the tenth century and found its political expression in a group of about fifty loosely organized states among which no semblance of union appeared during the Quitu period. These states were small and weak, and were unable to organize effective resistance against invaders who arrived in the closing years of the tenth century.

These invaders were the Cara or Shyri Indians, who apparently came south from the Caribbean region and completed the reduction of Quito by about the year 980. The Caras have been regarded as "superior to the native tribes at the time of their advent, more advanced in the arts of government, war, and peace, and ... of an intelligent and even noble character."[2] Under the guidance of the Caras, the kingdom of Quito rose to a measure of splendor, covering by the mid-fifteenth century an area roughly equivalent to that of the later republic of Ecuador.

The most spectacular political development in pre-Hispanic South America was the rise of the phenomenal Inca Empire. The Incas settled at Cuzco, in what is now Peru, at some time between the eleventh and thirteenth centuries. At the height of its power the Inca Empire embraced large parts of what are now the republics of Peru, Bolivia, Chile, and Ecuador. It has been estimated that about 25,000,000 persons lived within the Inca Empire, which developed a highly centralized administrative system and an economic pattern in which private ownership of land was unknown. It should be noted, however, that the Incas' reduction of the kingdom of Quito occurred quite late in the history of the Inca Empire—1487 is usually given as the date of the conquest—and that the Caras were never fully subjugated by the Incas.

Moreover, the conquest of Quito did not long precede the decline and fall of the Inca Empire. The Emperor Huayna Capac, under whose leadership the Incas added Quito to their domains, was a man of many

---

[2] C. Reginald Enock, *Ecuador* (London, 1914), p. 34.

wives and many children. Four members of his sizable family who were to play major roles in the Inca debacle were Coya, Huascar, Pacha, and Atahualpa. Coya was the emperor's legitimate wife, as well as his sister. Her oldest son was Huascar, who became the legitimate heir to the Inca throne. His claim was not to be uncontested, however. For Huayna Capac, finding the proud Cara aristocracy difficult to dominate, spent more time at Quito than at his own capital of Cuzco; and in an attempt to appease the Caras, added to his harem the Quito princess Pacha, daughter of the last Cara king. The oldest son of Pacha and Huayna Capac was Atahualpa, half-brother to Huascar. Atahualpa became the symbol of Cara rebellion against the Inca conquerors, and today his name ranks high among Ecuadoran national heroes. He is sometimes referred to as the first Ecuadoran, the "father of Ecuadoran nationality." Under his symbolic leadership, the resistance of the northern provinces against their Inca conquerors stiffened, and the Inca Empire had already begun to disintegrate when Huayna Capac lay near death in 1525.

The dying emperor divided his kingdom between Huascar and Atahualpa, the former to rule the southern section with Cuzco as his capital, and the latter to rule in the north with the city of Quito as his capital. Some historians consider that this action resulted from the Incas' inability to pacify the Caras, Atahualpa's appointment representing a concession to a species of home rule. It may also have resulted from Huayna Capac's reputedly great love for Pacha and Atahualpa.

Huayna Capac died shortly before war broke out between the two sections of the empire. For seven years the contest was bitterly fought until at length Atahualpa and his Quito legions decisively defeated the forces of Huascar. Thus was Quito liberated from the Incas. Many have speculated on the possible fate of the area, with the Inca Empire destroyed and the kingdom of Quito reborn, if outside forces had not intervened. Such speculation, however, is fruitless. Spaniards with other plans had already arrived.

Francisco Pizarro and his associates had planned relatively carefully for the conquest of "Peru," then a general term referring vaguely to the Pacific coast lands lying south of Panama. Two exploratory expeditions had already been carried out in 1524 and 1526 before Pizarro journeyed to Madrid to contract for the enterprise with the Emperor Charles V. The major expedition of Pizarro was organized in 1530. Early in the following year, the Spaniards arrived at the island of Puná, near what is now Guayaquil, Ecuador. They pushed south and east until they established contact with Atahualpa, who became their prisoner. Pizarro and his lieutenants at first intended to free Atahualpa, a large amount of gold having been paid for his liberty; but they later concluded that for reasons of policy it was necessary to kill the Indian king. Accordingly, a trial which has not been noted for its justice was held, and Atahualpa was declared guilty of eight crimes and doomed to be burned at the stake. He had "told his wives and followers that if his body were not burned, he would return to them even though he might be killed, because the Sun his father would restore him to life," Pedro Pizarro recorded. "On the day of his execution he was taken to the plaza, Fray Vicente de Valverde... instructing him in the faith, and urging him to become a Christian. He inquired whether they would burn him if he became a Christian, and they told him they would not. Whereupon he said that since he should not be burned he would be baptized. Therefore Fray Vicente baptized him, after which he was strangled, and the following day he was buried in the church which the Spaniards had built at Caxamalca."[3]

Pizarro's major operations had thus far been conducted to the south of Quito. The first member of his party to venture north was Sebastián de Benalcázar (sometimes written "Belalcázar"), who did so in violation of his orders after receiving accounts of the riches of Quito. On the plains of Riobamba, Benalcázar and his followers encountered the Indian defenders of the northern stronghold. These troops were under the brilliant generalship of the remarkable Ruminahui, a military radical whose "scorched earth" tactics almost defeated the Spaniards. However, Ruminahui's defense eventually collapsed, and on August 15, 1534, the victorious Benalcázar entered the northern capital, which he named Santiago de Quito. Thirteen days later the name was changed to San Francisco de Quito, honoring Francisco Pizarro. Ecuador's leading historian, Federico González Suárez, has adjusted the event to the perspective of world history thus: "The founding of our city of Quito took place, then, forty-two years after the discovery of America, and one year after the death of Atahualpa; Charles V and his insane mother Doña Juana ruled Spain, Pope Clement VII governed the Church, and Henry VIII had begun in England his persecution of the Catholics."[4]

During its history, Ecuador's political orientation has swung back

---

[3] Quoted in William H. Prescott, *History of the Conquest of Peru* (New York, 1890), Vol. II, 306. The reader may also wish to consult Pedro Pizarro, *Relación del Descubrimiento y Conquista del Perú* (Lima, 1917), and Pedro Cieza de León, *Crónicas del Perú* (Madrid, 1932).

[4] Federico González Suárez, *Historia General de la República del Ecuador* (Quito, 1890), Vol. II, 224.

and forth between the north and the south like a pendulum. The Incas' conquest of the kingdom of Quito in 1487 had anchored the area's political leadership in the south; the division of the Inca Empire in 1525 and Atahualpa's victory over Huascar in 1532 had freed Quito from southern rule; and the Spaniards, based on the Inca ruins in what is now Peru, reëstablished Quito's southward orientation. This directional flow of power was formalized in 1543 with the creation of the Viceroyalty of New Castille, the viceregal capital being established at Lima. Quito was not again freed from the south until 1717.

A royal decree signed in 1564 created the Royal Audiencia of Quito, with an area larger than that now occupied by the Republic of Ecuador, within the Viceroyalty of New Castille. King Philip V, who ascended the Spanish throne early in the eighteenth century, embarked upon a program of administrative reform for the overseas colonies. During the course of this program he established in 1717 the Viceroyalty of New Granada carved out of the northern part of Peru, with the viceregal capital at Santa Fé de Bogotá. The Royal Audiencia of Quito was suppressed in the same year, its area again being cut loose from the south; and Quito was thus bound to the north for the ensuing century.

In one sense Philip V's reforms created more confusion than they dissipated. With the reconstitution of the Royal Audiencia of Quito in 1722, this time within the Viceroyalty of New Granada, uncertainty over the location of its southern boundary laid the foundation for more than two hundred years of frontier disputes. Spanish colonial leaders were aware of the difficulty at the time of the resurrection of the Royal Audiencia of Quito, but the problem deceptively appeared to lose its significance two years later when, in 1724, the Viceroyalty of New Castille was abolished. However, the latter entity reappeared fifteen years later with a new name (the Viceroyalty of Peru); and the boundary difficulty remains a vexatious issue in the lives of twentieth-century Ecuadorans and Peruvians.

With the coming of the Latin American struggle for independence in the early years of the nineteenth century, Quito's fate became linked with that of New Granada. What is now Ecuador was known as the Department of the South within Gran Colombia, which dated its independence from 1819. The power of the Spanish royalist forces in the area, however, was not broken until the decisive Battle of Pichincha in May of 1824. General Simón Bolívar's Gran Colombia lived a politically tortured existence, centers of disaffection and secessionism being especially strong at Caracas and Quito. In 1830, the year of Bolívar's death,

Gran Colombia came to an end when Generals José Antonio Páez and Juan José Flores, placing themselves at the heads of secessionist movements at Caracas and Quito, respectively, established the republics of Venezuela and Ecuador. Since May 13, 1830—called in an old Ecuadoran saying "the last day of despotism and the first day of the same thing"—Ecuador has been, nominally at least, a sovereign, independent republic.

DEVELOPMENT OF THE REPUBLIC

In the years since 1830, Ecuador has been governed under no fewer than fifteen written constitutions.[5] For purposes of review, the constitutional history of the republic since the achievement of national independence may be said to fall into six periods: (1) the era of General Flores, which was brought to a close in 1845; (2) a period of intense nationalism and sporadic attempts to combat militarism, from 1845 to 1859; (3) the celebrated García Moreno era, from 1859 to 1875; (4) an epoch of particularly marked political instability and continued domination of the scene by the Church, from 1875 to 1895; (5) the era of Radical Liberal rule, from 1895 to 1944; and (6) the post-Radical Liberal period, since 1944.

ERA OF GENERAL FLORES, 1830–1845

General Juan José Flores, born in 1800 at Puerto Cabello in what later became Venezuela, was named Bolívar's military representative in the Department of the South in 1824. Flores remained at Quito to preside over the secession from Gran Colombia and to dominate Ecuadoran national politics until his overthrow in 1845. He was thirty years of age and almost illiterate when he became Ecuador's first president, and, having a police concept of government, he ruled the country largely by violence. He controlled the election of the constituent assembly which produced the nation's first constitution in 1830.

This constitution, which dubbed the country "Ecuador," was unique in that it provided for a confederation of three departments, Quito, Guayaquil, and Cuenca. Ecuadorans have had no opportunity to observe this decentralized arrangement in actual operation, however, as President Flores' dictatorship was highly centralized despite the text of the

---

[5] The texts of the constitutions of 1830, 1835, 1843, 1845, 1851, 1852, 1861, 1869, 1878, 1883, 1897, 1906, and 1929 may be found in Rodrigo Jácome Moscoso, *Derecho Constitucional Ecuatoriano* (Quito, 1931), pp. 233–595; for the 1945 charter see *Constitución Política de la República del Ecuador* (Quito, 1945); and the Constitution of 1946 appears in the *Registro Oficial* (Quito), No. 773, December 31, 1946. For an English translation of the 1946 document see Russell H. Fitzgibbon *et al.* (ed.), *The Constitutions of the Americas* (Chicago, 1948), pp. 321–365.

constitution; and the republic's subsequent fourteen charters have provided for a centralized and unitary type of organization. Like most other Latin American constitutions of the period, the Ecuadoran Constitution of 1830 envisaged a presidential system patterned after that of the United States, with powers divided among the familiar three branches of government—the executive, the legislative, and the judicial. The Church enjoyed a privileged position protected by the document. "The religion of the state is Catholic, Apostolic, Roman," the constitution declared. "It is the duty of the government, in the exercise of the right of *patronato*,⁶ to protect this religion, excluding any other."⁷

Flores governed Ecuador with little reference to the Constitution of 1830 or to its immediate successor, adopted in 1835, which dropped the confederate arrangement. More to his liking was the 1843 constitution, subsequently known as the "Charter of Slavery." This instrument, adopted primarily to prolong Flores' stay in power, lengthened the presidential term from four to eight years and stipulated that the bicameral congress would meet only once every four years unless special sessions were called by the president. The major aim of the 1843 charter was not accomplished, however, as opposition to Flores' rule stiffened markedly during the latter years of his regime. The financial chaos which settled on the nation after 1840 contributed to widespread unrest. Moreover, both Flores and many of his major collaborators had been born outside of Ecuador, and the nascent Ecuadoran nationalism of the period rejected the government as being dominated by foreigners.

Opposition to President Flores had been organized as early as 1833 by a strongly nationalist group at Quito which published a periodical called *El Quiteño Libre*. This antiforeign and antimilitarist group included among its leaders Francisco Hall, himself a foreigner born in England; Vicente Rocafuerte, who through an agreement with Flores had served as president of the republic from 1834 to 1839; and a young student named Gabriel García Moreno, who was little known during the Flores period. The people of Ecuador, however, were to have ample opportunity to become acquainted with García Moreno and his works somewhat later. This group formed the nucleus of the revolution which on March 6, 1845, overthrew the government of General Juan José Flores and drove him into exile.

---
⁶ This right to appoint high Church officials was conceded by the Vatican to the government of Gran Colombia in 1824, but the Holy See did not formally grant similar authority to the government of Ecuador until 1838. Cf. Antonio Bermeo, "Relaciones de la Iglesia y el Estado Ecuatoriano," *Boletín del Centro de Investigaciones Históricas* (Guayaquil, 1947), Vol. VII, Nos. 12–17, pp. 305–307.
⁷ *Constitución Política de la República del Ecuador* (Quito, 1830), Art. 8.

TABLE 2
ECUADORAN CHIEF EXECUTIVES, 1830–1948*

Chief executive	From	To
General Juan José Flores	May 13, 1830	Nov. 28, 1830
General Simón Bolívar	Nov. 28, 1830	Dec. 7, 1830
General Juan José Flores	Dec. 7, 1830	June 12, 1834
Felix Valdivieso	June 12, 1834	Sept. 10, 1834
Vicente Rocafuerte	Sept. 10, 1834	Jan. 31, 1839
General Juan José Flores	Jan. 31, 1839	Jan. 22, 1843
Provisional Junta	Jan. 22, 1843	Apr. 1, 1843
General Juan José Flores	Apr. 1, 1843	Mar. 6, 1845
Provisional Junta	Mar. 6, 1845	Dec. 8, 1845
Vicente Ramón Roca	Dec. 8, 1845	Dec. 15, 1849
Provisional Junta	Dec. 15, 1849	Mar. 2, 1850
Diego Noboa	Mar. 2, 1850	June 15, 1850
General Antonio Elizalde	June 15, 1850	Feb. 26, 1851
Diego Noboa	Feb. 26, 1851	July 24, 1851
General José María Urvina	July 24, 1851	Dec. 15, 1856
General Francisco Robles	Dec. 16, 1856	May 1, 1859
Provisional Junta	May 1, 1859	Sept. 17, 1859
General Guillermo Franco	Sept. 17, 1859	Sept. 24, 1860
Provisional Junta	Sept. 24, 1860	Apr. 2, 1861
Gabriel García Moreno	Apr. 2, 1861	Sept. 7, 1865
Jerónimo Carrión	Sept. 7, 1865	Jan. 20, 1868
Javier Espinosa	Jan. 20, 1868	Jan. 17, 1869
Gabriel García Moreno	Jan. 17, 1869	Dec. 9, 1875
Antonio Borrero	Dec. 9, 1875	Sept. 8, 1876
General Ignacio de Veintimilla	Sept. 8, 1876	Jan. 14, 1883
Provisional Junta	Jan. 14, 1883	Feb. 10, 1884
José María Plácido Caamaño	Feb. 10, 1884	Aug. 17, 1888
Antonio Flores Jijón	Aug. 17, 1888	July 1, 1892
Luis Cordero	July 1, 1892	June 5, 1895
General Eloy Alfaro	June 5, 1895	Aug. 31, 1901
General Leónidas Plaza Gutiérrez	Sept. 1, 1901	Aug. 31, 1905
Lizardo García	Sept. 1, 1905	Jan. 15, 1906
General Eloy Alfaro	Jan. 16, 1906	Aug. 31, 1911
Emilio Estrada	Sept. 1, 1911	Dec. 24, 1911
General Flavio E. Alfaro	Dec. 25, 1911	Dec. 28, 1911
General Pedro J. Montero	Dec. 28, 1911	Sept. 1, 1912
General Leónidas Plaza Gutiérrez	Sept. 1, 1912	Aug. 31, 1916
Alfredo Baquerizo Moreno	Sept. 1, 1916	Aug. 31, 1920
José Luis Tamayo	Sept. 1, 1920	Aug. 31, 1924
Gonzalo S. Córdova	Sept. 1, 1924	July 10, 1925
Provisional Junta	July 10, 1925	Apr. 1, 1926
Isidro Ayora	Apr. 1, 1926	Aug. 24, 1931

TABLE 2—Continued

Chief executive	From	To
Colonel Luis Larrea Alba	Aug. 24, 1931	Oct. 15, 1931
Alfredo Baquerizo Moreno	Oct. 15, 1931	Sept. 2, 1932
Alberto Guerrero Martínez	Sept. 2, 1932	Dec. 5, 1932
Juan de Díos Martínez Mera	Dec. 5, 1932	Oct. 20, 1933
Abelardo Montalvo	Oct. 20, 1933	Sept. 1, 1934
José María Velasco Ibarra	Sept. 1, 1934	Aug. 21, 1935
Antonio Pons	Aug. 21, 1935	Sept. 26, 1935
Federico Páez	Sept. 26, 1935	Oct. 23, 1937
General Alberto Enríquez Gallo	Oct. 23, 1937	Aug. 10, 1938
Manuel María Borrero	Aug. 10, 1938	Dec. 2, 1938
Aurelio Mosquera Narváez	Dec. 2, 1938	Nov. 16, 1939
Carlos Alberto Arroyo del Río	Nov. 16, 1939	Dec. 11, 1939
Andrés F. Córdova	Dec. 11, 1939	Sept. 1, 1940
Carlos Alberto Arroyo del Río	Sept. 1, 1940	May 28, 1944
Provisional Junta	May 28, 1944	May 31, 1944
José María Velasco Ibarra	June 1, 1944	Aug. 23, 1947
Colonel Carlos Mancheno	Aug. 23, 1947	Sept. 2, 1947
Mariano Suárez Veintimilla	Sept. 2, 1947	Sept. 17, 1947
Carlos Julio Arosemena	Sept. 17, 1947	Aug. 31, 1948
Galo Plaza Lasso	Sept. 1, 1948	

* This table is based largely on documentary materials made available by the Archivo y Biblioteca del Poder Legislativo at Quito during April of 1948. Cf. Carlos A. Rolando, "Los Presidentes del Ecuador," *Boletín del Centro de Investigaciones Históricas* (Guayaquil), Vol. IV, Nos. 4–6 (1946), pp. 234–246.

PERIOD 1845–1859

The revolutionists of 1845 endeavored to vindicate the twin principles of nationalism and antimilitarism. "In Ecuador there are three commanding generals," a revolutionary manifesto had declared in 1844. "The commander at Cuenca is a Venezuelan general, at Guayas an Irish general, and at Pichincha an English general. The Inspector General of the Army is a Frenchman. ... All of the principal officers are foreigners."[8] It was of major significance that Colombians and Venezuelans were for the first time spoken of as foreigners. Ecuadoran nationalism was beginning to be a reality, and an interest was awakening among the literate in the life and deeds of Atahualpa, the "father of Ecuadoran nationality."

In its opposition to militarism the revolution was less successful. Of Ecuador's six presidents during the period 1845–1859, four were army officers active in their military careers at the time they came to the presi-

[8] *Manifiesto No. 6* (Lima, 1844).

dency. The two civilian presidents of the period were unable to alter appreciably the pattern of military domination of the government; and the three written constitutions of this era immediately after Flores were largely patterned after the 1835 document.

ERA OF GARCÍA MORENO, 1859–1875

The overthrow of President Francisco Robles on May 1, 1859, ushered in the most bizarre epoch in Ecuadoran national history. The country was dominated during the ensuing sixteen years by the fabulous Gabriel García Moreno, who remains the most controversial figure in Ecuadoran national life. He is generally regarded as one of the two greatest presidents in the history of the republic. As Albert B. Franklin has noted, "every Conservative will tell you that García Moreno was the greatest President and grudgingly admit that Eloy Alfaro was the next greatest. Most [Radical] Liberals will say that Eloy Alfaro was the greatest President of Ecuador, but, if they do, will unfailingly admit that García Moreno was second only to him."[9]

García Moreno, born at Guayaquil on December 24, 1821, had been active in the revolutionary movement which overthrew President Flores in 1845. Fourteen years later he headed the provisional junta which governed the country after President Francisco Robles was deposed; and until 1875 Ecuadoran politics had meaning only as it related to García Moreno. Early in the 1860's he undertook the reformation of the Church in Ecuador. His intense Catholicism led him to seek an extension of rigid hierarchy to the social order, and his concept of the state was essentially authoritarian. For him such concepts as liberty and equality were synonyms for anarchy, and were evils to be eschewed at virtually any cost.

Two written constitutions were promulgated in Ecuador during the García Moreno period. The first of these, adopted in 1861, provided for a strong executive and for a weak congress, which was to meet regularly only once every two years. Roman Catholicism, the official religion of the state, was to be defended by the government, which was required to prohibit the exercise of any other faith in the country. García Moreno's second constitution, proclaimed in 1869, was subsequently known to his enemies as the "Black Charter" and the "Charter of Slavery to the Vatican." This extraordinary instrument allowed only practicing Roman Catholics to be Ecuadoran citizens, intensified the union of Church and State, and extended the presidential term from four to six years, the incumbent being indefinitely eligible for reëlection. García Moreno's

---

[9] Albert B. Franklin, *Ecuador: Portrait of a People* (New York, 1944), pp. 272–273.

critics have not been slow in citing his assaults against individual liberty; on balance, he may be regarded as a *caudillo* who employed the Church rather than the army as his primary instrument of power.

PERIOD 1875–1895

In 1875 Gabriel García Moreno was struck down by the assassin Faustino Lemos Rayo. The ensuing twenty years were marked by excessive political instability and frequent dictatorship. During this period Ecuador had two constitutions, one written in 1878, the other in 1883. These relaxed the theocratic authoritarianism of the preceding era, although the Church remained the dominant political force in national life.

RADICAL LIBERAL ERA, 1895–1944

A new epoch in the constitutional development of the republic came into being with the significant Radical Liberal revolution of 1895, led by the remarkable General Eloy Alfaro. During the Radical Liberal period, steps were taken to reduce the power of the Church and are evident in the texts of the constitutions of 1897, 1906, and 1929. The first of these documents banned religious orders in the country; and religious qualifications for the exercise of political and civil rights were terminated. Although Roman Catholicism remained the sole permitted religion, only native-born clergy were allowed to operate in the republic. The 1906 charter, suppressed in 1929 and reinstated in 1935, has been regarded as one of the most democratic constitutions of the Americas. Under its terms, freedom of worship was at last established. The Constitution of 1929 is notable primarily as Ecuador's first experiment with a semi-parliamentary type of government. During the Radical Liberal era, administrations were violently overthrown with decreasing frequency and the closing years of the period were marked by a sharp deterioration in the integrity of the electoral process.

PERIOD SINCE 1944

The remainder of this book deals primarily with conditions in Ecuador since the overthrow on May 28, 1944, of the government of Dr. Carlos Alberto Arroyo del Río, the most recent of the Radical Liberal presidents. It may be noted at this point, however, that the influence of political parties as such has declined since 1944, and that the Church has regained a portion of its former power. The Constitution of 1945 placed extreme checks on the authority of the president, but these were largely removed by the 1946 document. Both constitutions have introduced a radical alteration in the theoretical basis of the separation of powers, upon which the presidential system in Ecuador has traditionally rested.

CHAPTER II

THE ECUADORAN PATTERN

THE DIVISION of continental Ecuador into the three regions of the Sierra, the Coast, and the Oriente is far from being merely a physical one. On the contrary, this division is basic in the social, political, economic, and legal orientations of the country. Ecuadorans have long pointed out that the diversity of the regions has operated as a formidable obstacle to the development of a genuine national community of interests. The politics of the country normally reflects a struggle for power, occasionally quite acrimonious, between the Sierra and the Coast. The Oriente and the Galápagos Islands—a dependent Pacific archipelago—are largely undeveloped; and the people of these areas play an exceedingly minor role in Ecuadoran government and politics.

THE SIERRA

The Sierra may be regarded, from several points of view, as the most important region of Ecuador. An estimated 61 per cent of the nation's population resides in this region, which contains ten of the seventeen provinces of the republic and nine of its fifteen largest cities, including Quito, the national capital. Of the members of congress 59 per cent (twenty-four of the forty-five senators and forty of the sixty-four deputies) represent the Sierra, which cast more than 66 per cent of all valid ballots for president in the national election of June 6, 1948.

Geographically considered, the Sierra is a great valley of high elevation, hemmed in on the east and the west by the Andes, and extending from the Colombian to the Peruvian frontiers. The topography of the region almost defies description. Enormous mountains alternate with snow-clad volcanoes, some of which are active; ranges cut by impressive gorges follow huge stretches of paramo; and sunken tracts succeed verdant patches of vegetation, combining within a relatively small area to form incredible landscapes. A variety of climates and vegetation corresponds to the various gradations of altitude. The region knows two seasons a year: the rainy (called "winter") from December to May; and the dry (called "summer") from June to November.

The social and political organization of the Sierra rests upon a rigid class system. The three groups which this system includes are the so-called "whites"; the *cholos* or *mestizos,* the former term having greater currency in Ecuador; and the Indians. For the popular mind in Ecuador, these designations bear a racial connotation, but it is significant that the bases of differentiation among the groups are social rather than biological, that an individual's way of life rather than the physical characteristics of his body determines the group with which he is identified.

Dr. Alberto Arca Parró, director of the government statistical bureau at Lima, in discussing the Peruvian social classes has made the following statement, which is equally applicable to the Ecuadoran Sierra: "The way they live determines whether a family is Indian. There is a family of German descent near my home who live as 100 per cent Indians in a hut on a small *finca*. They speak only Quechua[1] and think only Quechua. Thus a language is another criterion of race. Speech determines culture. A Peruvian who knows no Spanish may be called an Indian."[2] Similarly, an Ecuadoran who knows no Spanish may be called an Indian. Some Ecuadoran anthropologists hold that an individual's style of dress is the sole determinant of whether he is a "white," a cholo, or an Indian. Persons may and frequently do move from one classification to another. When intermarriage occurs, for example, both parties to the marital contract generally become members of the same group, the determination depending on which partner's way of life becomes that of the household. In the small Sierra village of Nayón, to cite another instance, the writer met a schoolteacher, a former Indian, who said he became a "white" because he felt that the prestige of his new status was indispensable to the school's successful operation. In Indo-American countries such as Ecuador the matter of "race" is not a problem in the European sense of the word.

The so-called whites, who dress much like business and professional people in the United States, account for an estimated 28 per cent of the population of the Sierra. This Spanish-speaking group provides the region's large individual landholders, its political leaders and government officials, and the bulk of its voters. Considerable prestige attaches to the "white," who is, to his face, at least, treated with great respect and deference by the cholos and more especially by the Indians. The greater part of the formally educated people of the Sierra belongs to the "white" group, which enjoys a virtual monopoly on the liberal professions and the higher ranks in the army.

Despite the pride of a number of families, it is impossible for the bulk of the Sierra "whites" to demonstrate their unmixed Spanish descent. The group has sprung from "the most varied elements: the Span-

---

[1] Quechua is the language of the bulk of the Indians of the northern Andes.
[2] Quoted in W. Stanley Rycroft (ed.), *Indians of the High Andes* (New York, 1946), p. 33.

iards who, with or without titles and prerogatives, arrived in these lands during the conquest and during the colony; the leaders of our independence—generals descended from Spaniards and mulattoes and cholos; a small proportion of foreigners, largely British and Irish; a number of landholders and traders ... and finally, a portion of the Indians who had freed themselves from their sandals and ponchos."[3] Thus, the "white" class has not remained as biologically pure as some of its number might wish; but within the rigid class structure of the Sierra, the group is socially isolated from the cholos and the Indians.

The cholo or mestizo group represents an estimated 40 per cent of the population of the Sierra. As a cultural type, the cholo is a fusion, a species in the process of formation. He is an economic, cultural, and political entity, and his personality is rapidly acquiring characteristics of its own. He represents essentially a fusion of the cultures of the "whites" and the Indians.

Two aspects of the role of the cholo in the life of the Ecuadoran Sierra are of long-range significance. In the first place, the cholo group, as the vehicle of increasing union of "white" and Indian cultures, may well serve as a democratizing influence. The cholo's part in bringing all social levels closer together has become greater in recent years. Through him may come the eventual eradication of the artificial class barriers separating the groups of the Sierra from one another. Second, the cholo group may be expected to become proportionately larger in the population of the region. European immigration to Ecuador, since the achievement of the country's national independence, has been reduced to an insignificant population factor.[4] In view of this fact, the only logical direction of change in the republic's population structure is the continuing fusion of the groups now in the country. As an expanding force, the cholo may well preside over an eventual synthesizing of the cultural elements now divided in the Sierra.

At the bottom of the social scale of the Sierra are the Indians, who form an estimated 30 per cent of the region's population. The "whites" regard the Indians as a subject and abject race; and it is in the separation of the Indian from what in Ecuador is called the "national life" that the rigidity of the Sierra's class system finds its sharpest expression. A complete social separation between the Indian and the "white" is one

[3] Luis Monsalve Pozo, *El Indio* (Cuenca, 1943), p. 471. Cf. also Angel Modesto Paredes, *Problemas Etnológicos Indoamericanos* (Quito, 1947).

[4] About one thousand European refugees established their homes in Ecuador during the course of the Hitler period, a development which may be expected to retard somewhat but not radically alter the population dynamics of the country.

of the most marked cultural characteristics of the region. Different customs, dress, and values all tend to isolate them from each other unless brought together for the transaction of some business in which one finds the other indispensable. Friendless and hopeless in a basically hostile social environment, the Sierra Indian reminds the foreign visitor of nothing so much as a maladjusted and suppressed person.

Characteristic of the Indian's way of life are an intense love of the soil, a sentiment of fatalism and submission, a vigorous love for his intimates, a strong clannishness or group feeling, and a deep, abiding loyalty to the Roman Catholic Church. The Indian is predominantly an agricultural worker. Either he lives on a large landed estate, a hacienda owned by a "white"; owns his own small parcel of land; or is a member of a community which collectively owns and farms its land. The soil is the foundation of the Indian economy: an Indian separated from the land is like a disembodied spirit. His sentimental and mystic agrarianism knows little of the legal concept of landownership which the European culture has brought to his world. Though the earth is the center of his universe, the Indian has little interest in such things as "having title" to the land. The structure of landownership in the Sierra—vast haciendas owned by a relatively few "whites"—underlies the essentially feudal nature of the region's economy, in which the Indian frequently occupies a position strongly reminiscent of the serf of medieval Europe. "The servitude which the landowner has established is horrible," Moisés Sáenz declared in his significant study of the Ecuadoran Indian. "All the literature concerned with the social problems of Ecuador and the reform of prevailing conditions is a story of the hardships suffered by the agricultural worker at the hands of the *patrón* and a protest. . . . The hacienda has established a true slavery."[5] The Indian who is freed from this economy and journeys to an urban community to become a shoemaker, carpenter, mason, or mechanic is generally accepted as a cholo.

The fatalism and submissiveness of the Sierra Indians have deep ramifications affecting the Ecuadoran political pattern and go far toward establishing the orientation of most problems of government arising in the republic. The Indians have for centuries lived a life of civil obedience. With brief exceptions—as, for example, the Cara restiveness after the Inca conquest, a species of rebellion involving the ruling clique rather than the mass of the population of the old kingdom of Quito—the Indian has been submissive and obedient for centuries. In the pre-

---

[5] Moisés Sáenz, *Sobre el Indio Ecuatoriano* (Mexico, 1933), p. 103.

Hispanic period, life was controlled by indisputable law, and, essentially, the Spaniards did little more than continue this nondemocratic pattern. Nothing of self-government has existed in the history of the Sierra Indians: a kind of divine-right monarchy ruled the kingdom as well as the Audiencia of Quito, and it is to be noted that in a very real sense monarchy sleeps beneath the present-day republic. Visitors to the Sierra are repeatedly told that the Indians are "good people," by which it is meant that they are docile, submissive, and retiring. Yet the quality which renders them "good people" separates them in large part from active participation in the politics and government of their country.

The Sierra Indian is typically loyal to the Roman Catholic Church, and in his own way deeply religious. "The Indian would rather lose his material possessions than his essential characteristics," Sáenz has said. "His emotion and his sensibility persist; his fundamental attitudes about life and the universe are eternal. The Indian soul is immortal in a sense no doubt different from the theological but perhaps more real. Despite all the vicissitudes of history, despite exploitations, repression, and failure, the Indian soul—emotion, sensibility, attitude—continues alive."[6] It is to be noted, in comparing the Sierra Indians with the indigenous peoples of Guatemala and Mexico, that the survival of pre-Hispanic usages and rites is weaker in Ecuador than in either of the two middle American states, and that Catholic rituals and concepts are therefore stronger among the Ecuadoran Indians.

Moreover, the influence of the Church in the Ecuadoran Sierra is more coherent and systematic than in somewhat analogous situations in other Latin American countries with large indigenous populations. The Ecuadoran clergy is closer to the Indian. In the typical Sierra village the churchman participates fully in the life of the community. It is not uncommon to see the local clergymen joining their people in fiestas, taking part in the dances and in the drinking of *chicha*, a kind of corn beer widely consumed by the Sierra Indians. The Ecuadoran rural clergy is not an absentee class, as in Guatemala and Mexico; it is, on the contrary, very close to most phases of the Indian's life.

Ecuador's Constitution of 1946, like most of its predecessors, recognizes the equality of all Ecuadorans, including Indians, before the law. Though written into legal texts, this equality is not implemented in actual practice. The interests of the "white" generally triumph against those of the Indian, who lives as an inferior and undervalued being.

---

[6] Sáenz, *The Indian, Citizen of America* (Washington, 1946), p. 4.

Under Spain's Laws of the Indies, the Indian was in a legally inferior but protected position; he lost his *legal* inferiority—and protection—with the coming of Ecuadoran independence early in the nineteenth century, when he was declared to be free and equal with his fellow Ecuadorans. But unimplemented legal pronouncements have not been sufficient to change the condition and status of the Indian.

His relationship to the state leaves much to be desired. Typically, the Indian comes into contact with the government of Ecuador almost exclusively through its tax collectors and policing officials. Generally, the Indian hears about the state only in connection with his being punished for some delinquency or other. The Sierra Indian normally dislikes intensely the national and provincial governments and their representatives, and takes no active interest in politics.

The Constitution of 1946 has established a literacy qualification for voting. It has been estimated that 95 per cent of Ecuador's Indians are illiterate; accordingly, illiteracy legally bars the Indian from any major participation in political life. In the opinion of Senator Pío Jaramillo Alvarado, dean of Ecuador's *indigenistas*,[7] the Indian's position in the rigid Sierra class system "has produced the failure of all democratic reforms which have affected only the political, economic, and social periphery, establishing in fact an antagonism of classes. A nucleus, a minority ... continues to dominate the Indo-American situation."[8] The exclusion of the Indian from participation in national political life provides a significant background against which political instability has developed in Ecuador.

It has long been recognized in the republic that the Indian is one of the few true resources upon which the Ecuadoran nation can rely, but it is only recently that the country's chief executives have begun to take a serious and active interest in the problem. Galo Plaza Lasso, who became president of Ecuador on September 1, 1948, told the writer: "The Indian is indeed a problem, and no government can solve it in the space of four years. I do not believe that much can be done with the present Indian generation. But with an educational program including instruction in agriculture and domestic industry and the inculcation in the Indian child of habits of hygiene and the necessities of civilized life, there can be developed a generation which will produce miracles."

An over-all view of the class system of the Sierra indicates that the

---

[7] Scholars and other persons in Ecuador interested in the problems of the Indian are known as *indigenistas*.

[8] Pío Jaramillo Alvarado, *El Régimen Totalitario en América* (Guayaquil, 1940), p. 117. See also his *El Indio Ecuatoriano* (Quito, 1936), and *Cuestiones Indígenas del Ecuador* (Quito, 1946), the latter edited by him.

"whites," forming a little more than one quarter of the region's population, maintain their undisputed domination of the cholos and Indians by means of at least seven fairly well-defined instruments of power: (1) An almost feudal system of landownership retains the Indian in a condition of virtual economic bondage. (2) The Roman Catholic Church in Ecuador maintains a powerful hold on the loyal and devout Indians through the intimate contact established by the lower clergy; the latter

TABLE 3

The Sierra Provinces: Selected Data for the Election of June 6, 1948

Provinces	Population (1947)	Registered voters[a]	Valid ballots cast for president[b]	Strongest political organization[b]
Totals	*2,066,160*	*288,794*	*187,803*	
Carchi	84,702	17,921	13,110	Conservative
Imbabura	156,045	18,939	16,230	Conservative
Pichincha	341,353	78,190	53,230	M.C.D.N.[c]
Cotopaxi	211,436	15,493	11,545	M.C.D.N.[c]
Tungurahua	219,299	31,022	22,776	Conservative
Chimborazo	292,492	25,510	15,616	Conservative
Bolívar	118,680	14,301	8,298	Conservative
Cañar	131,524	13,135	9,167	Conservative
Azuay	278,987	34,515	21,285	Conservative
Loja	231,622	37,723	16,546	Conservative

[a] Figures furnished by Supreme Electoral Tribunal, Quito, June 3, 1948.
[b] Data supplied by Supreme Electoral Tribunal, Quito, August 17, 1948.
[c] National Civic Democratic Movement (*Movimiento Cívico Democrático Nacional*).

are, of necessity, at the disposal of the "white"-dominated higher ranks of the Church hierarchy. (3) The armed forces of the republic stand ready to suppress the infrequent and desultory cholo and Indian rebellions. (4) The class system involves a division of labor which places posts of power and influence exclusively in the hands of the "whites." (5) The status system interwoven with the class structure confers considerable prestige and its concomitant prerogatives upon the "whites." (6) The "white" group enjoys a virtual monopoly within the region on formal education, a situation which facilitates "white" control of the Sierra. (7) Certain legal arrangements (e.g., the disfranchisement of almost all of the Indians and the bulk of the cholos) assure "white" domination of the region. Slightly more than 9 per cent of the estimated population of the Sierra cast valid ballots for president in the national election of 1948; these voters were almost exclusively "whites."

Traditionally, the Sierra has been Ecuador's stronghold of social and political conservatism. Hoary traditions and social usages, exaggerated formality in speech and conduct, and colonial customs and practices remain very much alive in the region. "The Sierra ... lives an intimate, silent, and solemn life: its cities are syntheses of Ecuadoran history, as are its customs and its mores; the colonial spirit still vibrates in its temples," Pérez Guerrero has said. "In the inter-Andean peoples tradition remains intact, with all its beauty and pomp, with its hates and its beliefs, its fears and its enthusiasms."[9] Politically, the Sierra is the traditional stronghold of the strongly Catholic Conservative party, a situation which has become more marked since 1944. In eight of the region's ten provinces, Conservative party candidates received more votes than their rivals in the presidential and vice-presidential election of 1948. Fifty-two per cent of the members of the Sierra delegation in the 1947–1949 congress—twelve of the region's twenty-four senators and twenty-one of its forty deputies—were members of the Conservative party. The localization in the Sierra of Conservative strength heightens the tension between this region and the Coast, and increases political instability in Ecuador.

THE COAST

The region known as the Coast lies to the west of the Sierra, being bounded on the east by the western cordillera of the Andes, and on the west by the Pacific Ocean. The Coast is about 350 miles in length, measured from the Colombian frontier at the north to the Peruvian frontier at the south; the region's width, from east to west, averages about eighty-five miles. On the whole, the Coast is low in altitude, with a hot and humid climate and essentially tropical vegetation. As in the Sierra, the "winter," or rainy season, extends from December to May; and the "summer," or dry season, from June to November. In the northern section of the region, the temperature decreases from the Pacific coast to the interior, whereas a reverse gradation is normal in the central and southern sections of the Coast.

This region contains an estimated 33 per cent of the population of Ecuador, five of the country's seventeen provinces, and six of its fifteen largest cities, including Guayaquil, the nation's commercial center and biggest city. About 30 per cent of the members of congress (fourteen of the forty-five senators and nineteen of the sixty-four deputies) represent the Coast, which cast 32 per cent of all valid ballots for president in the national election of June 6, 1948.

---

[9] Alfredo Pérez Guerrero, *Ecuador* (Quito, 1948), p. 62.

The Coastal class system differs markedly in both nature and content from that of the Sierra. The rigidity of the Sierra class structure is nowhere apparent in the Coast, where the various elements of the system mix relatively freely and easily. Communication and contact among these groups are widespread in the Coast, which does not experience social isolation on nearly as large a scale as is prevalent in the Sierra. In the Coast, as in the Sierra, the "whites" stand at the top of the social pyramid; but other groups of the region are essentially different from the cholos and the Indians of the Sierra. The second position in the class structure of the Coast is occupied by a group called the *montuvios,* and the lowest position is that of the Negroes. Although an Indian cultural admixture is not foreign to any of Ecuador's social groups, it can be said that no Indians reside in the Coast if the term "Indians" is understood to refer to people of non-European dress who speak a language which is not Spanish.

The "whites" account for an estimated 27 per cent of the population of the Coast. This group contains the Coast's large individual landholders, its government officials and political leaders, and the greater part of its voters. Most of the formally educated people of the Coast and the bulk of its higher army officers and members of the liberal professions are "whites." Because of the greater informality of Coastal social usages and the reduced social distance among classes, the "white" in this area does not receive the extreme degree of prestige and deference enjoyed by his counterpart in the Sierra.

An estimated 20 per cent of the Coast's population is accounted for by the so-called montuvios. In the popular mind this is a biological and racial term. There are those who have concocted a recipe for a montuvio: 60 per cent Indian, 30 per cent Negro, and 10 per cent white. Social and cultural factors, however, rather than biological ones, determine whether or not a man is a montuvio. A montuvio may be defined as a rural dweller of the Coast who "speaks Spanish, dresses like a 'poor white' peasant, and overtly partakes of Ecuadoran [as opposed to Indian] culture."[10]

About 60 per cent of the land on which the rural montuvios live and work consists of large haciendas owned by "whites." The montuvios fall into three categories: those who work and live on the haciendas, those who possess their own small parcels of land, and those who are tradespeople—a small minority. Considered as a citizen, the montuvio partici-

---

[10] John Murra, "Historic Tribes of Ecuador," *The Andean Civilizations* (*Handbook of South American Indians,* Vol. II) (Washington, 1946), p. 786.

pates in Ecuadoran national politics in two ways: as a guerrilla fighter and as a voter. The great majority of Ecuador's revolutions and civil wars are launched in the Coast, and when these occur the montuvio is prominent as an irregular fighting man. His role as a voter operates largely in conjunction with the lack of integrity which characterizes many of Ecuador's elections. The montuvio is frequently counted as having voted whether he actually did so or not; and he is sometimes regarded as having cast a ballot if he merely registered.

Negroes, rare in the Sierra, constitute an estimated 15 per cent of the population of the Coast. Most of them are in the northern Coastal provinces of Esmeraldas and Manabí, where they live an exclusively rural life. Their culture retains many African elements. Few of the Coastal Negroes vote or otherwise actively participate in the government and politics of Ecuador.

Although the Coast is dominated by the "whites," their instruments of control are not so rigidly iron-bound as in the Sierra. Conditions of landownership, armed force, a system of division of labor placing positions of power in the hands of the "whites," and "white" possession of the benefits of formal education safeguard the position of Coastal "whites" as they do that of Sierra "whites." The Roman Catholic Church, so closely linked to "white" interests in the Sierra, does not play a similar role in the Coast, where it has been deprived of much of its former political power since the Radical Liberal revolution of 1895. The vote, though the montuvio enjoys it to a limited extent, is exercised largely by the "whites" in the Coast. Slightly less than 8 per cent of the estimated population of the Coast cast valid ballots for president in the national election of 1948. The overwhelming majority of those voting were "whites."

Social and political liberalism, as manifested in Ecuador, has for the most part been centered in the Coast. The Sierra's emphasis on tradition is absent in the western region, where informality of social usages and a disregard of the older social forms are much in evidence. In 1948 the style of dress in the Sierra was strongly reminiscent of nineteenth-century customs, but in the larger cities of the Coast, especially Guayaquil, the latest fashions in feminine dress had taken hold almost as strongly as in the United States. "In the Coast, tradition is not meat of the meat and soul of the soul as it is in the Sierra," Pérez Guerrero has observed. "The Coast is open toward the outside, toward novelty, toward foreign ways. Its cities are modern cities, correct and uniform.... Perennial unrest agitates it, the perennial change of ideas and fervors.

It is the open eye of Ecuador, always in search of what other peoples have to make them stronger, richer, and happier. From the Coast comes liberalism as action and as government."[11]

During most of the twentieth century, the Coast has been the stronghold of the Radical Liberal party, which came to national power in 1895 as an expression of protest against clerical tendencies in Conservative rule. Whatever progress Socialists and Communists have made in recent years has been made largely in the Coast, where the members of these

TABLE 4
THE COASTAL PROVINCES: SELECTED DATA FOR THE ELECTION OF JUNE 6, 1948

Provinces	Population (1947) estimate	Registered voters[a]	Valid ballots cast for president[b]	Strongest political organization[b]
Totals................	1,136,535	166,358	90,549	
Esmeraldas...........	64,639	11,754	2,408	Coalition[c]
Manabí...............	367,263	44,455	30,246	M.C.D.N.[d]
Los Ríos..............	144,294	9,760	4,523	M.C.D.N.[d]
Guayas...............	469,315	83,370	43,566	M.C.D.N.[d]
El Oro................	91,024	17,019	9,806	Conservative

[a] Figures furnished by Supreme Electoral Tribunal, Quito, June 3, 1948.
[b] Data supplied by Supreme Electoral Tribunal, Quito, August 17, 1948.
[c] Coalition formed for the election of 1948 by the Radical Liberal and Socialist parties.
[d] National Civic Democratic Movement (*Movimiento Cívico Democrático Nacional*).

parties have endeavored to arouse political consciousness in the montuvios. In the national election of 1948, a new anti-Conservative political organization, the National Civic Democratic Movement, carried three of the Coast's five provinces; a coalition formed by the Radical Liberal and Socialist parties received more votes than any of its rivals in a fourth province of the region; and only one Coastal province, El Oro, reported a Conservative victory. Sixty-one per cent of the Coastal delegation in the 1947–1949 congress—eight of the region's fourteen senators and twelve of its nineteen deputies—was Radical Liberal. Except for two Conservatives, every non-Radical Liberal congressman from the Coast in 1948 was a Socialist, a Communist, or an independent. The political divergence between this region and the Sierra is a factor of considerable weight in political instability in the republic: as has been noted previously, most of Ecuador's revolutions originate in the Coast provinces.

[11] Pérez Guerrero, *op. cit.*, pp. 62–63.

THE ORIENTE

Many of the fundamental problems which have arisen during the course of Ecuador's history are as yet unsolved. One of these is the Sierra Indian. Another is the Oriente, the third continental region of Ecuador. The Oriente is the republic's largest region, occupying more than 60 per cent of the estimated continental territory of the country. Yet only about 5 per cent of the nation's population is in the Oriente.

This fabulous and paradoxical region, Ecuador's share of the Amazon jungle, is at once one of the country's most exasperating problems and its hope for a brilliantly satisfying future. It is in this region lying east of the Andes that the republic's frontier disputes with Peru have arisen. The Oriente is low in altitude, flat, hot, humid, honeycombed in many sections by large and small rivers, and lush with jungle vegetation. Transportation is virtually nonexistent in the region, as few roads exist. Communication is extremely difficult. The Oriente is so sparsely populated that it is possible to travel for hours and even days without encountering signs of human life. The land must be populated and cultivated, Ecuadorans agree. Without roads or means of communication, the colonizing work has been practically nil, to the great jeopardy of the wealth and future of the nation.

The Oriente, a vast and baffling hiatus in the Ecuadoran pattern, was essentially untouched by the Inca and Spanish conquests. Inca influence did not extend east of the Andes, and few of the conquistadors ventured there. The small groups of Indians residing in this region, completely isolated from Ecuadoran national life, have been associated by anthropologists with Amazonian rather than Andean culture patterns. Historically, three major Indian groups lived in the Oriente—the Yumbos, the Zaparos, and the Jivaros. Of these, the Yumbos are now extinct as an ethnic unit, although the word *yumbo* has worked its way into the language of the Ecuadorans as a term referring to jungle Indians generally. Today the Zaparos live in small and scattered groups in the northern part of the Oriente, whereas the Jivaros occupy southern areas.

Political organization among the Jivaros, the best-known of the Oriente Indians, is loose and flexible. They are divided into so-called tribes. These divisions, however, exist in the minds of anthropologists rather than in the consciousness of the Jivaros themselves. The basic unit of organization is the family group living under one roof and having no permanent political ties with other groups. The Jivaros frequently make war among themselves—it is said that the most important thing in life to a Jivaro is war—and during such hostilities, further political organization appears in the form of temporary alliances in which a number of houses in the same general vicinity place themselves under the jurisdiction of a common war leader called a *curaka*. His power is purely advisory and is limited to warfare.

The Jivaros' custom of severing and shrinking human heads has aroused considerable interest in their way of life and has inspired most students of their practices, including the present writer, to conduct their inquiries at a safe distance. The practice is closely interwoven with the Jivaro system of blood-revenge warfare. The shrunken heads, known as *tsantsas,* have religious significance, and the ceremonies held with the tsantsas are in part demonstrations for the benefit of departed relatives. Few visitors in Ecuador are able to escape the opportunity to purchase a tsantsa at a price considerably lower than that paid by the original owner.

Two provinces, Napo-Pastaza and Santiago-Zamora, have been created in the Oriente, entitling the region to two senators and four deputies in congress. Oriente residents cast approximately one per cent of all valid ballots for president in the national election of 1948, less than 2 per cent of the region's estimated population voting.

The government of Ecuador until recently had done virtually nothing to colonize and otherwise develop the Oriente, potentially rich in natural resources. To many Ecuadorans, development of the Oriente appears to be a vast and hopeless task. "Reality has disabused us of the optimistic dream which we had regarding this region," the dean of the Quito press has said editorially. "The highways are being built at a hopelessly slow pace. Already they have arrived at a point in the jungle, but it is not enough. Already we have organized provinces in this region; already they send us legislators; already there exists some semblance of administration—but the basic work of colonization remains to be done. A large and rich territory remains a little less than useless in contributing to the progress of the nation."[12]

THE GALÁPAGOS ISLANDS

The Ecuadoran tricolor also flies over a group of some sixty Pacific islands between five and seven hundred miles off the country's coast. Officially designated as the Archipelago of Columbus, the islands have also been known as the Enchanted Isles, Pirates' Paradise, and the Galápagos; and it is by the last of these names that they are popularly

---

[12] *El Comercio*, Quito, May 11, 1948.

referred to in Ecuador. The utmost confusion reigns about the names of the individual islands in the archipelago. They have been named and renamed several times, and have widely divergent popular and official designations in Ecuador. To add to the chaos, they are known in the United States and the United Kingdom by names unrecognized by Ecuadorans.

The islands' visitors during the course of their history have been few but, for one reason or another, distinguished. The remarkable roster includes the names of Charles Darwin, Herman Melville, William Dampier, and Alexander Selkirk, the prototype of Robinson Crusoe.

It was during a voyage to the Galápagos that Melville conceived the inspiration for his celebrated *Moby-Dick*. In his little-known *Piazza Tales*, he described the archipelago thus: "Take five-and-twenty heaps of cinders dumped here and there in an outside city lot; imagine some of them magnified into mountains, and the vacant lot the sea; and you will have a fit idea of the general aspect of the ... Enchanted Isles. ... It is to be doubted whether any spot on earth can, in desolateness, furnish a parallel to this group."[13]

The first recorded representative of European civilization to put in at the islands was Fray Tomás de Berlanga, the third Bishop of Panama, who planted the cross and the Spanish flag in the archipelago on March 10, 1533. During the ensuing three centuries, until the assertion in 1832 of Ecuadoran sovereignty over the group, the islands' chief visitors were pirates and whalers. The Galápagos are regarded as "one of the few places on earth where aboriginal man never existed; there surely is no other place where man has so much adventured, and which has yet remained for the most part a desert."[14]

Early visitors to the islands were astonished by the animal life of the archipelago. They encountered tortoises, turtles, iguanas, penguins, flightless cormorants, fork-tailed gulls, hawks, and doves. It was from the tortoises that the islands received their popular name, *galápago* being Spanish for "tortoise"; these creatures are now becoming extinct in the islands. Among a group of British pirates who put in at the archipelago in 1684 was the remarkable William Dampier, navigator, philosopher, naturalist, and buccaneer, who wrote: "The Spaniards, when they first discovered these islands, found multitudes of guanoes [sic], and land turtle or tortoise, and named them the Gallipagos [sic] islands. I do believe there is no place in the world that is so plentifully stored with these animals. The guanoes here are as fat and large as any that

---

[13] Herman Melville, *Piazza Tales* (New York, 1948), p. 149.
[14] William Beebe et al., *Galápagos: World's End* (New York, 1924), p. 332.

I ever saw; they are so tame that a man may knock down twenty in an hour's time with a club. The land turtle are here so numerous that five or six hundred men might subsist on them alone for several months, without any other sort of provision."[15] The fauna of the Galápagos have attracted natural scientists to the archipelago in great numbers, among them Charles Darwin and William Beebe.

Permanent settlements exist on thirteen of the islands, the population of which was estimated in 1947 at 737 persons. The archipelago, governed through the Ministry of National Defense, cast a grand total of sixty-three valid ballots for president in the national election of 1948. A major issue in recent Ecuadoran politics has been the existence of United States naval and air bases in the islands during World War II. Negotiations for their postwar retention were opened in 1944, but Ecuadorans, jealous of their sovereignty, brought about a decision in 1946 to withdraw United States personnel from the Galápagos, a process which was completed in August, 1948. Fear of United States intentions toward the archipelago caused the writers of the Constitution of 1946 to insert in that document the proviso that "the national territory is inalienable, and no pact may be negotiated which affects its integrity or which diminishes national sovereignty, without prejudice to the duties imposed by the international juridical community."[16]

REGIONALISM IN ECUADOR

Ecuadoran national politics frequently presents the spectacle of a struggle for power between the Sierra and the Coast, virtually no role in the contest being taken by the residents of the Oriente and the Galápagos Islands. "Regionalist problems arise," it has been noted, "where there is a combination of two or more such factors as geographical isolation, independent historical traditions, racial, ethnic, or religious peculiarities, and local economic or class interests."[17] All these factors are present in the Ecuadoran pattern. The Andes geographically isolate the Sierra, the Coast, and the Oriente from one another, and the introduction of the airplane is only beginning to break down this formidable barrier to interregional communication. The historical traditions associated with the Incas and with Pizarro and Benalcázar belong to the Sierra rather than to the Coast or the Oriente; the Roman Catholic Church is an intimate and ever present force in the life of the people

---

[15] Quoted in Beebe et al., op. cit., pp. 204–205.
[16] *Constitución Política de la República del Ecuador* (Quito, 1946), Art. 4.
[17] Hedwig Hintze, "Regionalism," *Encyclopaedia of the Social Sciences* (New York, 1937), Vol. VII, 209.

of the Sierra in a fashion which is certainly not true of the Coast or the
Oriente; and the differing ethnic and class structures have added to
the extreme difficulty in establishing class interests which could cross
the ruggedly mountainous regional lines. The economy of the Sierra
is predominantly agricultural, whereas the Coast in large part lives on
commerce.

The Coast and the Sierra are expressions of a species of dualism by
which Ecuador is divided. Guayaquil is the capital of one region, Quito
of the other; and the tension frequently produces strains of separatism
at Guayaquil. Together—when they are together—the Sierra and the
Coast rule Ecuador. The combined population of these two regions is
estimated at 94 per cent of the people of the republic. The residents of
these regions cast almost 99 per cent of all valid ballots for president
in the national election of 1948; and 88 per cent of the members of
congress represent the Sierra and the Coast.

The metaphor of a one-foot tail wagging a nine-foot dog is suggested
by the small percentage of the estimated population of the Sierra and
the Coast normally voting in elections. In the national election of 1948,
in which the turnout of voters was slightly larger than usual, less than
9 per cent of the estimated combined population of the two dominant
regions cast valid ballots for president.

Efforts to secure a measure of unity between the ruling classes of the
Sierra and the Coast may be inferred from a number of the legal and
political arrangements in force in the country. For example, there is a
constitutional provision enfranchising literate Ecuadorans over the age
of eighteen and making balloting compulsory for males in this category.
This provision may be viewed as an attempt to force the "whites" of
the two regions to vote while excluding the lower classes from the electorate. Again, it may be said that one function of national political
parties in Ecuador is to secure a modicum of agreement and unity of
the "whites" on both sides of the western cordillera, although this function is vitiated by the inability of the Conservatives to maintain strength
in the Coast and the weakness of the Radical Liberals' position in the
Sierra. Yet these unifying factors are at best artificial and only semieffective. The excessive political divergence between the two dominant
regions of the republic remains basic in political instability in Ecuador.

The disastrous results of the national election of 1931 illustrate the
role of regionalism in the republic's political pattern. Neptalí Bonifaz,
the Church-supported Conservative candidate for president, received
an overwhelming majority of the votes cast in the Sierra, whereas

Commandant Ildefonso Mendoza, the anti-Church standard-bearer of the Radical Liberal party, swept the Coast. Since more votes were counted in the Sierra than in the Coast, Bonifaz was declared the president-elect. However, under the Constitution of 1929, which was in force at the time, congress had the authority to review the electoral tally and to rule on Bonifaz' eligibility for the presidency. The legislature, dominated by Radical Liberals, desperately sought grounds for his disqualification. The pretext was found in the assertion that Bonifaz was not an Ecuadoran by birth and was thus constitutionally ineligible for the office to which he had been elected.

"Bonifaz was a man with a ninth-century mind, and we knew he could not govern the country," the writer was told by a political leader who had been a member of the senate at the time. "And so it was said that he was a Peruvian, in order that he could be disqualified. I voted against the disqualification because the charge that he was a foreigner was absurd and false." The majority of the congressmen voted otherwise, however, and Bonifaz was declared ineligible for the presidency. The tragic result of this action is known in Quito annals as the "Four Days' War." Sierra Conservatives rose in violent rebellion against the decision of the Radical Liberals in congress, but were bloodily overcome by montuvio guerrilla forces brought from the Coast. "Walking down the street, I saw the dead bodies," a survivor of the "Four Days' War" told the writer, years later. "Some had been piled along the sides of the road for group burial, while others still lay where they had fallen at the barricades."

In rationalizing their struggle with the Sierra, the people of the Coast usually rely on what they call economic arguments. They point to Guayaquil, the republic's one major port and commercial center, and assert that their region deserves a political preëminence commensurate with its position in Ecuadoran commerce. In the Sierra, on the other hand, one hears historical rather than economic justifications. In this region it is emphasized that the kingdom of Quito was centered at what is now the city of Quito, and that the Audiencia of Quito had its seat there. It is argued in the Sierra that the entire republic ought to be called "Quito" instead of "Ecuador," and that the Sierra is justified in resting on the laurels of Quito's position as a center of Spanish colonial society and civilization.

The Coast continues to be restive and somewhat resentful against governmental authority issuing from Quito, the capital of the republic. Most of the country's rebellions have originated in the Coast, and have been centered at Guayaquil. This city's municipal council holds a political position of crucial significance. Within its jurisdiction lives a good half of the metropolitan public of Ecuador. This group, liberal, sophisticated, and modern, is frequently irritated by governmental orders and instructions emanating from what it regards as the small, conservative, silent, religious, and "backward" capital in the Sierra.

Ecuadoran national leaders have endeavored, frequently unsuccessfully, to bridge the immense gulf between the two regions. In election campaigns it is not unusual to find a political party nominating a Sierra man for president and a Coastal leader for vice-president—or vice versa—in an attempt to make the ticket popular with voters in both regions. Indeed, one of the arguments advanced in the constituent assembly of 1946 on behalf of including the office of vice-president in Ecuador's new constitutional system was that the Sierra and the Coast could then be simultaneously represented by high executive officials. In forming their cabinets, most Ecuadoran presidents have tried to achieve a balance between Sierra and Coastal ministers. Shortly before he became president in September of 1948, Galo Plaza Lasso told the writer: "I am now in the process of completing my cabinet. And in doing so, I have wished to comply with the following political formula: in the cabinet there will have to be represented the Coast and the Sierra." A similar regional distribution is normally found within the membership of Ecuador's fifteen-man supreme court.

Regionalism thus constitutes a fundamental aspect of the background against which political instability has developed in Ecuador.

CHAPTER III
POLITICAL INSTABILITY IN ECUADOR

ECUADOR, as many of its presidents have affirmed, is not an easy country to govern. Although none of the fifteen written constitutions it had between 1830 and 1949 ever provided for a presidential term of less than four years, its forty-four chief executives within that period remained in office an average of 2.74 years. Only ten presidents (23 per cent of the total) were able to serve out the full terms for which they were chosen; and by 1949 no chief executive had been able to accomplish that feat since President José Luis Tamayo, who governed the country from 1920 to 1924. During the nine-year interval ending in 1940, Ecuador had no less than fourteen presidents, four of them during the single month which ended on September 17, 1947. Instability is likewise dramatized on the cabinet level: twenty-seven different ministers occupied eight cabinet posts between May 29, 1944, and August 23, 1947. Twelve foreign ministers attempted to administer Ecuadoran foreign policy in the two-month period between August and October of 1933.

This fluid condition has sprung in part from the nature of the adjustment which Spanish and Indian culture patterns have made to each other in the generations since Francisco Pizarro and his followers initially upset the balance of Indo-American society. Two elements of this adjustment may well be stressed. (1) The institution of divine-right monarchy was fundamental in the governmental systems of both Spaniards and the Indians, and contributed to the joint acceptance of continuing authoritarianism in government. (2) The Indo-American tradition of submissiveness and obedience adjusted itself readily in a complementary relationship with such elements of the Spanish culture as haughtiness and a disdain among "gentlemen" for manual labor, laying much of the basis for the class system noted in the preceding chapter.

IN THE WAKE OF MONARCHY

Monarchy sleeps beneath the republic. The indigenous population of the kingdom of Quito and the Inca Empire had been accustomed to divine-right monarchy long before the Spanish variant of the same institution was introduced in South America. The Ecuadoran Indian's role in government has been basically and uninterruptedly the same since the Quitus' arrival at the area which received their name. For the Ecuadoran Indian, life has been controlled by indisputable law for at least a thousand years, regardless of whether the particular political unit happened to be called the kingdom of Quito, the Inca Empire, the Audiencia of Quito, the Presidencia of Quito, the Department of the South, or the Republic of Ecuador.

The institution of monarchy, moreover, was embedded with equal firmness in the Spanish culture. The conquistadors, the Creoles, and their twentieth-century counterparts have lived in a monarchical tradition; they have known no other. In a sense, the monarchical system was only partially altered by the region's political severance from Spain.

The idea that the separation of the Spanish overseas colonies from the mother country signified the substitution of democratic republics for the older monarchy is in large part a delusion. Most major leaders in the wars for independence against Spain believed that the former colonies should continue in monarchy. Augustín de Iturbide established a throne in Mexico, and General José de San Martín endeavored to do the same in Peru. It is a fact too often ignored that *only one* major leader of the independence movement, the Liberator, General Simón Bolívar, advocated republics as opposed to monarchies. An almost blind cult of Bolívar worship has unfortunately obstructed South American scholars' inquiries into the Liberator's political ideas. It is, however, apparent that Bolívar was at best a quondam republican: his ideas differed at various stages in his career.

During the latter years of his life, from about 1825 to 1830, Bolívar entertained "republican" ideas bearing a significant relationship to monarchy. Consider, for example, the Constitution of 1826 which he wrote for Bolivia: it provided for a president with not only lifelong tenure but also the authority to choose his successor. "The President of the Republic becomes in our Constitution the sun, which, firm in the center, gives life to the universe," Bolívar wrote. "This supreme authority should be perpetual...." The Liberator felt that "a life-term President with the power of naming his successor is the most sublime addition to the republican system." This arrangement, he said, had the advantage of avoiding "the changing administrations caused by party government and the excitement that too frequent elections produce." On one occasion, Bolívar said: "I have never been an enemy of monarchy, as far as general principles are concerned; on the contrary, I consider monarchies essential for the respectability and well-being of new nations."[1] Hear

---
[1] Quoted in Víctor Andrés Belaunde, *Bolívar and the Political Thought of the Spanish American Revolution* (Baltimore, 1938), pp. 243, 244, 246, and 283. See also Vicente Lecuna, *Cartas del Libertador* (New York, 1948), Vol. XI, 44, 50–51, 189, 222–223, and 267.

the Liberator: "The new states of America ... need kings with the name of presidents."[3] Thus spoke the sole top-level republican of the independence period. His contemporaries, collaborators as well as rivals, were, by *contrast,* monarchists.

The Ecuadoran saying that the date of national independence was "the last day of despotism and the first day of the same thing" thus is not entirely facetious. For most of the people in all social classes there was no effective difference between the colonial monarchy and the new republic. Where they had formerly accepted the proposition that sovereignty of kings came from God, some of them later subscribed to the doctrine that this power resided in the people; but they had done little more than substitute one dogma for another. In Ecuador, the republic follows the lines laid down during the monarchical period.

Although most of the country's written constitutions have declared that sovereignty resides with the people, the mass of the republic's population has never yet exercised that power. The lower classes, so far as they are identified with the culture of the Indians, have been "good people"—that is, docile and obedient to an extent which shocks the foreign observer. These characteristics cannot be laid to the Spanish conquest, having been organically integrated with the Ecuadoran Indian's way of life since the days of the kingdom of Quito. Against this background, the lower classes have never contested the privileged position of the "whites" on anything like an organized basis.

THE CAUDILLO

The monarch in republican dress who carries on Ecuador's monarchical tradition is called the *caudillo.* Both monarchical systems upon which the Ecuadoran political process partly rests—the system of the non-American Spaniards and that of the pre-Hispanic Americans—contained the hereditary principle of legitimacy as the vehicle for replacing defunct monarchs. With the coming of independence from Spain, Ecuador was cut loose from this hereditary principle, and not having adopted Bolívar's formula for Bolivia that the dying ruler name his successor, found itself without any principle of succession with sufficient root in either the Spanish or the Indo-American culture to become legitimate. *Caudillismo,* unplanned and unpremeditated, sprang from the Ecuadoran cultural milieu spontaneously and chaotically as a method of selecting "natural" rulers, a substitute vehicle of succession.

[3] Quoted in Jaramillo Alvarado, *El Régimen Totalitario en América* (Guayaquil, 1940), p. 107.

The Ecuadoran caudillo—the "natural" leader, the "man with a mission"—arises from the "white" group and is produced by a species of sociopolitical interaction which operates within the ruling class. Among themselves, the "whites" enjoy what has been called "democracy in the Greek sense, in which the people are not the lower classes but rather the men of education and culture."[3] Coexistent within the "white" group with its "democracy in the Greek sense" is a measure of anarchy. The ruling class conducts a constant intra-class struggle for power. In this chaotic rivalry, certain of the "whites" rise to greater power than is enjoyed by other members of the group. This intra-class contest appears to be conducted along at least three lines of division. The first and most significant of these is personal rivalry, Ecuadoran politics being notoriously laden with *personalismo*. Second, regionalism enters into the struggle to no small extent, Coastal "whites" frequently being pitted against those of the Sierra. Third, doctrinal or ideological differences enter into the contest somewhat, but these are exceedingly minor in the process when compared with personal rivalry and regionalism.

It would appear that the caudillo—he who rises to the top in the chaotic intra-class struggle—possesses certain more or less well-defined characteristics. (1) He is, for example, usually but not necessarily an army officer. Generals Juan José Flores and Eloy Alfaro would serve as examples of major military caudillos, and Gabriel García Moreno is Ecuador's classic instance of a nonmilitary caudillo. (2) The intellectual capacity of the caudillo generally compares favorably with those less successful in the contest. This does not necessarily mean that he has had an extensive formal education—witness Flores—although he frequently is well educated and may even, like Dr. José María Velasco Ibarra, hold a doctorate. (3) In his own view, the caudillo is an indispensable man. He normally feels that he is the only figure on the national scene who can "save the country." He is exceedingly conscious of his own significance, and bears a striking resemblance to Max Weber's "charismatic" leader, who feels an "inner call." He is recognized by his followers as "the innerly 'called' leader of men," Weber has pointed out. "Men do not obey him by virtue of tradition or statute, but because they believe in him." He governs through a species of divine right, but "his divine mission must 'prove' itself in that those who faithfully surrender to him must fare well. If they do not fare well, he is obviously not the

---
[3] Jácome Moscoso, *op. cit.*, p. 33. See also Angel Modesto Paredes, *Naturaleza del Poder Público y del Sometimiento del Hombre a las Autoridades del País* (Quito, 1929), *passim*.

master sent by the gods.'"[4] (4) The caudillo is a man of more than average vitality. He is generally a physically dynamic person, and normally he makes a great number of speeches during his career. (5) The caudillo is a man of some reputation: he is not unknown to a large sector of the "whites" on the eve of his assumption of national power.

Caudillismo lives in a symbiotic relationship with militarism. Among the caudillo's instruments of power, the Ecuadoran army occupies a high place. Of the country's presidents, 31 per cent have been army officers. Not all of these have been caudillos, but every major caudillo, except for Gabriel García Moreno, has been a military man. "The last step in a military career is the presidency of the republic" is among Ecuador's more significant political maxims, and the army has been a major force in Ecuadoran national life. It was with almost heroic effort that the civilian administration of President Carlos Julio Arosemena was able to reduce the army's share of the 1949 budget to only 20 per cent of the total. The army and the national police force, in continual rivalry, have carried on a struggle which has exaggerated the prestige of the former and made the policeman an object of scorn in Ecuadoran eyes. An emphasis on militarism is evident almost everywhere in the Sierra and the Coast. Military parades, complete with fixed bayonets, the latest surplus United States Army equipment, and blaring bands playing in the weird and plaintive five-tone minor scale of most Ecuadoran music, are held apparently at the slightest provocation, whether the occasion be one of the republic's numerous national holidays or the presentation of a newly arrived diplomat's credentials.

It is against this essentially fluid and at times chaotic background that political instability operates in Ecuador. Caudillos come and go; they are made and unmade. The caudillo, having come to power, may lose it. So long as he retains control of his followers and his region, so long as he possesses the major part of the caudillo's characteristics, and so long as he retains mastery of an appreciable portion of the instruments of power, he may remain dominant. Some caudillos—for example, García Moreno and Alfaro—die while politically powerful, but this is rare. Normally the caudillo, through the fluidity of the process, loses his hold and is overthrown, but remains alive, frequently in exile.

Caudillismo is by its nature uncertain and unpredictable. Occasionally two or more caudillos exist at the same time, their rivalries heightening the instability of the political process; a caudillo may remain powerful

---

[4] Max Weber (Gerth and Mills, tr.), *From Max Weber: Essays in Sociology* (New York, 1946), pp. 79, 249.

for only a short period of time, again intensifying the unstable character of the situation; there may be a period of considerable length during which only one caudillo exists on the national scene and is able to retain undisputed control of a fundamental power instrument, in which case it is said that the republic experiences a measure of stability; or there may be prolonged periods (stable or unstable, depending on other factors) in which no caudillo exists on the national level and some "whites" fall into the normally non-Ecuadoran habit of familiarizing themselves with the contents of whatever written constitution happens to be in force at the time.

Caudillismo, unlike divine-right monarchy, makes some use of a written constitution. This document relates to the Ecuadoran political process in a twofold manner. One, the constitution adds a measure of legal protection, albeit weak, of the power instruments which are bound up in the process. The structure of landownership, for example, is thus defended by the Constitution of 1946: "The right of owning property is guaranteed, reconciling it with its social function. Confiscation of property is prohibited. . . ."[5] The following treatment of the Church as an instrument of power has appeared, in one form or another, in several of Ecuador's constitutions: "The religion of the state is Catholic, Apostolic, Roman. It is the duty of the government... to protect this religion, excluding any other."[6] Under García Moreno's extraordinary Constitution of 1869, be it remembered, only a practicing Catholic could be a citizen of Ecuador. Armed force as an instrument of power is handled by the Constitution of 1945 in the following manner: "The members of the armed forces enjoy special exemption [*fuero*]. They may not be sued or deprived of their ranks, honors, and pensions, except in a form and under circumstances to be determined by law. . . . The police force is a civil institution destined principally to guarantee internal order and individual and collective security. Its members do not enjoy special exemption."[7] Moreover, the literacy requirement contained in the 1946 document limits the suffrage virtually exclusively to the "whites."

Two, the second significant relationship between caudillismo and the written constitution lies in the uncertainty and unpredictability of the political process. As has been noted, Ecuador occasionally experiences longer or shorter periods when no caudillo exists on the national level, when there is no monarch to wear the republican dress. In such times, the written constitution steps into the breach by providing the basis for

---

[5] *Constitución Política de la República del Ecuador* (Quito, 1946), Art. 183.
[6] *Ibid.* (Quito, 1830), Art. 8.
[7] *Ibid.* (Quito, 1945), Arts. 118, 120.

the organization of an interregnum. The official who presides over this interim government may be called, for the purposes of the present analysis, a "constitutional president." That is, he is normally selected in a manner related to the text of the constitution, and his administration generally adheres scrupulously to constitutional forms. The government of President Carlos Julio Arosemena, a representative "constitutional president," read the Constitution of 1946 so literally—the document provided that presidential terms begin on September 1 of years in which administrations change—that the inauguration of Arosemena's successor was held *exactly at midnight* on August 31, 1948. The "constitutional president," judging by the speed with which he is forgotten by historians, is a remarkably minor figure in national politics when compared with the caudillo. The "constitutional president" is generally named for a term of four years or an unexpired portion thereof, and is occasionally able to serve out the entire period for which he was chosen. When he is unable to do so, the explanation may lie either in the rise of a new caudillo before the legal termination of the presidential period, or insufficient strength on the part of the "constitutional president" to prevent the interregnum from passing to other "constitutional" hands.

Apart from this twofold relationship to the written constitution, caudillismo operates in a manner largely independent of the document and frequently in violation of it. The specific Ecuadoran instances of conflict between the facts of caudillismo and the text of a written constitution have generally been resolved by disregard for, and even destruction of, the latter. Little else can be expected, since caudillismo is deeply embedded in Ecuadoran history, tradition, and culture, and is an organic and integral part of the republic's way of life. Absolute monarchy lay in both the Indian and Spanish backgrounds; this, combined with the Indian culture pattern of humility, docility, and submissiveness, on the one hand, and the traditional upper-class superiority of the Spaniards, on the other, has formed the complex that is contemporary Ecuador.

CONSTITUTIONS AND REVOLUTIONS

The frequently noted distinction between "real" and "written" constitutions is of assistance in isolating some fundamental aspects of Ecuadoran constitutional problems. A "real" constitution may be defined as the existing system of power relationships operating within a state: Aristotle once defined a constitution as the "arrangement of the inhabitants of a state."[8] A "written" constitution is that document which has

---

[8] Aristotle (Benjamin Jowett, tr.), *Politics* (London, 1920), p. 100.

been declared by the legally competent authorities to be the supreme law of the land. The "written" constitution may or may not approximate the contents of the "real" constitution.

Ecuador's "real" constitution includes at least these seven basic elements: (1) A small minority, perhaps not more than 15 per cent of the population, called "whites," controls exclusively the organs of, and avenues to, public power. (2) This minority is divided within itself along regionalist lines, the normal condition being an open struggle or an uneasy truce between Sierra and Coastal "whites." (3) The monarchist tradition, deeply embedded in the Spanish and Indian cultures, underlies a continuing authoritarianism in government. (4) Although the hereditary principle in selecting new rulers has been rejected, no effectively formalized vehicle of succession has replaced it. (5) Within the dominant "white" group exists a modicum of "democracy in the Greek sense" which combines with such anarchistic elements as regionalism and personal rivalries to produce the "caudillist process" as the prevailing though nonformalized principle of succession. (6) The vast majority, perhaps 85 per cent of the inhabitants of the state, is excluded from active participation in government and politics on a national scale. (7) The political system is maintained by such instruments of power as landownership, the Roman Catholic Church, armed force, the class distribution of literacy, and to a lesser extent, the laws of the republic.

In contrast, the "written" constitution of Ecuador may be identified as that document (or any faithful transcription of it) which possesses the three following characteristics: (1) It is the most recent sheaf of papers which has been placed in a large and impressive wooden box in the Archivo y Biblioteca del Poder Legislativo at Quito. (2) The document bears the title, Constitución Política de la República del Ecuador. (3) The initial deposit of the document in the above-noted receptacle was accompanied by the legally required formal ritual.

It is probably true that no constitution, Ecuadoran or otherwise, functions wholly in the manner in which it is written. Textual references to Ecuador's "real" constitution are exceedingly rare in the republic's "written" constitution. Many of the country's political leaders have readily declared that the Constitution of 1946 is, to use one of their more common expressions, "divorced from reality." A prominent Ecuadoran "jungle senator" has said: "Our idiosyncrasy has been to omit from our constitutions any traces or indications of the complex which characterizes our nationality."[9] This has been in large measure true of

---

[9] Jaramillo Alvarado, *El Régimen Totalitario en América*, p. 73.

the bulk of Ecuador's fifteen "written" constitutions. Of these, the 1843 and 1869 charters approximated the "real" constitution more closely than the other thirteen. The remainder have been, for the most part, translations into Spanish of ideas and practices—such as the rights of man and the separation of powers—which, in the opinion of Ecuadoran constitution writers, met with some success in other countries, particularly the United States and France.

An Ecuadoran political scientist, in assessing his country's constitutional ills, has said: "It can happen that the system of rules set forth in the [written] constitution does not coincide with the existing political conditions in the state, in which case the objective law created by constitutional norms cannot have actual, effective validity. In such a case there is produced a frank discrepancy between the constitutional order and the political order. . . . This discrepancy, if not adjusted in logical and realistic terms, can produce changes and unrest in the social order, to the extent that passive as well as active resistance movements result in the reform or the elimination of the written constitution."[10] This passage describes a chronic condition in Ecuador.

In the rural and isolated—"uncivilized," Ecuadorans say—inter-Andean basin of the southeastern Sierra, there resides in dull contentment a group of Indians cut off from the "national life." These people suffer from an assortment of chronic and recurring ills, from which relief is sought by laying the more weighty problems before a respected gentleman known as a *brujo*. He is admittedly a species of medicine man. With one chicken he is able to make minor problems disappear; three chickens accomplish staggering feats; and the results achieved with ten chickens are appalling and suggestive of much.

In the urban and cultured center of civilization in the north central Sierra, there resides in satisfied superiority a group of "whites" who are the "national life." These people suffer from an assortment of chronic and recurring ills, from which relief is sought by laying the major questions before a respected gentleman known as a constitution writer. He normally does not think of himself as a medicine man. With ten articles, however, he is able to make minor problems disappear; thirty articles accomplish staggering feats; and the results achieved with fifty articles are appalling and suggestive of much.

The constitution writer does not believe that the methods of the brujo are effective. He points out that ills theoretically cured by the medicine have a habit of recurring, frequently regardless of the number of chick-

---

[10] Aurelio García, *Ciencia del Estado* (Quito, 1947), Vol. II, 259–260.

ens expended by way of remedy. He states with finality that the approaches of the brujo to the problems of Ecuadoran life are subject to the most severe censure, since they are "divorced from reality."

It is manifest that Ecuadoran administrations frequently change in a manner not provided for by the text of the "written" constitution. When this occurs, it is generally said that a "revolution" has taken place. This usage of the term, it should be noted, differs from the meaning of the word "revolution" as it has been developed by definition writers in the United States. Although these writers have variously defined the term, the bulk of them would probably agree that in "revolution" as they understand it "a major change in the political order—not merely a shift in the personnel of the government or a reorientation of its concrete policies—must be preceded or accompanied by a drastic change in the relation among the different groups and classes in society. Thus a recasting of the social order is . . . a far more important characteristic of revolutions than a change of the [written] political constitution or the use of violence in the attainment of this end."[11] Although some case may be made for calling the Ecuadoran upheavals of 1830, 1845, 1895, and 1944 "revolutions" in this sense, most of the transformations in Ecuador's government have not carried with them alterations of far-reaching significance for the social order. Perhaps no Ecuadoran "revolution" has achieved this since Sebastián de Benalcázar upset the balance of Quito society in the sixteenth century. Neither have most of Ecuador's "revolutions" been *coups d'état* as this term has been understood in the United States, where it is held that *coup d'état* applies to unconstitutional governmental changes made by people already in office.[12] The term "revolution" as it appears in these pages is used in the Latin American sense to refer to any change in government effected, with or without violence, in defiance of the written constitution and initiated either by those who already hold public office or by those who seek it.

The typical Ecuadoran revolution is not a mass movement, as it affects only the members of the "white" group. The overwhelming majority of the people of Ecuador—Indians, cholos, montuvios, and Negroes—are not normally directly affected by a revolution. Indian uprisings, when they occur, are quite another matter. Ecuadoran revolutions are always made by the "whites"—by the landholders, the military leaders, and the

---

[11] Alfred Meusel, "Revolution and Counter-Revolution," *Encyclopaedia of the Social Sciences* (New York, 1937), Vol. VII, 367.

[12] Cf. Henry R. Spencer, "Coup d'État," *Encyclopaedia of the Social Sciences* (New York, 1937), Vol. IV, 508–510; and Carl J. Friedrich, *Constitutional Government and Democracy* (New York, 1946), pp. 127 and 150 ff.

men of formal education. The Ecuadoran caudillo is in every case a "white." The republic's revolutions are frequently characterized by an alliance of the formally educated leaders with the commanders of the armed forces. The humble Indian plays no active part in the process, and his way of life goes on as it has for centuries, regardless of what government happens to be in power, how it achieved office, and what specific points may be included in its program. The Indian's existence is markedly isolated from the "whites" and from the political process which is theirs and theirs alone, for he is cut off from the "national life."

A CASE STUDY IN CAUDILLISMO: JOSÉ MARÍA VELASCO IBARRA

May 29, 1944, was not unlike any other relatively uneventful day in the life of the Sierra Indian. He was awake at an hour when he knew the sun was rising, although he could not see the sun because "winter"— the rainy season—was unduly prolonged that year, and the days were cold and rainy. He went to the market early in the morning, as was his custom, for there would be little that he could do there if he arrived later than half-past seven. Later, he returned to his beloved fields, which were the heart of his way of life. His agriculture was so basic that conquest by the Incas and the Spaniards had not been able to turn him from the soil; and on May 29, 1944, as on almost all the other days of his life, he carried on within his ancient pattern of planting and harvesting, still deeply in harmony with the earth, the cold Andean rains, and the lonely peaks that bounded his world. Perhaps he would drink too much chicha and, under its influence, rail against the patrón; but this would most likely not occur until the next three-day fiesta.

May 29, 1944, for Ecuadorans cut off from the "national life," did not differ from the other days of the dreary "winter"; and within the Sierra Indian's frame of reference there was no point in attempting to establish a distinction.

For the "whites" of the larger cities of the republic, May 29, 1944, was a day which would not soon be forgotten. A reporter for *El Comercio*, the capital's largest newspaper, knew that he could never fully describe that day's events, but hoped that future historians might gain some idea of what had happened in the life of Quito when they read his account: "Citizens in general, when they learned that the revolutionary movement had triumphed in the port of Guayaquil and that [President] Arroyo del Río had resigned, organized delirious demonstrations in which they cheered Dr. Velasco Ibarra, sang the national anthem, and carried the national tricolor and portraits of Dr. Velasco Ibarra. Some of these demonstrations, after moving through their respective neighborhoods, advanced on the Plaza de la Independencia and in front of the statue to Liberty sang the national anthem with great emotion. Various orators spoke in the Plaza de la Independencia, cheering the triumphant revolution at Guayaquil and expressing their satisfaction with the resignation [of the president].... The heated speeches of the orators ... raised the fervor of the enormous throng congregated in the Plaza to the point of delirium.... It can be affirmed that by about ten o'clock at night, close to half the population of the city was milling through the streets shouting cries of satisfaction...."[13]

Dr. José María Velasco Ibarra, the "Great Absentee," had returned to Ecuador after years in exile. The "National Personification" had at last come home, and the people of the larger cities seemed delirious.

Dr. Carlos Alberto Arroyo del Río, the president who was overthrown in the revolution of May 28, 1944, had foreseen the event for months. "I hated Velasco Ibarra," Arroyo del Río told the writer. "I knew that if he were to come to the presidency, he would ruin the country." The plot to depose the Arroyo del Río government had taken definite form as early as mid-December of 1943, and news of the conspiracy reached the administration shortly thereafter. "It was known in the ministry of government that a revolution was afoot," one of the conspirators wrote. "Arroyo knew it, the people knew it, but nobody could localize it. It was an underground movement which was undermining the edifice of despotism.... It is certain that Arroyo and his ministers did everything in their power to discover where this revolution was."[14] In March, 1944, a group of leftist parties—the Socialist, Communist, Socialist Revolutionary Vanguard, and Democratic organizations—formed a coalition, the Ecuadoran Democratic Alliance, for the purpose of supporting the candidacy of the exiled Velasco Ibarra in the presidential election scheduled for June 2 and 3. The government was suspicious of the coalition's motives, and on April 8 President Arroyo del Río dispatched a circular telegram to the provincial governors. "Since the Ecuadoran Democratic Alliance began its apparently electoral work, the government has received information that it is pursuing ends contrary to public order," the telegram declared. "The government has made this known to the country; but, as was natural, the interests involved in the plot have denied the existence of these reprehensible endeavors. Today the government has in its hands documentary proof which confirms its

---
[13] *El Comercio*, Quito, May 30, 1944.
[14] Sergio Enrique Girón, *La Revolución de Mayo* (Quito, 1945), pp. 134–135.

suspicions, and which makes evident the true temper of this group and its plans."[15]

Arroyo del Río has been severely criticized for his handling of the 1944 campaign. A presidential election had been scheduled for June, and the president exercised complete control over the selection of legal candidates. He headed the Radical Liberal party, which had been in power since 1895, and used his twofold role as chief of state and leader of his party with disastrous results. His primary aim was to prevent Velasco Ibarra, who had been president from 1934 to 1935, from returning to power. As chief of state, Arroyo del Río declared Velasco Ibarra's candidacy illegal and denied him permission to return to Ecuador. Exiled since 1940, Velasco Ibarra nevertheless persisted in his campaign, which he conducted from the Colombian border. As leader of his party, President Arroyo del Río personally hand-picked the Radical Liberal—and sole legal—candidate to succeed him. Although the president did consult other Radical Liberal leaders in the matter of designation of a legal candidate, he chose to ignore their advice and to deny them voice in the formulation of Radical Liberal policy.

A group of Radical Liberals led by Gonzalo Zaldumbide, then ambassador to Brazil, believed that it was both impossible and unwise to obstruct the election of Velasco Ibarra. "To attempt to halt the advance of Velasco Ibarra is to attempt something impossible," Zaldumbide declared. "Velasco Ibarra is one of the great manifestations of nature in these times."[16] A second Radical Liberal faction, represented by Dr. José Vicente Trujillo, believed that the party might be able to win a fair election if it nominated a strong candidate to run against Velasco Ibarra, and suggested Captain Colón Eloy Alfaro, then ambassador to the United States. Arroyo del Río, however, was determined to keep Velasco Ibarra out of the country and to control the 1944 election. Accordingly, the president's nominee, seventy-year-old senate president Miguel Angel Albornoz, became the Radical Liberal standard-bearer.

As the campaign developed, Albornoz was the sole legal candidate. The majority of the Radical Liberal leaders had not desired his selection and this fact, coupled with Albornoz' weakness, ineffectiveness, and unpopularity as a campaigner, plunged the republic into crisis as the scheduled election date approached. Opposition to Arroyo del Río's tactics became widespread among political leaders and contributed to

---

[15] From documentary materials made available to the writer by Dr. Arroyo del Río at Guayaquil during July, 1948.
[16] Quoted in Girón, *op. cit.*, p. 110.

the weakening of the regime during the early months of 1944. Many of the nation's voters, in the wake of the Albornoz nomination, acquired a new sympathy for Velasco Ibarra and his cause. The Ecuadoran Democratic Alliance readily exploited this situation by means of various propaganda devices. The coalition's illegal candidate became known as the "Great Absentee," and manifestoes dramatized the difficulty involved in contacting the exile. "With grief and bitterness, with profound grief and bitterness, the journey was made to the neighboring republic of Colombia, refuge of liberty, of respect for human rights, of profound and authentic democracy, because of the fact—unprecedented in the history of our republic—that the Ecuadoran people, by means of their representatives, have had to leave the country to interview the candidate of their choice," a typical manifesto asserted. "This demonstrates in incontrovertible relief that we Ecuadorans have lost our liberty, the practice of the law, and have been transformed into an enslaved, humiliated, and scorned nation."[17]

Arroyo del Río and Albornoz rapidly lost control of the situation. On May 20, Velasco Ibarra declared from his campaign headquarters in Colombia that only electoral fraud could deprive him of the presidency. He warned that he would fight tirelessly against the regime if such fraud should take place.

There was no electoral fraud because there was no election. The military garrison at Guayaquil launched a rebellion at ten o'clock on the night of May 28, 1944, publishing the following proclamation:

PEOPLE OF GUAYAQUIL

The entire military garrison of this city, with the support of all the people, principally students, workers, and intellectuals, has risen to put an end to the hateful tyranny of traitors whom we can no longer tolerate.

The government of Arroyo has been an interminable orgy of crimes, thievery, and infamous mistakes which have brought the country to its ruin....

This sinister clique has been preparing to retain power, mocking the will of the people by means of the terror which has been unloosed and by the most scandalous of frauds planned for the coming election. The murder of the people had been planned.... The citizens are urged to remain tranquil and to refrain from joyous celebrations until after all the delinquents and provocateurs have been disarmed. Order must be maintained at all costs.

The army has no desire for power. This will be placed in the hands of civilians who will guarantee an immediate return to normality. As soon as the republic is pacified, a presidential election will be called, initiating an era of well-being and progress for our beloved country.[18]

---

[17] Alianza Democrática Ecuatoriana, *Manifiesto a la Nación*, April 2, 1944.
[18] *El Telégrafo*, Guayaquil, May 29, 1944.

Captain Sergio Enrique Girón, one of the officers of the Guayaquil garrison, asserted that "we, the military men who made the revolution, did not receive orders from anybody.... Nobody was 'director,' nobody was chief.... We did not subvert order. We transformed it. We did not make a barracks revolt. We made a true revolution, supported and inspired by the people, to whom we belong and whom we obey.... We, the men of the people, captured the government, and we set up a popular regime, the most democratic in this America."[19]

The military "men of May 28," upon the resignation of President Arroyo del Río and his cabinet, delivered the power of government to the Ecuadoran Democratic Alliance. This organization announced a six-point political program involving the establishment of "true democracy," aid to agriculture and industry, stimulation of labor unions, development of sanitation and hygiene, continued collaboration with the other American republics, and coöperation with the United Nations. This program was accepted by Velasco Ibarra, who by virtue of a decree dated June 1 became president of the republic, his term to expire on September 1, 1948. The revolution was almost uniformly hailed by the press of the Western Hemisphere, editorial endorsement being given the Velasco Ibarra regime by such newspapers as *El Tiempo* of Bogotá, Colombia; and in the United States by the *Washington Post*, the *Baltimore Sun*, and the *New York Times*.

Dr. José María Velasco Ibarra is probably one of the most widely misunderstood figures in contemporary Ecuadoran national politics. Given the circumstances of the time, it was easy to forget in mid-1944 that he had been the president of Ecuador once before, and that his earlier presidency had ended in disaster. Inaugurated in September, 1934, he had been able to hold office for less than a year before he was overthrown. His first administration had been authoritarian in character, culminating in his dissolution of congress because the senate had opposed his policies. Critics who pointed out that his attack on the legislature was in violation of the Constitution of 1929, then theoretically in force, were met with the rejoinder that the senate had also defied the document by remaining out of session for more than three days without the consent of the chamber of deputies. Deposed in 1935, Velasco Ibarra lived in exile in Colombia until 1940, when he returned to Ecuador to run again for the presidency. He was defeated in that contest by Arroyo del Río; and the "Great Absentee" resumed his exile, this time in Chile, after his followers staged an abortive revolt. Early in

---
[19] Girón, *op. cit.*, pp. 10, 54–55, 122.

1944, he journeyed to Colombia to establish campaign headquarters near the Ecuadoran border. During his second exile, the "Great Absentee" was required to wear the additional halo of the "National Personification," the brilliance of which clouded the vision of the faithful.

Measured against the records of such leaders as Flores, García Moreno, and Alfaro, Velasco Ibarra was only a minor caudillo. It has already been noted that the characteristics of the Ecuadoran caudillo include intellectual ability, vitality, reputation, and a consciousness of his own significance. An examination of the extent to which Velasco Ibarra possessed these traits may prove of value in assessing his role in Ecuadoran government and politics.

Dr. Velasco Ibarra's academic career was distinguished. The greater part of his formal higher education was acquired at the University of Paris, and upon his return to Ecuador he served as professor of law intermittently at the University of Guayaquil and the Central University at Quito. He has written prolifically, and a part of the riddle that is Velasco Ibarra approaches solution when viewed in terms of his published work.

His political ideas rest in part upon a denial of the existence of absolute truth, although he has pursued it. He has said that history has meaning only as "an experiment in relative truths," and therefore that man has "a perfect right... to attempt various approaches to the human problem."[20] He proclaimed himself a liberal, an advocate of "the liberalism of the eighteenth century: individualist and opposed to the intervention of the state in the name of social justice."[21] He asserted that he was "devoted to the liberty of man, liberty as understood in its deepest sense: liberty of man as a citizen, that is, political democracy; liberty of man as an integrated person, that is, biological, economic, and cultural opportunities for self-expression."[22] He repeatedly affirmed that he thought of man and his problems in individualistic rather than collectivistic or societal terms. "Everything in universal history moves toward the individual person," he declared. "Economics and ethics must be definitely subordinated to the individual person."[23]

Velasco Ibarra thus rejected both communism and fascism, viewing

[20] José María Velasco Ibarra, *Un Momento de Transición Política* (Quito, 1935), p. 8.
[21] Velasco Ibarra, *Conciencia o Barbarie* (Buenos Aires, 1938), p. 65.
[22] Quoted in Girón, *op. cit.*, p. 345. Cf. also William Rex Crawford, *A Century of Latin-American Thought* (Cambridge, 1944).
[23] Velasco Ibarra, *Mensaje Presentado a la Honorable Asamblea Nacional Constituyente, ... 10 de Agosto de 1946* (Quito, 1946), p. 58.

them as instruments of regimentation, as enemies of the liberty of man as an individual. "What difference is there between communism and fascism?" he wrote. "The same mechanical conception of man, the same material absorption of man.... Fascist fanaticism reduces man to a conceit for the national organism, according to the capricious norms of the Caesar of the moment."[24] This sector of his thought is of considerable significance in an analysis of his 1944–1947 administration as president of Ecuador. He felt that socialism and communism, as manifested in the republic, were little more than "words for the exploitation of workers."[25] Velasco Ibarra was brought to power in 1944 by the essentially leftist Ecuadoran Democratic Alliance, in which the country's Socialist and Communist parties figured prominently. Yet the "National Personification" believed that "all the injustices which are committed in other countries in the name of conservatism are committed in Ecuador in the name of leftism.... For this reason I do not belong to any of the political parties of Ecuador. My political school is liberal, genuinely liberal."[26]

Though he professed a great love for liberty as he defined it, Velasco Ibarra believed that his liberalism was impossible in the Ecuador he knew. "The conflict between dreams and reality ... has been the tragedy of Spanish America," he said. "Unified by the Spanish soul, Americans have desired union, and have come up against infinite distances, gigantic mountains, varied climates, unhealthful valleys, and perpetually extended rivers and plains."[27] Overwhelmed by his South American environment, man was, in Velasco Ibarra's view, incapable of achieving genuine liberty, and almost always fell hopelessly into a regimented way of life. "In America there exist almost all formulae and systems; almost all are men in regimentation."[28]

Given these peculiarly South American obstacles to individual liberty, what was the true role of the liberal politician, the political leader who believed in the liberalism of Velasco Ibarra? The task of such a statesman was to create "a new democracy, ... a democracy adapted to the psychology of the American 'white.' "[29] The humble Indian, as always, was to be omitted from the new order. To bring about an environment which would render more perfect Ecuador's "democracy in the Greek

---
[24] *Idem, Conciencia o Barbarie*, p. 16.
[25] United Press dispatch, July 13, 1945.
[26] Velasco Ibarra, *Conciencia o Barbarie*, p. 11.
[27] *Idem, Experiencias Jurídicas Hispanoamericanas* (Buenos Aires, 1943), pp. 137–138.
[28] *Idem, Conciencia o Barbarie*, p. 15.
[29] *Idem, Experiencias Jurídicas Hispanoamericanas*, p. 66.

sense," it was necessary for the state to plunge actively into a staggering public works program directed toward the removal of the physical obstacles to the liberty of the "whites": the state must build roads, conquer mountains, clear jungles. Thus Velasco Ibarra fell hopelessly into the exasperating dilemma of many another Latin American liberal thinker: the democrat "opposed to the intervention of the state" had to embark upon a program of state intervention of unprecedented proportions in order to establish an environment conducive to liberty.

Velasco Ibarra recognized that the South American obstacles to individual liberty were not exclusively nonhuman. The politician, in his view, must take a firm hand in dominating those human traits which obstructed the achievement of individual liberty for the "whites." The politician, Velasco Ibarra believed, "has to dominate the insurrections of creative interests, of disorderly aspirations, which take for their banners noble ideals which are based on obedience to animal instincts of a simply vegetable life."[30] Thus, Velasco Ibarra did not reject dictatorship as such:

> Evil is not essentially in dictatorship, and good is not necessarily in democracy. Evil lies in attempting oppression with a perverse or vain intent. Good lies in making effective the rights of man and of the citizen and in the creation of institutions which guarantee them.... If there is no juridical institution [to do this], dictatorship designed to establish one is humane and just.... But, if there are juridical institutions which guarantee the rights, ... dictatorship is senseless and criminal.[31]

José María Velasco Ibarra was fully aware of his own significance as the indispensable man, the "man with a mission." He did not hesitate to admit that "my destiny is indestructibly tied to the destiny of my country";[32] he was "absolutely convinced that the people are with me, they are all with me.... See me acclaimed by waves of humanity proclaiming democracy!"[33] He once admitted that only 80 per cent of the population of Ecuador supported him. "This figure of eighty per cent is modesty on my part in giving my enemies twenty per cent.... This eighty per cent does not belong to any political party, these men are with me because they know that I do not rob them, I do not lie to them, I work for them day and night."[34] What was the significance of the 1944 revolution in the over-all scheme of the universe? Hear Velasco Ibarra: "On the 28th of May, the people expressed confidence in me, in me

---

[30] *Idem, Conciencia o Barbarie*, p. 27.
[31] *Idem, Experiencias Jurídicas Hispanoamericanas*, pp. 64–65.
[32] *El Comercio*, Quito, March 10, 1944.
[33] Quoted in Girón, *op. cit.*, p. 341.
[34] Quoted in *New York Herald Tribune*, June 13, 1946.

principally. Human waves acclaimed me and urged me to be their leader and president. ... It is certain that I was the center of popular gravitation."[35] When the voters elected a congress hostile to the president, the "National Personification" made clear his position thus: "Circumstances will determine if there will be a congress this year."[36] And if a group of citizens should protest administrative changes in the provinces, what then? "You have absolutely no right to protest because the government has decided to change the governor of Manabí," Velasco Ibarra asserted, and went on: "We are creating a true chaos in Ecuador. Everybody protests against everything."[37] Thus spoke the "National Personification," José María Velasco Ibarra, described by one of the army officers who supported him as a "man of the people, a pure man, the man who is ... the soul of Ecuador. ... Velasco Ibarra was a force of nature, and we had to submit ourselves to that force. The people wanted him and they waited for him and they clamored for him. The army had to identify itself with this will."[38]

Velasco Ibarra's vitality and personal magnetism were best expressed by his phenomenal ability as an orator. He produced an almost hypnotic effect not only upon massed audiences but also upon the members of congress. It was not unusual for throngs to stand entranced in the Plaza de la Independencia listening to the president and apparently oblivious to the pouring rain. "I have been mesmerized by experts," the writer was told by a veteran of Hitler's Germany and Mussolini's Italy, "and I rank Velasco Ibarra high among them." A member of the senate during Velasco Ibarra's first administration told the writer that he too had at times fallen under the president's spell. "I was violently opposed to his policies and uniformly voted against them," he said. "One day, however, President Velasco Ibarra came to congress to deliver personally a message urging passage of one of his projects. ... Never before had I heard such a speech! When it was finished, the president and congress were unashamedly in tears, and we stood up and voted unanimously for his bill. ... On my way home, I scolded myself many times, for I had been such a fool, such a fool, to vote for his insane measure!"

Velasco Ibarra had three major weaknesses as a caudillo. First, he could not command the certain support of leaders of the political parties, all of which he alienated within two years after the 1944 revolution.

---

[35] Velasco Ibarra, *Mensaje Presentado a la Honorable Asamblea Nacional Constituyente, ... 6 de Febrero de 1945* (Quito, 1945), p. 5.
[36] *El Telégrafo*, Guayaquil, June 3, 1947.
[37] *El Comercio*, Quito, September 13, 1944.
[38] Girón, *op. cit.*, pp. 54, 124.

Second, he was unable to straddle the regionalist gulf between Sierra and Coastal "whites." His revolution had been made at Guayaquil, but he was not of the Coast. His Sierra confreres rejected him, partly because he came to power through a Coastal revolution directed against the government with headquarters in the Sierra; Coastal "whites" were opposed to him, partly because he was of the Sierra, and partly because his revolution had unseated the Radical Liberal party (with which Coastal destinies had been intimately associated) and had deposed President Arroyo del Río, a man of some stature and following in the Coast. Third, Velasco Ibarra was not a military man and never could depend with certainty upon the loyal support of the army. Indeed, it was the military that accomplished his second overthrow on August 23, 1947.

THE CONSTITUTIONS OF 1945 AND 1946

Two constitutions were written in Ecuador during the 1944–1947 administration of President José María Velasco Ibarra. The first of these was promulgated on March 6, 1945, and suspended on March 30, 1946; the second entered into force on December 31, 1946, and continued in effect up to the time this book went to press.

Shortly after the 1944 revolution, President Velasco Ibarra announced that a constituent assembly would be elected on July 23 of that year for the purpose of writing a new constitution. The parties which had formed the Ecuadoran Democratic Alliance—the essentially leftist coalition which was responsible for the revolution—were victorious in the election and dominated the constituent body when it convened on August 10. The assembly of 1944–1945 proceeded to confirm Velasco Ibarra as the president of the republic, and from August, 1944, until March, 1945, it labored in desultory fashion to produce the unique document known as the Constitution of 1945.

Like many another written constitution of Ecuador, the 1945 charter was divorced from reality. The short-lived instrument imposed a number of severe checks on the executive, rendering the cabinet partially responsible to congress, establishing a court of constitutional guarantees and a permanent legislative commission to serve as watchdogs against the president, and radically curtailing his veto power. The constitution stated that the "three political tendencies" of the republic—the right, the left, and the center—were to be equally represented as such in the permanent legislative commission and the independent superior electoral tribunal. September 1, 1948, was set as the date on which President

Velasco Ibarra's term would expire, although full and ample power to depose him before then was conferred upon congress in the event that sufficient impeachment charges were brought by the court of constitutional guarantees, the permanent legislative commission, or both. This constitution was promulgated on March 6, 1945. President Velasco Ibarra refused to take a ceremonial oath to support the document, although he "signed it against my personal convictions and only to save the country from evil times."[39]

The work of the constituent assembly of 1944–1945 marked a definitive break between Velasco Ibarra and the leftist elements which had made possible his return to power. The president had told the assembly's opening session that "I am a man of the left, but as a governor I must place myself in the center";[40] and before the constitution makers had been at their labors for many weeks it became apparent that a basic conflict had developed between the predominantly leftist constituent assembly and the more conservative administration of President Velasco Ibarra. In November, 1944, the assembly sent greetings to the government of the Soviet Union on the anniversary of the Russian revolution of 1917, and later passed a resolution of "adhesion to socialism,"[41] both measures being acknowledged by the Soviet government. The break between Velasco Ibarra and the constituent assembly became so serious in the closing months of 1944 that the president threatened to resign if a reconciliation could not be reached.

The Communist and Socialist parties formally resolved in January, 1945, to abstain from participating in the administration of President Velasco Ibarra, a move which signified the dissolution of the Ecuadoran Democratic Alliance, the coalition which had brought about the 1944 revolution. As Communists and Socialists proceeded to resign in large numbers from government posts, the president asserted with some defiance that "bureaucrats who do not agree with the administration can continue resigning." The "National Personification" declared that he would "be no one's puppet. The postulates of the May revolution are clear, and this was done by all the Ecuadoran people, not by any one sector."[42] Widespread rioting and demonstration by rival groups for and against the leftist constituent assembly occurred in the streets of Guayaquil and Quito in January and February. The assembly at length adjourned on March 11, 1945, while a hostile mob milled about outside

---
[39] United Press dispatch, March 6, 1945.
[40] Velasco Ibarra, *Mensaje Presentado a la Honorable Asamblea Nacional Constituyente, ... 10 de Agosto de 1944* (Quito, 1944), p. 3.
[41] *El Comercio*, Quito, November 11, 1944.
[42] *Ibid.*, February 2, 1945.

its doors. Carlos Guevara Moreno, the minister of government, charged the assembly with responsibility for fomenting discontent, infringing on the executive's prerogatives, and hindering the progress of the nation; while President Velasco Ibarra asserted in a radio address that "Ecuadoran leftism is headed toward failure."[43]

The Constitution of 1945 remained in force for a little more than a year, being suspended by presidential decree on March 30, 1946. A few days later the 1906 Constitution was substituted for it on a temporary basis. The leftist parties, which had resolved to defend the 1945 document, joined with the Radical Liberals in publishing on March 31 a joint manifesto signed by the directors of the Socialist, Communist, and Radical Liberal parties, declaring: "Velasco Ibarra, by a voluntary and personal act, on March 30, 1946, has ceased to be the constitutional president of the republic, in directing a manifesto to the nation and publishing a supreme decree by means of which he abandoned the legal order and installed an executive dictatorship, unequivocal and totalitarian in form.... The government of Ecuador... has preferred to destroy institutional order, placing itself above the constitution, ignoring it, and assuming dictatorial functions by its own authoritarian will."[44]

Meanwhile, the Conservatives stepped into the breach by proposing that a new constituent assembly be called to write another constitution. "The maintenance of order and the health and prestige of the republic demand the meeting of a constituent assembly," Conservative party leader Mariano Suárez Veintimilla declared in a letter to Velasco Ibarra. "We petition for the convocation of a constituent assembly under conditions which will make possible the greatest participation of all the citizens."[45]

Velasco Ibarra, announcing that he would "submit absolutely to the pronouncement of the Ecuadoran national will,"[46] signed a decree calling for the election of a new constitution-writing body. The leftist parties, stubbornly wedded to the 1945 charter, resolved to abstain from participation in the election of the new assembly. While Velasco Ibarra might have expected their action, the *coup de grâce* came when the Radical Liberals announced their decision to join forces with the leftists in abstention. Velasco Ibarra's maneuver had boomeranged: it had dropped him into the lap of the Conservative party, the only

[43] United Press dispatch, July 13, 1945.
[44] *El Telégrafo*, Guayaquil, March 31, 1946.
[45] *El Comercio*, Quito, April 9, 1946.
[46] United Press dispatch, April 10, 1946.

organization participating in the 1946 election on a national scale. "It would be absurd to suppose that the Radical Liberals could forget so easily the origin of their political misfortunes," *El Comercio* said editorially, in reference to the revolution of 1944. "Liberalism must march in its own direction and with its own flag."[47]

The voters who went to the polls on June 30, 1946, found that in most provinces it was impossible to vote for any but Conservative candidates for membership in the body which was to write the Constitution of 1946. "The Socialist party, always the sentinel of democracy," this party emphasized in a manifesto published in July, "points out to the Ecuadoran nation and to the progressive nations of the continent that the supposed constituent assembly which will convene on August 10, 1946, is nothing more than an assembly of the Ecuadoran Conservative party, with a few reactionary elements from the present fascist dictatorship, and that, above all, it neither incarnates nor can incarnate the sovereignty or the free and sacred expression of the great Ecuadoran people."[48]

The 1946 constituent assembly, convening in August, confirmed Velasco Ibarra in the presidency until September 1, 1948, and turned to the task of giving the republic its fifteenth constitution. Promulgated "in the name of God," on December 31, the Constitution of 1946 was a moderate instrument. This document is considered at some length in later chapters of this book, but it may be observed at this point that the president was freed from such encumbrances as the court of constitutional guarantees and the permanent legislative commission. Of cardinal significance for the immediate future was the resurrection of the office of vice-president of the republic, absent under the 1945 charter. It was also significant that the Conservative party's chieftain, Dr. Mariano Suárez Veintimilla, was named to that post and charged with the responsibility of succeeding to the presidency in the event that Velasco Ibarra might disappear from the scene.

THE MONTH OF FOUR PRESIDENTS

The bizarre month which came to a close on September 17, 1947, encompassed a period which, in the opinions of a number of Ecuadoran political observers, will drive historians mad. During this brief space of time, the republic's presidential chair was occupied by no fewer than four chief executives: Velasco Ibarra, Colonel Carlos Mancheno, Dr. Mariano Suárez Veintimilla, and Carlos Julio Arosemena.

---

[47] *El Comercio*, Quito, May 22, 1946.
[48] *Ibid.*, July 7, 1946.

The death warrant of the Velasco Ibarra administration was in effect signed by the abstention of the non-Conservative parties from the 1946 election. However, it was not until August 23, 1947, that the president departed in some haste. He was on that date removed from office by a "one-shot revolution" led by Colonel Carlos Mancheno, who had been minister of defense in the Velasco Ibarra cabinet. Mancheno assumed the presidency on the announced ground that "the members of the armed forces see ourselves in the necessity of taking over the government temporarily."[49]

Mancheno, calling himself president and erroneously believing that he had the support of the Radical Liberal party, asserted that "the new government, which is transitory, desires to direct the country along the road of more authentic democracy and respect for the essential guarantees of citizenship, the only manner of achieving the economic, social, and cultural improvement of the Ecuadoran people. To this end I invoke and ask the support of the country's people and armed forces, who at all times and in every emergency have known how to give unequivocal proof of their high patriotic spirit."[50]

However, the Conservatives, under the leadership of Suárez Veintimilla, refused to accept the Mancheno move. Insisting that he was president under the constitution by virtue of Velasco Ibarra's ouster, Suárez Veintimilla issued a call for a special session of congress to meet in September. The Conservatives and other anti-Mancheno partisans of the Constitution of 1946, dubbing themselves "Constitutionalists," organized in support of Suárez Veintimilla, who offered assurances that he sought only to rescue constitutional processes and that he would present his resignation from the presidency when congress met. "For perfectly known reasons and in compliance with the duties placed upon me by the constitution, I have had to assume the office of president of the republic, with the support of the citizenry," Suárez Veintimilla asserted in a circular letter to provincial and local authorities. "The only way to maintain constitutional government ... is to require the meeting of ... congress, which I have convoked."[51]

An attempt to reconcile the rival points of view was made on August 28, when Mancheno met with Suárez Veintimilla to discuss the issues. But no common ground could be reached, and force of arms was to decide the controversy. On September 1 a communique of the Mancheno

---

[49] Associated Press dispatch, August 24, 1947.
[50] *El Comercio*, Quito, August 28, 1947. The texts of executive decrees normally appear in the *Registro Oficial*, which was not published during the Mancheno period. *El Comercio*, however, carries the full texts of most measures of major consequence.
[51] *El Comercio*, Quito, August 28, 1947.

regime reported that "in the city of Riobamba there appeared yesterday a small seditious center, whose leaders are the directors of the Conservative party. The government maintains absolute control of the situation in the rest of the republic."[52] The "small seditious center" grew rapidly, however, and Mancheno declared a state of siege on the night of September 1, assuring his supporters that his regime possessed sufficient strength to dominate the opposition forces. To Mancheno's dismay, the strategic Ninth Infantry Battalion, stationed at Guayaquil, joined the "Constitutionalists," radically altering the military picture. The anti-Mancheno revolt was general in five major provinces by daybreak on September 2. On the following day, Mancheno resigned and departed for Argentina, his minister of labor, Luis Maldonado Tamayo, observing with some hopelessness that "I have been left in charge of a rear-guard political action."[53]

"Constitutionalist" forces entered Quito in triumph late on September 2, installing Suárez Veintimilla in the executive office. He reiterated his intention to present his resignation to congress, which convened on September 15.

The "caudillist process" had run a representative sector of its course. It stood in a position which clearly revealed the underlying nature of Ecuador's "real" constitution: the lowly Indian, though he had missed the excitement, and the superior "white" had, each in his own way, created the curious matrix of the political system of Ecuador. The Indian had figuratively come from his fields and the Spaniard had come from his ships, and together they had welded a new political order. Each had contributed the only governmental system he knew—absolute monarchy. Yet the product of this cultural fusion in twentieth-century Ecuador was something less than monarchy: Huayna Capac and Charles V had ruled empires which emerged from a firm and stable pattern of legitimacy. This hereditary principle had been lost by their cultural heirs. Rejecting the formulas of San Martín and Bolívar, Ecuadorans lived in the remnants of absolute monarchy, which—shorn of the hereditary principle and containing no formalized system to replace it as a method of succession—they called a republic. The legislators who gathered in the bar of the Hotel Majestic at Quito on September 15, 1947, were in the habit of saying that the Indian was cut off from the "national life." They greatly revered Aristotle, but they had forgotten his observation that a constitution was the arrangement of the inhabitants of a state.

[52] *Ibid.*, September 1, 1947.
[53] Associated Press dispatch, September 3, 1947.

These legislators could be forgiven for ignoring such things on September 15, 1947, for a more immediate problem commanded their attention. In all of Ecuador there was no caudillo, no monarch to wear the republican dress. It was necessary to find a "constitutional president," and Carlos Julio Arosemena had been most uncoöperative. He had painstakingly pointed out that he was no politician and had neither thirst for power nor political ambition. He was a banker and a philanthropist, he lived at Guayaquil, he loved the Coast. He did not wish to journey to the lonely, silent, and "backward" Sierra. He had thought it highly quixotic of the congressional delegation to insist that those were the very reasons why he ought to become the president of the republic. At length he acceded to the legislators' pleas, but on the very firm and definite condition that he would be absent from the Coast only until the expiration of what was to have been Velasco Ibarra's four-year term, and not one day more, even if it meant leaving the presidency utterly and completely vacant. "I am unable to offer grandiose programs, nor do I wish to make gallant promises," President Arosemena said in his inaugural address on September 17, 1947. "Detached from all political aggrandizement, I come to the presidency with no obligation other than my contract with the republic."[54]

During his brief administration, Carlos Julio Arosemena performed a service of large significance for the nation, as described in the latter part of the following chapter. But it seems certain that the determiners of public policy who sip rum in the bar of the Hotel Majestic a generation or two in the future will be able to recall with facility the name of José María Velasco Ibarra, while that of the little banker-philanthropist from the Coast will have slipped from the memory of man.

[54] *El Comercio*, Quito, September 18, 1947.

CHAPTER IV
PARTIES AND ELECTIONS

PARTY POLITICS in Ecuador mirrors more or less accurately the social and economic structure of the republic. Only "whites"—a small percentage of them—are active in the political parties. The great mass of the people of the country—Indians, cholos, montuvios, and Negroes—exercise no direct influence on national politics.

ECUADORAN PARTY POLITICS

In the absence of a national population census, only estimates of the "white" percentage of the population are available. Most of Ecuador's more competent students of social problems calculate that the "whites" number somewhere between 350,000 and 500,000; and few estimates place the figure at more than 20 per cent of the country's people. Relatively few of the members of this upper class actively participate in national politics. Prieto, whose estimate places the number of "whites" at 400,000, has endeavored to subdivide this figure to determine what proportion of the "whites" is engaged in government and politics. He calculates that 150,000 of the "whites" are children; that 50,000 are "non-productive adults"; that 170,000 are engaged in agriculture, commerce, industry, and letters; and that 30,000 are "bureaucrats." The term "bureaucrats," as employed by Prieto, includes all officials and employees of the national, provincial, and local governments; all persons holding posts in the hierarchies of the various political parties; and all members of the armed forces, not including the noncommissioned personnel of the national police force. It is probably true, regardless of the validity of Prieto's figures, that not more than 350 or 400 Ecuadorans, all of them "whites," are active members of the political parties of the republic.

Since national politics and the political parties belong exclusively to the "white" group, they are in a sense little more than vehicles for the conduct of the intra-class struggle which is the essence of the Ecuadoran political system. "The soul of the people remains indifferent toward this fight," it has been said. "It would be absurd to imagine national liberal or conservative policies: we know the Sierra group and the Coastal group; ... militarism and civilism; ... but to think of a joint

---
[1] Jorge Prieto A., *Bases de Reconstrucción Nacional* (Guayaquil, 1945), pp. 19–20. It may be noted in this connection that Ecuador's 1949 budget placed the number of employees of the eight executive ministries at 36,705 persons.

aspiration or a polarization of these groups toward a political objective is to think of something which does not exist."[3] Ecuadoran politics reflects few issues beyond personal rivalries and regionalism.

Personalismo, adherence to a leader through personal and individual motivations rather than because of common support of an idea or political program, is a fundamental characteristic of the country's politics. Most government workers are commonly regarded as the direct employees of the president of the republic; expenditures decreed by him are frequently viewed as his personal gifts. This aspect of Ecuadoran politics dominates the organization and function of the country's political parties.

Regionalism also plays its part in politics. The divisive nature of this factor has long been recognized by Ecuadorans as an evil, and the national parties have frequently regarded the bridging of the regionalist abyss as one of their leading objectives. No Ecuadoran political party has yet successfully straddled the western cordillera of the Andes. The Sierra and the Coast continue to go their own ways in politics as in other matters: parties which strive for an interregional base generally find that they have been captured by one or the other of the major regions of Ecuador. Though a party employ any of a number of devices (as, for example, running a representative of each of the two major regions for president and vice-president, respectively, on the same ticket) in an attempt to become "national," failure in this project has been a frequent result. Ecuador's two major political parties have not bridged the gap; regardless of protestations to the contrary, the Conservatives are the party of the Sierra and the Radical Liberals are the party of the Coast.

Power, for an individual or for a region, is the immediate end of all Ecuadoran politics. It must be said in justice to some political leaders that they are concerned with larger matters than personal and regional benefits, but these leaders are inevitably caught up in the system. Thus, a man who raises the abstract ideas which a broad political program normally entails is, as Ecuadorans like to say, "divorced from reality." The elite eschew the politician wedded to doctrinal and ideological ideals as a new and frequently dangerous Don Quixote.

Within the Ecuadoran pattern, the basic function of a political party is to coördinate the activities of the "whites" as they relate to government. The two principal aspects of this function are (1) an attempt to bridge the regional barriers between Sierra and Coastal "whites"; and

---

[3] Pérez Guerrero, *op. cit.,* pp. 103–104.

(2) an attempt to preserve a harmonious relationship among the instruments of power serving the "whites," and thus guard the group's dominant position. The extent to which the interregional attempt has failed has already been suggested. One measure of its success lies in the inescapable fact that one state exists where there easily might have been two. Moreover, the political parties have been relatively successful in securing a consonant relationship among the "whites'" major instruments of power. Spokesmen for such institutions as landownership, the armed forces, formal education and the professions, and the Roman Catholic Church are so distributed among the major Ecuadoran parties as to provide a species of political equilibrium.

The republic's political parties are thus to be considered against a threefold background: (1) They provide a vehicle for the operation within the "white" group of the intra-class struggle which forms the chaotic and unstable base of Ecuadoran politics. (2) Party politics, like the intra-class struggle it reflects, is conducted on the basis of personal and regional rivalries rather than ideas or ideals. (3) The basic function of Ecuadoran political parties is to coördinate the activities of the "whites" as they relate to government.

Political Parties

The Ecuadoran party system sidesteps the familiar dichotomy of bi-party and multi-party systems. It may be said with equal truth, depending on the emphasis adopted, that *both* bi-party and multi-party systems exist in Ecuador, or that *neither* of these systems exists. The paradox stems from the fact that the political organizations in Ecuador are not all "political parties" in the same sense, although that term is indiscriminately applied to most of them.

Ecuadoran political parties may be classified into three groups: "major" parties, "third" parties, and "ad hoc" or temporary parties. The two "major" parties are the Conservative and the Radical Liberal parties. Ecuadorans refer to them as the country's "historic" parties. Their organization is relatively stable and formalized, and they have been in existence for a sufficiently long time to have acquired significant roles in the political history of the republic. Historians generally refer to the period before 1895 as the era of Conservative rule, and to the years between 1895 and 1944 as the period of Radical Liberal rule. Neither "major" party has been in power on a national scale since 1944.

Two "third" parties, the Socialists and the Communists, exist in Ecuador. They resemble the "major" parties in having been in operation for a relatively long time and having an organization that is somewhat stable and formalized. They are unlike the "major" parties in that they normally are weak and draw only small percentages of the votes cast in elections.

The picture is completed by a number of "ad hoc" parties, brought into brief existence for the purpose of achieving short-range political objectives. Representative of "ad hoc" parties which have been active in recent years are the National Civic Democratic Movement (popularly known as M.C.D.N.), the Socialist Revolutionary Vanguard, the Ecuadoran Nationalist Revolutionary Association (A.R.N.E.), and the Ecuadoran Nationalist Revolutionary Union (U.N.R.E.). A combination of some "ad hoc" parties with the "third" parties staged the revolution of 1944, and an "ad hoc" organization won the presidential election of 1948.

THE CONSERVATIVE PARTY

The Ecuadoran Conservative party, which dominated national politics until the revolution of 1895, has been gaining in strength since 1944. In 1948, 34 per cent of the members of congress were Conservatives; and the party's candidate, Manuel Sotomayor y Luna, was elected vice-president of the republic.

The structural organization of the Conservative party roughly reflects the nation's governmental and administrative subdivisions. Party organs exist on the national level and in the provinces, cantons, and parishes. Two organizational units of the party, the general assembly and the general directorate, operate on the highest of these four levels.

The general assembly, which meets regularly once every two years, is roughly analogous to the national convention of one of the major parties of the United States. It nominates the Conservative candidates for the presidency and the vice-presidency of the republic, determines the general policy and strategy of the party with reference to national issues, and elects the members of the party's general directorate. The general assembly contains at least seventy-two members, including four representatives from the party's organs in each of the seventeen provinces, and one delegate from each of Ecuador's four universities. Also, at times when the party has formed a coalition or other working arrangement with one or more other political parties, each coöperating organization is entitled to send two delegates to the general assembly of the Conservative party.

The party's general directorate exercises functions similar to those of the national committee of either major party of the United States.

The general directorate, within policy lines laid down by the general assembly, instructs lesser organs and affiliates of the party in their duties and tactics, convokes emergency sessions of the general assembly, and serves as the agency of liaison between the party and those of its affiliates who may hold positions in the government. The general directorate is composed of seven members, including and presided over by the director general of the Conservative party. The members are elected for two-year terms by the general assembly.

The Conservative party maintains a provincial assembly and a provincial directorate in each of the seventeen provinces of Ecuador. The membership of the provincial assemblies varies in size, depending on the number of cantons in each province. The provincial assembly, meeting regularly once each year, is composed of three delegates from each canton, elected for two-year terms by the cantonal assemblies. The provincial assembly nominates the party's candidates from the province for the national senate[3] and chamber of deputies, directs the party's affairs within the province, and elects the members of the provincial directorate.

The provincial directorate of the Conservative party in each province is composed of seven members, who are charged with the tasks of designating the party's candidates for the provincial council, coördinating the activities of the party's cantonal directorates within the province, and calling emergency or special meetings of the provincial assembly. The provincial directorate submits an annual report on its activities to the provincial assembly, and a monthly report to the general directorate.

Cantonal assemblies and directorates are theoretically maintained by the Conservative party in all cantons of the republic, but either or both are lacking in many Oriente cantons and in other areas where Conservative voters are virtually nonexistent. All Conservative voters resident in a given canton theoretically constitute the party's assembly for that canton, and are expected to meet in this capacity at least once each year. The cantonal assembly nominates the party's candidates for the cantonal council, sends three delegates to the appropriate provincial assembly, and elects the members of the cantonal directorate.

In each canton where it exists, the cantonal directorate of the Conservative party convokes meetings of the cantonal assembly, if there is one; submits a monthly report to the appropriate provincial directorate; appoints the Conservative parish chiefs to the parishes under its juris-

---

[3] Conservative candidates for senators representing provinces are nominated in this way, but Conservative aspirants for the posts of "functional senators" are not. Cf. p. 106, below.

diction; and in general coördinates and directs the political activities of Conservative residents of the canton.

Each canton is divided into a number of parishes. A Conservative parish junta and parish chief theoretically exist in each of these, but are actually lacking in many. The parish junta is composed of all the Conservative voters in the parish, and meets at least once a year to consider parish problems as they relate to the party. The parish chief, if any, directs Conservative activities in the parish, presides over meetings of the parish junta, and keeps the appropriate cantonal directorate informed of the political situation in his parish.

Observers who have watched the Conservative party in operation are generally impressed by the extent to which custom and tradition govern the party machinery. The Conservatives are the oldest and best-established party, and their written statutes have done little more than transcribe practices dictated by generations of usage. The rank-and-file members have a greater voice in decisions than do those of any of the other parties. The strength of custom and tradition, however, generally causes them to pay considerable deference to the views and wishes of "old guard" leaders—persons who have been active as party regulars for a great number of years, and who have been Conservative in terms of their family and regional heritages. This "old guard" normally dominates the general directorate, which plays a major role in the determination of the party's destinies. Yet the Conservative general assembly exercises greater influence in its party than the allegedly deliberative bodies of the other parties do in theirs.

The Conservative party, its strength localized in the Sierra, has long been the political spokesman of the Church, and has regarded the proclerical Gabriel García Moreno as the greatest of its heroes. "Man is essentially a religious being and religion, consequently, is a natural phenomenon," a prominent party leader has written, in exposition of Conservative doctrine. "The end of man is God, whom he should serve and adore in order to enjoy after death the beatified possession of divinity. . . . The purpose of the state is to facilitate religious action so that its subjects will not lack the necessities of the spirit and will be able to obtain in the next life the happiness which can never be achieved in this."[4] The Conservatives hold that there is an innate right to private property, and that man is civilized so far as he possesses tradition.

The days of Conservative domination appeared to have ended with the revolution of 1895, but the party's fortunes took a turn for the better

---

[4] Jacinto Jijón y Caamaño, *Política Conservadora* (Riobamba, 1934), Vol. I, 26, 32.

after the Velasco Ibarra revolution of 1944, which removed the Radical Liberals from power. Among the first to sense the long-range significance of that upheaval was deposed President Carlos Alberto Arroyo del Río himself, who declared: "With the fall of [Radical] Liberalism, the Conservative party will be the one to gain from the situation, ... Dr. Velasco Ibarra has had the sad honor of playing the role of the Trojan horse for the penetration of clericalism and the resurrection of the religious problem."[5] Participation by the clergy in political affairs has increased markedly, notably in the Sierra, since 1944; and in 1949 the Conservatives were probably stronger than they had been at any other time since 1895.

Conservative leadership since 1944, largely in the hands of Mariano Suárez Veintimilla and Jacinto Jijón y Caamaño, has been both astute and fortunate. Joining the leftist Ecuadoran Democratic Alliance on the eve of the Velasco Ibarra revolution, the Conservatives played only a minor part in that coup; but the new president, in paying his political debt to the parties of the alliance, conferred the post of treasury minister in his cabinet upon Suárez Veintimilla. The Conservative party formally withdrew from the alliance within two weeks after the 1944 revolution, but Suárez Veintimilla retained his post in the Velasco Ibarra cabinet for more than a year, during which he was influential in the formative stages of the new administration. In mid-1945 he resigned from the cabinet on the express orders of the general directorate of the Conservative party.

Nationwide municipal elections in November of 1945 resulted in a resounding Conservative victory in many areas, particularly in the Sierra, where Jijón y Caamaño was elected mayor of Quito. The political composition of the capital city's municipal council early in 1946 (eight Conservatives, two Socialists, and one Communist) set the pace for continued rapid increases in Conservative strength among the voters, a trend illustrated by the congressional election in June of 1947. The Conservatives enhanced their position by supporting in the constituent assembly of 1946 a motion to retain Velasco Ibarra in the presidency, and further entrenched themselves by electing Suárez Veintimilla to the vice-presidency in January, 1947. The Conservatives were thus able to emerge in triumph from 1947's chaotic "month of four presidents." Nationwide municipal elections in November of that year gave new successes to Conservatives, as did the election in 1948 of their candidate, Manuel Sotomayor y Luna, to the vice-presidency of the republic.

---

[5] Arroyo del Río, *Bajo el Imperio del Odio* (Bogotá, 1946), p. 37; and Arroyo del Río, *En Plena Vorágine* (Bogotá, 1948), p. 47.

THE RADICAL LIBERAL PARTY

The Radical Liberal party of Ecuador, in power almost uninterruptedly from 1895 to 1944, has been significantly weakened since the latter date. In 1948 only 34 per cent of the members of congress were Radical Liberals. Traditionally the party of the Coast, the Radical Liberals have been weakened and demoralized since their overthrow in the revolution of 1944.

The structural organization of the Radical Liberals, like that of the Conservatives, is patterned after the territorial divisions of the republic. A Radical Liberal assembly and a supreme junta exist on the national level; there is a provincial junta in each of the seventeen provinces; and cantonal and parish juntas are theoretically located in all cantons and parishes of Ecuador.

The assembly, nominally the supreme authority of the party, is composed of fifty-one delegates, three being chosen for two-year terms by each of the provincial juntas. The assembly, meeting regularly once every two years, nominates the Radical Liberal candidates for president and vice-president, and determines the national strategy and tactics of the party.

The supreme junta of the Radical Liberal party is composed of seven members, including the director general of the party, who presides over meetings of the junta. The members are elected for two-year terms by the assembly. There are in addition five advisers to the supreme junta, appointed by the junta itself. This body represents the Radical Liberal party in all national political matters, and determines the strategy of the party when the assembly is not in session. The supreme junta keeps Radical Liberal members of congress informed of the party's attitude on matters before the legislators, and when necessary calls special sessions of the assembly. The supreme junta maintains control of provincial and local units of the party by supervising and distributing instructions to the Radical Liberal provincial juntas.

The number of members in each of the seventeen provincial juntas varies according to the size and social complexity of the province, and the number of cantons in it. Members of the provincial junta (including the provincial director, who presides over its sessions) are elected for two-year terms, the junta being renewed by halves in Radical Liberal primaries held on June 5 of each year. The integrity of these elections varies according to the political situation in each province. The provincial junta nominates the province's Radical Liberal candidates for the senate,[6] the chamber of deputies, and the provincial council. The junta also carries out in the province instructions received from the assembly, the supreme junta, and the director general of the party, and defends Radical Liberal interests in the province. A large part of this last function consists of supervising the work of the cantonal juntas.

Juntas are theoretically established in all cantons of the republic except those which contain provincial capitals, where the provincial junta operates on both provincial and cantonal levels. Actually, however, there are no juntas in many cantons of the Oriente and other areas where Radical Liberal strength is almost nonexistent. The size of the cantonal junta varies considerably from canton to canton, and members are elected for two-year terms, each cantonal junta being renewed by halves in the annual primaries on June 5. The cantonal junta nominates the Radical Liberal candidates for the cantonal councils, and executes in the canton the orders and instructions received from the assembly, the supreme junta, and the appropriate provincial junta. The cantonal junta also controls Radical Liberal activities in the parishes under its jurisdiction by appointing the chairmen of parish juntas and overseeing their work.

The lowest position in the hierarchy of the Radical Liberal party is occupied by the parish junta, which is established in all parishes containing party followers. All Radical Liberals in the parish theoretically constitute this junta, but for practical purposes all party authority on the parish level is vested in the chairman of the parish junta, who is appointed and supervised by the appropriate cantonal junta.

The Radical Liberals' tables of formal organization are to a certain extent misleading. Although it is asserted that the assembly possesses supreme authority within the party, in actual practice this body is normally subservient to the supreme junta, and frequently does little more than rubber-stamp the previous decisions of the latter. This became the case with increasing notoriety during the twenty years immediately preceding the revolution of 1944, with the result that the party's formal machinery became a mere tool in the hands of the president of the republic, who normally dominated the supreme junta. This condition contributed to political corruption and electoral fraud on a steadily expanding scale which culminated in the fiasco that was to have been the election of 1944. President Arroyo del Río's manipulation of the party machinery in the campaign of that year has been noted in the

---
[6] Radical Liberal candidates for senators representing provinces are nominated in this way, but Radical Liberal aspirants for the posts of "functional senators" are not. Cf. p. 106, below.

preceding chapter. The demoralization and disintegration of the Radical Liberals in the years since their overthrow in 1944 have tended to reduce the supreme junta's hold on the party, and the assembly was able to exercise considerable initiative in the nomination of candidates for the election of 1948.

Principles formally endorsed by the Radical Liberal party include the right to life, liberty of conscience, free expression of thought, liberty of labor, and the right of association. The party has also defended the principle of private ownership of land and other forms of property.

The major doctrinal difference between the Radical Liberals and the Conservatives has revolved around the question of the Church, the Radical Liberals championing the separation of Church and State. The principal difference between these two major parties, in terms of the realities of the power situation in Ecuador, resides in regionalism. The Conservatives are based in the Sierra, the Radical Liberals in the Coast. From the standpoint of the national economy, both parties rest on the institution of landownership, although the Conservatives do so more exclusively than the Radical Liberals, who have been more interested in the development of trade and industry in Ecuador, and the attraction of foreign capital to the country.

The Radical Liberal party of Ecuador was founded on September 8, 1878, by General Ignacio de Veintimilla. Its fortunes since that date have ranged between jubilant victory and demoralizing and humiliating defeat. The party counts some fifteen variously glorious revolts as major milestones in its history. Outstanding among these is the definitive and decisive revolution of 1895, in which the Radical Liberals, led by the redoubtable General Eloy Alfaro—the party's major historic hero—put an end to generations of Conservative rule.

The party remained in power for almost half a century, during which it endeavored to reduce the political influence of the Church and to add to landownership such elements of economic strength as commerce and the rudiments of industry. For the Radical Liberals, however, power eventually brought ossification and degeneration. Carlos Alberto Arroyo del Río, the most recent of the Radical Liberal presidents, inherited an aging and decrepit party, and his administration did little to improve it. Against this background of institutional decadence, the Radical Liberals were deposed by the Velasco Ibarra revolution of May 28, 1944.

The years since that debacle have brought continued disruption and despair to the Radical Liberals, a condition which no amount of reshuffling of the party's assembly and juntas has been able to alter. The elections since 1944 have reflected a persistent decline in Radical Liberal strength, and many politicians have deserted the party. This phenomenon has become the subject of editorials and political cartoons in the nation's press. One newspaper, following the Radical Liberal rout in the nationwide municipal elections in November of 1947, published a cartoon depicting the party as a ship from which the crew were departing in large numbers, ignoring the plea of the faithful that "the fact that we cannot see the horizon is no reason for abandoning the ship."[7]

"THIRD" PARTIES

The "third" parties, the Socialists and the Communists, formed the nucleus of the Ecuadoran Democratic Alliance, which staged the Velasco Ibarra revolution. These parties enjoyed a brief period of power immediately after that upheaval, but since 1946 have suffered a fate similar to that of the Radical Liberals.

The Socialist party of Ecuador was founded on July 9, 1925, and throughout most of its history has been an opposition party. Sixteen per cent of the members of congress in 1948 were Socialists. This party, according to its own pronouncements, "is a Marxist political organization of a permanent character ... which fights, under norms of collective discipline, for the integral elimination of the exploitation of man by man."[8] The Socialists are the only party in the republic whose tables of organization recognize the existence of the Ecuadoran Indians. Within the forty-eight-man Socialist congress, provision is made for two "functional representatives" of the Indians. These representatives are not themselves Indians, be it noted; for the Socialists, like the Conservatives, Radical Liberals, and others, have agreed that the Indian is cut off from the "national life." Nevertheless, many of Ecuador's *indigenistas*, interested in aiding the Indian, have become affiliated with the Socialists on the ground that this is the only party indicating a concern with the problem of the Indian.

Perhaps nowhere in the country's politics is the verbalistic nature of Ecuadoran political doctrines better illustrated than in the Socialist party. The party's program, according to one of its spokesmen, reflects "the influence of Soviet socialism. ... Reference is made to 'big business,' to 'capitalist concentration,' etc., phenomena which can be studied in capitalist countries like the United States, Germany, and England, but"—and here is localized the doctrinal dilemma of the Socialists of

---

[7] *El Telégrafo*, Guayaquil, November 17, 1947.
[8] XIII Congreso del Partido Socialista Ecuatoriano, *Estatutos del Partido Socialista Ecuatoriano* (Quito, 1946), Art. 1.

Ecuador—"which do not exist in our country, with its incipient industry and its predominantly agrarian and pastoral economy."⁹ Velasco Ibarra has said: "The Socialist party does not really exist in Ecuador. Of course, there are many who are called Socialists and who are said to be members of the Socialist party. But there is no real socialism. . . . Above all, socialism is a sentiment, a sentiment of piety, of generosity."¹⁰

The small and weak Communist party of Ecuador controlled three members of congress in 1948. In recent domestic politics the Communists have intermittently coöperated with the Socialists, but in matters of foreign affairs the Communists have uniformly urged Ecuadoran-Soviet collaboration. In 1945 the party took the lead in pressing for Ecuadoran ratification of the Charter of the United Nations. On August 21 of that year, the Communists petitioned the foreign office at Quito to demand immediate withdrawal of United States military and naval forces from bases in the Galápagos Islands, and repeatedly raised this issue until the United States relinquished the bases in 1948. The Ecuadoran Communists have agitated consistently against "Yankee imperialism" since the end of World War II.

The Socialists and Communists dominated the constituent assembly of 1944–1945, which wrote the Constitution of 1945. Their decline was symbolized by Velasco Ibarra's destruction of the 1945 charter in March, 1946, since which time the frustrated Socialists and Communists have returned to impotent opposition. The suspension of the Constitution of 1945 marked the second time within a decade that Socialists and Communists had achieved power only to lose it shortly after their victory. In 1938 they had won an election; but their leftist congress, unable to agree on one of its members to serve as president of the republic, in tragic desperation "awoke Aurelio Mosquera Narváez, the *titular head of the* [*Radical*] *Liberal Party,* and informed him, to his utter and absolute amazement, that they had elected him constitutional President of Ecuador!"¹¹

Perhaps from the leftist point of view the tragedy of 1944–1946 was even greater than that of 1938. Achieving the stewardship of the nation in the hard-won revolution of 1944, they again delivered the presidency to a non-leftist, Velasco Ibarra, only to suffer cruel treatment at his hands. So far as leftist aspirations were embodied in the Constitution of 1945, they were ruthlessly crushed in 1946. The story is poignantly

---
⁹ Luis Maldonado Estrada, *Socialismo Ecuatoriano* (Guayaquil, 1935), p. 36. Also, cf. *idem, Bases del Partido Socialista Ecuatoriano* (Quito, 1938).
¹⁰ Velasco Ibarra, *Conciencia o Barbarie,* pp. 50–51.
¹¹ Franklin, *op. cit.,* p. 305.

told by the position of the Socialist party a year after the revolution of 1944. Asked if his group would participate in a planned national observance of the first anniversary of the revolution, a Socialist spokesman declared flatly: "This party does not see any reason for popular rejoicing or for any big celebration."[12] The Socialists, with the Communists, had returned to opposition and a species of oblivion.

"AD HOC" PARTIES

Ecuadoran "ad hoc" parties, extremely fluid organizations created for the purpose of achieving short-range political objectives and disappearing when these ends have been accomplished or defeated, exist in varying numbers at different times. It is normally impossible—and unrewarding—to determine the exact number of these organizations operating at any given moment. Nine of them were probably in existence on the eve of the election of 1948. Entities such as these prompted the inspired observation in 1942 that "in these times, nothing is simpler than to found a political party. To form a political party only three people and one object are necessary: a president, a vice-president, a secretary, and a rubber stamp. The party can get along even without the vice-president and the secretary.... There have been cases in which the existence of only the rubber stamp has been sufficient."[13] These organizations may be of the extreme right or the extreme left, and are occasionally located near the center of the political spectrum. Rightist "ad hoc" organizations are typified by the Ecuadoran Nationalist Revolutionary Union (U.N.R.E.) and the Ecuadoran Nationalist Revolutionary Association (A.R.N.E.); leftist groups are exemplified by the Socialist Revolutionary Vanguard and the Popular Union; and the National Civic Democratic Movement would serve as an example of a transitory party closer to the political center.

A discussion of the National Civic Democratic Movement (popularly known as the M.C.D.N.[14]) would illustrate the role played in Ecuadoran politics by "ad hoc" parties. The M.C.D.N. was established on May 16, 1947, for the specific purpose of preventing the Conservative party from returning to power after the fall of the Radical Liberals. The disruption of the latter party and the disappearance of the Ecuadoran Democratic Alliance, itself a transitory organization, had threatened to leave the

---
[12] United Press dispatch, May 22, 1945.
[13] Luis Terán Gómez, *Los Partidos Políticos y su Acción Democrática* (La Paz, 1942), pp. 60–61. The quoted observation was made with reference to political parties in Ecuador, Peru, and Bolivia.
[14] *Movimiento Cívico Democrático Nacional*.

field open to the Conservatives. All politicians interested in forestalling the Conservatives' resumption of national domination were invited to join the M.C.D.N. The new organization ran candidates for the first time in the congressional election of June 1, 1947; though the results were disappointing to M.C.D.N. affiliates, the Conservatives were prevented from obtaining a majority in either chamber of the national legislature. A second election (nationwide municipal contests in November of 1947) resulted in most areas in crushing defeats for the M.C.D.N. and victories for the Conservatives, the latter occurring primarily in the Sierra.

The battered M.C.D.N. then marshaled its forces for what its leaders regarded as the crucial test—the presidential and vice-presidential election scheduled for June 6, 1948. All anti-Conservative elements were urged to adhere to the M.C.D.N. as the campaign began to take form. Dissident Radical Liberals, many Socialists, and even some liberal Conservatives allied with the M.C.D.N. as the date of the election approached. When the official results of the election were made known, it was apparent that the M.C.D.N. was only partially successful in its attempt to impede the Conservative advance. The M.C.D.N. had, in the view of anti-Conservatives, rescued the presidency; but the Conservatives had captured the vice-presidency. Leaders of the M.C.D.N. announced in August of 1948 that their organization would remain in existence as long as necessary to hold the presidency beyond Conservative reach.

The long-range significance of the M.C.D.N. remained uncertain at the time this book was written. It appeared, however, that this "ad hoc" organization would perform either of two functions in the post-1944 development of Ecuadoran politics: (1) The M.C.D.N., if eventually successful, might fight a heroic delaying action, giving the broken and demoralized Radical Liberals time to regroup and revitalize their forces preparatory to reëstablishing something of the pre-1944 equilibrium. (2) Failing this, the M.C.D.N. might be expected to ease the post-1944 transition from Radical Liberal to Conservative rule. Such a function might conceivably reduce the political instability in contemporary Ecuador. At any rate, the historic significance of the revolution of 1944 appeared to depend on what would happen to the M.C.D.N. in the years after 1948.

ELECTIONS

Ecuadoran elections, superficially considered, have been characterized by a chronic lack of integrity. Some Ecuadorans have voiced perplexity that otherwise honest men frequently exhibit few or no scruples in accepting public offices conferred upon them through manifest electoral fraud. It seems obvious, however, that elections have been provided for only by the country's "written" constitutions. Under the "real" constitution, as has been indicated in an earlier chapter, national officials are often chosen in quite another manner. The politician who acquires public office after a fraudulent election is not necessarily depraved. The fraudulent election is an accommodatory device, an instrument of adjustment which permits Ecuador to retain a "written" constitution in addition to the "real" constitution. The caudillo and his associates frequently acquire public office through revolution or fraudulent election; the "constitutional president" and his collaborators normally achieve office by means of the electoral process as established by the written laws of the republic.

The Constitution of 1946 and supplementary legislation entrusted the administration of the "electoral function" to an autonomous set of tribunals and boards. These hierarchically organized bodies are the supreme electoral tribunal, seventeen provincial electoral tribunals, parish registration boards, and local electoral boards.

The seven members of the supreme electoral tribunal are chosen in a manner designed to implement the autonomy of the body, three members being elected by congress, two appointed by the president of the republic, and the remaining two designated by the supreme court.[15] Members of the tribunal have four-year terms, and may not resign without the consent of the organs of government which selected them. The supreme electoral tribunal is charged with general supervision of the electoral process, and is empowered to interpret the laws treating of elections, investigate and determine the disposition of cases involving irregularities or fraud, and count the votes in elections of president and vice-president of the republic. The supreme electoral tribunal designates the members and supervises the work of the provincial electoral tribunals.

One provincial electoral tribunal, composed of five members designated for two-year terms, is established in the capital of each of the seventeen provinces. The provincial electoral tribunal supervises the conduct of elections in its province, serves as a court of first instance in all cases involving electoral irregularity or fraud, and counts the ballots in elections of provincial senators, deputies, provincial councilors, and mayors.

---

[15] Each appointing or electing authority also designates two *suplentes* or alternates for each incumbent member it names to the supreme electoral tribunal. Any incumbent member who dies, resigns, or for any other reason is unable to participate in the work of the tribunal is replaced by the appropriate suplente.

A parish registration board theoretically exists[16] in each parish of the republic. This body, composed of three persons designated by the appropriate provincial electoral tribunal, issues identification cards to qualified voters and maintains an up-to-date list of registered voters of the parish.

One local electoral board is maintained in each district containing roughly six hundred voters. Electoral districting generally follows parish lines, electoral districts frequently being territorially coterminous with parishes. The local electoral board, composed of three members chosen by the appropriate provincial electoral tribunal, operates one polling place (popularly called a *mesa*) on election day, and makes a preliminary count of the votes at the close of the balloting.

The question of who may vote in Ecuador rests upon the distinction in the republic's constitutional law between "nationality" and "citizenship." The former, connoting an essentially passive relationship between the individual and the state, signifies little more than membership in the state. The Ecuadoran "national" is a person who lives in the country, is subject to its laws, and owes no obedience or allegiance to the government of any other state. Citizenship, on the other hand, presumes greater activity in the relationship. The Ecuadoran "citizen" participates in political affairs: he votes, and he runs for and holds office. "Nationality indicates the *experiencing* of political rights," a constitutional lawyer has explained, "and citizenship the *exercise* of them."[17] For most purposes, it may be said that the Ecuadoran citizen is the national who has the obligation or privilege of voting. All Ecuadoran citizens are nationals; a very small percentage of the country's nationals are citizens. Moreover, the citizens are almost exclusively "whites."

Under the Constitution of 1946, every Ecuadoran national, regardless of sex, who is over eighteen years of age and able to read and write Spanish is a citizen. The vote is compulsory for male and optional for female citizens. The only citizens who may not vote are judges and members of the armed forces.[18] Normally, about 5 per cent of the estimated population votes: 8.32 per cent voted in the election of 1948.

Women citizens vote in small numbers. They have specifically been given the privilege to vote by four of Ecuador's fifteen constitutions: the Constitution of 1883, which was in force for fourteen years; the

---

[16] Oriente parishes containing no voters contain no parish registration boards.

[17] Francisco Zevallos Reyre, *Lecciones de Derecho Constitucional* (Guayaquil, 1947), p. 133. Italics mine.

[18] For legal purposes the national police force is not regarded as a part of the armed forces.

Constitution of 1929, in force for six years; the Constitution of 1945, operative for one year; and the Constitution of 1946, which continues in force. It had, then, been permissible for women to vote during twenty-three years, sporadically distributed through the history of the republic. The provision has not operated without interruption long enough to accustom women citizens to the practice of voting. Of political significance is the fact that women citizens employed by the Church, for example, nuns, are expected by the Church to vote in elections in which that organization has an interest. Strong Church pressure on behalf of the Conservative party was reflected in the election of 1948 by the long lines of nuns waiting to vote at various mesas of the Sierra. Few women other than these vote in Ecuador, for the practice is strongly frowned upon by the mores, especially in the Sierra. Woman suffrage as it exists in Ecuador functions almost exclusively to the benefit of the Conservative party.

As optional voting for women has created a definite politically oriented bloc of voters, so compulsory voting for men has also produced a bloc. The official penalties for nonvoting by male citizens include their dismissal from government posts; disqualification for one year from public employment; and fines ranging from the equivalent of $1.20 to $303.[19] All government workers and aspirants for public posts are therefore impelled to vote; other male citizens may stay away from the polls with impunity.

The structure of the Ecuadoran electorate thus presents a picture of a set of laws designed to force male "whites" to vote and to prevent the great mass of the population—Indians, cholos, montuvios, and Negroes—from casting ballots. As enforced, these laws produce two blocs of voters who give each election its fundamental course and character. Government employees and persons hoping to join their ranks constitute one group, partisans of the government in power. The other, the Church bloc, is composed of Church employees and the merely faithful, the distinction resting on the location of the world in which they receive their remuneration. When the Church supports the government, the election results are crudely one-sided; when the two are opposed, the contest is heated and close.

The provincial electoral tribunals are required to publish, on or before the seventh day before an election, complete lists of candidates and offices involved in the contest. Each provincial electoral tribunal

---

[19] In Ecuadoran currency, the range is from 20 to 5,000 *sucres*, here converted at the rate of 16.50 sucres to the dollar.

prints all ballots to be used in its province and is responsible for distributing them to the local electoral boards before the polling places, or mesas, open. Ballots must be printed in black ink on white paper, except that they may be typewritten in districts in the Oriente and the Galápagos Islands if printing presses are not available.

The mesas are required by law to be open to the voters from seven o'clock in the morning to five o'clock in the afternoon of election day. Voters approach the mesas (generally located in the open air) singly, present their registration certificates, and vote theoretically in secret,[20] after which their hands are stamped with indelible ink to prevent repeating. After the mesas close, each local electoral board counts the ballots in its box, records the results, and sends the votes to the appropriate provincial electoral tribunal. The latter makes the final count unless the president and vice-president of the republic are to be elected. In this event, the final count is conducted by the supreme electoral tribunal.

The organization of Ecuadoran election machinery has traditionally presented innumerable opportunities for fraud. These still exist despite the revamping of the machinery in conformity with the provisions of the Constitution of 1946. Central counting in each province has been partly motivated by suspicion, usually well-founded, of the motives of the members of the local electoral boards. Chicanery on the local level has remained rampant even though the control of the provincial electoral tribunals has been expanded. The local boards are still substantially free to violate the integrity of the ballot box before dispatching its contents to the appropriate provincial body. The latter tribunal, in reviewing the local count, almost invariably makes its "corrections" in favor of its own political interests.

Proportional representation, the principle of which is proclaimed in the Constitution of 1946, is used where each voter casts his ballot for more than two members of the same body. Thus, the system is employed in the election of members of the chamber of deputies representing the Sierra and Coastal provinces; members of provincial councils;[21] and members of cantonal councils.[22] Proportional representation is achieved by means of a list system. Political organizations, singly or in combination, nominate lists of candidates for these posts; the voter, unable to split his ballot, votes for an entire list. The count is conducted

---

[20] Voters generally hold their ballots against the side of a building or similarly convenient object while recording their choices, and anyone interested in watching the process is normally free to do so.
[21] See p. 151, below.
[22] See pp. 157–158, below.

by dividing the total number of valid ballots cast by the number of offices to be filled, the result of this process being known as the first quota. Any list of candidates receiving a number of votes totaling less than half of the first quota is eliminated at that point. A second quota is arrived at by dividing the total number of valid votes cast for the remaining lists by the number of offices to be filled. The number of valid ballots cast for each list involved in the computation of the second quota is then divided by that quota, the result for each list being the number of seats it has won on the body to be elected.

As it has operated in Ecuador, proportional representation has contributed to the political apathy of the people. Election results are normally announced between three and six weeks after the balloting, and such popular interest in the contests and the issues as might have existed at the time of the voting has usually subsided when the results are made known. Proportional representation has not been an effective method, from the standpoint of the electorate, of recording popular decisions, largely because the system of counting is complex and is not understood by the bulk of the voters. The general feeling that the ballots are in the hands of the politician, who is free to do with them as he pleases, has intensified apathy as well as cynicism on the part of the electorate. Indeed, a case might well be made for a simplified method of counting which would be understood by the voters. Such a reform might conceivably give a renewed significance to the power of the ballot.

The Election of 1948

The major task confronting the administration of President Carlos Julio Arosemena, in office from September 17, 1947, until September 1 of the following year, was the creation of a political environment in which a president and vice-president could be elected for the period from 1948 to 1952. In this work Arosemena was eminently successful. The orderly conditions under which the election of June 6, 1948, was held contrasted markedly with the political chaos which had brought Arosemena to the presidency less than nine months earlier.

The first presidential aspirant to announce his availability was Senator Galo Plaza Lasso, who had served as ambassador to the United States from 1944 to 1946. Plaza's announcement came on October 6, 1947. He had not intended to enter the race so early, but his hand was forced when President Arosemena expressed interest in Plaza's reappointment as chief of the Ecuadoran diplomatic mission at Washington. In a public statement, Plaza declined the appointment "because numerous citizens throughout the republic have resolved to advance my name in candidacy for the presidency."[23] These citizens were the directors of the M.C.D.N., who believed that Plaza offered more promise of forestalling a Conservative triumph than any other available national figure.

Galo Plaza Lasso is unique among Ecuadoran politicians. He was born in New York on January 18, 1906, when his father (former President General Leónidas Plaza Gutiérrez) and mother were temporarily in the United States, a country with which the younger Plaza became perhaps as familiar as with Ecuador. He was brought to Quito while an infant, but returned to the northern republic for his higher education. Galo Plaza Lasso attended the University of California, Berkeley, the University of Maryland, and Georgetown University. On the football field his performance was more distinguished than in the classroom, a fact which led the irate general to cut off his son's allowance. This disaster striking the younger Plaza simultaneously with the depression of the 1930's, he sold apples on the streets of New York before working his passage back to Ecuador on a Grace Line steamship. In 1938 and 1939 he served as minister of national defense in the cabinet of President Aurelio Mosquera Narváez, after which he retired from politics to administer his family's large hacienda in the Sierra.

In 1944 President Velasco Ibarra named Plaza ambassador to the United States. Plaza remained until 1945 at Washington (where he became popular with newsmen after he told them that "I never have worn striped pants and I never will"). Returning to Ecuador, he was elected senator from Pichincha in 1947. "I believe that the essential task of government is to maintain and perfect the exercise of human rights and the fundamental human guarantees," he declared when asked to summarize his political philosophy. "I believe that a government of liberties and individual initiatives is not incompatible with tactful intervention by the state in the interests of the collectivity, to prevent some men from being converted into the slaves of others."[24]

Though Plaza had announced his presidential candidacy six months earlier, the M.C.D.N. did not nominate his running mate until April 15, 1948, when it chose Dr. Abel A. Gilbert, noted Guayaquil physician and surgeon, as its vice-presidential candidate. In his own way, Dr. Gilbert—whose campaign photographs bore an interesting resemblance to portraits of Daniel Webster, a resemblance not apparent on personal contact—was unusual among Ecuadoran politicians. He was primarily a medical man, and did not become interested in politics until quite

[23] *El Comercio*, Quito, October 7, 1947.
[24] *Ibid.*, November 22, 1947.

late in his career, when he had already earned a reputation as one of the republic's most skilled physicians and surgeons. His first sortie into politics resulted in 1947 in his election to the senate; he ran unsuccessfully for mayor of Guayaquil later in the same year. Long known as one of the outstanding members of the faculty of the University of Guayaquil, he was reëlected vice-rector of that institution on August 3, 1948.

While the candidates on the M.C.D.N. ticket were unusual as Ecuadoran politicians, one aspect of the nominations reflected a traditional approach to Ecuadoran regionalism. One candidate, Galo Plaza, was from the Sierra and was expected to draw strong support from that region for the M.C.D.N.; the other candidate was from the Coast, was a respected member of its intellectual elite, and was expected to draw considerable support from that region for the ticket.

The Conservative party's candidates were nominated by the general assembly of that party, which convened at Quito on January 3, 1948. Persuaded that their optimum prospects for victory lay in nominating two candidates who were (1) openly favorable to the Church and (2) from the Sierra, the Conservative stronghold, the general assembly on January 6 named Dr. Manuel Elicio Flor and Manuel Sotomayor y Luna as the Conservative candidates for president and vice-president, respectively. Dr. Flor, a noted constitutional lawyer, had been a member of congress from 1938 to 1940, one of the signers of the ill-fated Constitution of 1945, and president of the supreme court. His running mate, Sotomayor y Luna, was Ecuador's representative at the Vatican at the time of the nominations. "A Catholic cannot vote for any but Catholic candidates," former President Mariano Suárez Veintimilla explained on behalf of the Conservative party's ticket. He warned that Galo Plaza was "liberal, with a tendency to the left," and said, "It is better to be victims of a dictatorship, suffering for a noble and grand cause, than to surrender ... to liberalism, which has done so much damage to the country."[25]

Indications that the Radical Liberals and Socialists were drifting toward coalition had been evident as early as June, 1946. The Radical Liberal assembly, convening at Quito on November 21, 1947, formally received two Socialist delegates in an effort to negotiate an "understanding" between the two parties. The demoralized and disoriented Radical Liberals, however, were divided into at least four factions which could not agree on the coalition issue. This party at length rejected the

---

[25] *Ibid.*, March 30, 1948.

Socialist bid, and on November 23 nominated for the presidency Dr. José Vicente Trujillo, a leading constitutional and international lawyer. Trujillo, who had been foreign minister from August 20, 1945, until October 17, 1947, when he resigned to seek the presidency, was unable to appease the Radical Liberal dissident elements. With dissension mounting within the party in consequence of his nomination, Trujillo withdrew his candidacy on December 15.

The Socialists renewed their bid for a coalition when the Radical Liberal assembly reconvened on January 23, 1948. The Radical Liberal supreme junta, more receptive to the proposal than it had been in November, requested that the Socialist congress meet at the same time as the Radical Liberal assembly, and the path was cleared for coalition. The agreement was formally announced on January 23: under its terms, the presidential candidate would be a Radical Liberal chosen by that party's assembly, and the vice-presidential nominee would be a Socialist, selected by the Socialist congress; the coalition would seek leftist support; and if the coalition won the election, cabinet posts would be equally divided between members of the two parties.

Accordingly, the Radical Liberals named former President General Alberto Enríquez Gallo as the coalition's presidential candidate, and the Socialists selected Carlos Cueva Tamariz as his running mate. Enríquez Gallo had presided over an uninspired administration from October, 1937, until August of the following year. He was a relatively colorless and politically weak candidate, and did not prosecute a vigorous campaign in 1948. Cueva Tamariz, the Socialist, was a more driving and colorful campaigner. As Socialist representative in the Ecuadoran Democratic Alliance, he had led the revolutionists of 1944 in the Sierra province of Azuay. As a member of the constituent assembly of 1944–1945, he had signed the short-lived Constitution of 1945, and later rebelled against Velasco Ibarra when the latter suspended that constitution. Cueva Tamariz had attempted to wrest leadership from Velasco Ibarra in April, 1946, and was jailed at that time.

The campaign as it developed reflected the fundamental fact that only a small proportion of the population was interested in or affected by the contest. The poverty of the country likewise found expression in the campaign. Lack of party resources precluded the printing on any large scale of campaign leaflets and posters; and campaign propaganda, such as it was, appeared largely in the form of brief slogans painted on walls and buildings. Plaza, the only presidential candidate with substantial financial resources, introduced a few United States campaign methods, such as radio addresses and a nationwide campaign tour. His advisers, however, considered it prudent that he hold these activities to a minimum in view of the economic inability of other contestants to duplicate them. Plaza and Gilbert campaigned vigorously; Flor and Sotomayor y Luna, somewhat less so; and Enríquez Gallo and Cueva Tamariz, virtually not at all until the last two weeks before the election.

So far as the writer was able to determine, election day, June 6, was on the whole orderly, peaceful, and without untoward incident. "The Ecuadoran people have given the world an example of high political culture," President Arosemena declared afterward, "constituting an unequivocal manifestation of their intellectual and civic maturity."[26]

All ballots reached Quito by June 10, those cast in the Oriente and the Galápagos Islands being flown to the capital. The supreme electoral tribunal then embarked upon the official count, which was not completed until July 13. The work of the tribunal was prolonged and eventful. This body, empowered to annul ballots submitted by local electoral boards which had not followed the proper procedure, exercised this power freely in the early days of the count. By June 14 the votes cast at thirty-four mesas had been invalidated. As the greater number of these mesas were in the provinces of Pichincha and Guayas where M.C.D.N. strength was concentrated, there arose a suspicion that the supreme electoral tribunal was attempting to falsify the results to produce a Conservative victory. The situation became heated, and a prolonged debate within the tribunal was followed by the resignations of four of the body's seven members between June 15 and 20. Unable to proceed for lack of a quorum from June 20 to 28, the tribunal became the object of severe criticism conducted by the nation's press and other opinion media. *El Comercio,* Quito's leading daily, felt editorially that "no motive can justify" the supreme electoral tribunal's behavior: "the country wants to know the result [of the election], ... and the peculiar norms adopted in the count have agitated public opinion."[27] *El Universo* of Guayaquil editorially declared that "the tribunal has forgotten that it holds in its hands and in its charge nothing less than the fate of a nation.... This delinquency constitutes a grave fault and a responsibility which history will record."[28] This newspaper also published a political cartoon depicting a young lady agreeing to marry her impulsive swain on condition that he promise never to become a member of the supreme electoral tribunal.

[26] *Ibid.,* June 8, 1948.
[27] *Ibid.,* June 21, 1948.
[28] *El Universo,* Guayaquil, June 30, 1948.

TABLE 5
Official Results of the Election of June 6, 1948*

Regions and provinces	M.C.D.N.[a] candidates		Conservative candidates		Coalition[b] candidates	
	Plaza (for president)	Gilbert (for vice-pres.)	Flor (for president)	Sotomayor (for vice-pres.)	Enríquez (for president)	Cueva T. (for vice-pres.)
Totals........	*115,835*	*113,188*	*112,052*	*114,008*	*53,601*	*54,067*
Sierra.........	*71,501*	*69,732*	*92,491*	*93,991*	*23,811*	*24,051*
Carchi.......	2,030	2,036	8,060	8,064	3,020	3,011
Imbabura....	6,865	6,730	7,449	7,584	1,916	1,917
Pichincha....	27,909	26,662	16,317	17,566	9,004	8,999
Cotopaxi.....	5,489	5,458	4,259	4,290	1,797	1,796
Tungurahua..	7,807	7,779	13,826	13,853	1,143	1,136
Chimborazo.	7,154	7,138	7,719	7,735	743	743
Bolívar......	2,211	2,211	5,144	5,144	943	943
Cañar.......	1,669	1,652	6,845	6,846	653	669
Azuay.......	7,262	6,976	12,636	12,688	1,387	1,614
Loja.........	3,105	3,090	10,236	10,221	3,205	3,223
Coast.........	*42,425*	*41,547*	*18,739*	*19,195*	*29,403*	*29,629*
Esmeraldas..	306	302	715	714	1,387	1,378
Manabí......	16,151	16,152	6,369	6,369	7,726	7,726
Los Ríos.....	2,120	2,116	890	893	1,513	1,532
Guayas......	20,775	19,904	6,764	7,218	16,027	16,261
El Oro.......	3,073	3,073	4,001	4,001	2,732	2,732
Oriente........	*1,848*	*1,849*	*821*	*821*	*386*	*386*
Napo-Pastaza ...	901	902	308	308	366	366
Santiago-Zamora....	947	947	513	513	20	20
Galápagos.....	*61*	*60*	*1*	*1*	*1*	*1*

* The writer wishes to acknowledge the painstaking assistance of officials of the supreme electoral tribunal at Quito in making available the data upon which this table is based.
[a] National Civic Democratic Movement (*Movimiento Cívico Democrático Nacional*).
[b] Coalition of the Radical Liberal and Socialist parties.

Resuming the tally, the reconstituted body voted on June 28 to rehabilitate thirty-two of the thirty-four disqualified mesas, an action which restored approximately 5,000 votes apiece for Plaza and Gilbert and 3,000 apiece for Flor and Sotomayor y Luna, the totals for Enríquez Gallo and Cueva Tamariz not being materially affected by the decision. The count was at length completed on July 13.

The official results of the election conferred the presidency upon Plaza, who was given 115,835 votes against 112,052 for Flor and 53,601 for Enríquez Gallo. The vice-presidency was won by the Conservative candidate, Sotomayor y Luna, who received 114,008 votes against 113,188 for Gilbert and 54,067 for Cueva Tamariz. A total of 281,488 Ecuadorans—8.32 per cent of the estimated population of the republic—had cast valid votes for the presidency. The election figures reflected a familiar pattern: the Conservatives had carried the Sierra while the Coast was swept by anti-Conservative parties.

Authority to review the work of the supreme electoral tribunal rested with the national congress, and considerable interest attended the convening of the latter body at Quito on August 10. "The presidential election of June 6, 1948, was the most free, pure, and ample which has taken place in Ecuador since the beginning of its republican life," outgoing President Arosemena told the legislators' opening session. "This was what I promised when I assumed the presidency, and this was my chief ambition during the days which preceded the election."[29] A six-man joint committee of congress, named to study the supreme electoral tribunal's figures and report thereon, recommended on August 13 that congress accept the tribunal's action as final. This the legislators agreed to do, and formally proclaimed Plaza and Sotomayor y Luna as president-elect and vice-president-elect, respectively.

The formal inauguration was held exactly at midnight on August 31. "The government which I represent from this moment forward," declared Galo Plaza Lasso, forty-fourth president of Ecuador, "understands that in the recent election campaign there were no victors and no vanquished."[30]

---

[29] *El Comercio*, Quito, August 11, 1948.
[30] *Ibid.*, September 1, 1948.

CHAPTER V

THE NATIONAL ADMINISTRATION

THE CONSTITUTION of 1946 has retained a significant change, inaugurated in the 1945 document, in the theoretical basis of presidential government in Ecuador. The separation of executive, legislative, and judicial powers familiar in the United States had been written in virtually identical form into the republic's first twelve constitutions. The first indications of an Ecuadoran break with this traditional doctrine appeared in the text of the Constitution of 1929, but the departure did not take on a definitive and decisive form until the promulgation of the country's fourteenth constitution in March of 1945.

THE PRESIDENTIAL SYSTEM IN ECUADOR

The assumption underlying the earlier documents had been that a division, on paper at least, of national governmental organs into separate, autonomous, and mutually exclusive executive, legislative, and judicial branches was essential to the existence of the presidential system in Ecuador. The three branches (called "powers" in the constitutional law of the republic before 1945) were held to be independent of one another, each supreme within its own sphere of action. It is perhaps unnecessary to observe that this legal arrangement was divorced from reality during most of the constitutional history of Ecuador, but the citizenry had become accustomed to this unreality as a characteristic of written constitutions.

Proponents of the doctrine of the separation of powers still exist in appreciable numbers in Ecuador, and are not likely to disappear in the foreseeable future. It is a curious fact that partisans of this formula invariably draw their arguments from the experiences of nations other than Ecuador. An Ecuadoran is hard pressed for an answer when asked about the benefits which his country may have derived from the separation of powers. The doctrine was written into Ecuadoran constitutions during the first hundred years of the country's independent national existence. Yet few of the nation's political experiences during that century can be organized into a case for Ecuadoran retention of the formula. The arguments must come from abroad.

It is unquestioned dogma among most of Ecuador's constitutional lawyers that the separation of powers has operated with complete success in the United States. Moreover, the admiration on the part of

Ecuador's intellectual elite for French cultural achievements has contributed to perhaps unduly heavy references to Montesquieu's *Esprit des Lois* as a further defense of the formula. Thus, Francisco Zevallos Reyre, whose *Lecciones de Derecho Constitucional* was used as a textbook on constitutional law at the University of Guayaquil in 1948, has relied entirely on Montesquieu and the Constitution of the United States in pronouncing the doctrine to be a salutary constitutional device. "The proper advancement of public services and a proper administrative life demand the separation of powers as an absolute thing," Zevallos has concluded. "When each one of the powers conducts itself with the most complete independence of the others, the efficiency of the organs [of government] redounds in a harmony of the whole, within a just equilibrium and the necessary control.... The equilibrium, carefully maintained among the branches of public power, is... of great utility in avoiding the excessive influence of one single interest group in public affairs, a supremacy which operates to the detriment of the other groups and of the political aspirations of the great majority of the citizens."[1] But Zevallos has pointed to nothing in *Ecuadoran* constitutional experience which might demonstrate the validity of this view.

It is only in recent years that some Ecuadorans have begun to doubt that the traditional separation of powers deserves a place in their country's written constitutions. A new school of Ecuadoran thought, represented by Angel M. Paredes and Pío Jaramillo Alvarado, has attacked the hallowed formula, gaining sufficient force in the republic to influence substantially the ideas of the writers of the constitutions of 1945 and 1946. "The separation of powers fits into only a theory of the republic, to be destroyed completely in actual practice," Paredes has written. "The various factors of our life are so intimately interwoven that every dividing line is violated and overcome."[2] Jaramillo Alvarado has argued that "in truth power has not been and cannot be divided, although there may exist various functions for the better exercise of power, which by the law of political gravitation has to fall upon the executive.... We can speak of the coöperation of different powers, but not of a division of them, the classical concept which has induced the battle between executive and legislative powers which have been considered as autonomous and jealous of their mutually exclusive functions. Modern political science [*derecho político*] considers the power to govern as having a unified form expressed in distinct functions."[3]

---

[1] Zevallos, *op. cit.*, p. 229.
[2] Paredes, *Naturaleza del Poder Público y del Sometimiento del Hombre a las Autoridades del País*, p. 316.
[3] Jaramillo Alvarado, *El Régimen Totalitario en América*, pp. 62, 63, 114.

Conceding the validity of this approach, the writers of the Constitution of 1945 embarked upon a significant departure from traditional Ecuadoran usage, a departure which was retained in the Constitution of 1946. Ecuador's first thirteen constitutions had referred to the executive, the legislature, and the judiciary as "powers." In the 1945 and 1946 constitutions, these organs are no longer "powers," but have become "functions." The constitutional emphasis before 1945 was on the *separation* of "powers"; under the republic's latest two constitutions, the stress has been placed upon the *coördination* of "functions." Where constitutional law before 1945 had held that the three powers were coördinate or equal, the position since then has been that the three functions are *not* equal, the executive and judicial functions being subordinate to the legislative. "The state operates, by reason of its sovereignty, as the owner of its organs, which are considered as instruments for the exercise of this sovereignty," García has explained, in summarizing the law of the 1945 and 1946 constitutions. "The state is the proprietor of the organs and exercises over them such rights as an owner has over his house or land.... In every [such] case, the property is subject to the will of the owner."[4]

Thus, in laying the theoretical basis of presidential government in Ecuador, the constitutions of 1945 and 1946 represent a fourfold departure from the republic's previous usage.

1. The nomenclature has been changed in that the three organs of government, formerly referred to as "powers," have been called functions since 1945. It was not possible at the time this study was made to assess the full significance, in terms of constitutional practice, of this change in terminology: the Constitution of 1945 had been in force for only a year before it was suspended, and the latest constitution had been in force for only two years by the end of 1948, little having been done in that period to indicate the extent of the change involved. It is unfortunate that the alteration in terminology was not debated on the floor of either the constituent assembly of 1944–1945, which wrote the Constitution of 1945, or the constituent assembly of 1946, which produced the most recent constitution. Some constitutional lawyers with whom the writer discussed the matter (e.g., Fernando Barredo Hidalgo) feel that little more than a change in words has been accomplished; others (represented by Dr. José Vicente Trujillo) believe that the new nomenclature will have far-reaching ramifications if (a) the Constitution of 1946 enjoys a measure of longevity, or (b) its successor retains the terminology adopted in 1945.

[4] Aurelio García, *op. cit.*, Vol. II, 111.

2. The law of the constitutions of 1945 and 1946 constitutes the Ecuadoran version of the proposition that power cannot be divided. It is contended in some quarters that official acceptance of this doctrine may have the long-run effect of injecting an unprecedented degree of realism into the republic's written constitutions. The realities of Ecuadoran politics have rarely embodied the three-way division of authority declared by earlier constitutions to exist; and the hope has been expressed that the Constitution of 1945 has ushered in an era in which written constitutions will be less divorced from reality than they formerly were.

3. The pre-1945 doctrine that the three branches of government were equal has been discarded under Ecuador's two latest constitutions. The current constitutional law holds that the three functions are *not* equal, the legislative function being above the executive and judicial functions. Although this point is further discussed on other pages, it may be noted here that what may have been gained in the direction of realism on other counts could well be more than nullified by placing the executive function in a subordinate position. The vision of a chastened president defies the Ecuadoran imagination: to be sure, he has existed, but he is rare. Moreover, the allegedly subordinate executive function was assigned no less than 89.64 per cent of the 1949 budget.

4. The emphasis in constitutional law since 1945 has been on the coördination of functions rather than on the autonomy or separation of the organs of government. It is true that each of the functions is assumed to enjoy a measure of autonomy in its field, but the legal implications of this assumption have been deliberately minimized under the Constitution of 1946, which stresses the desirability and necessity of coöperation and harmony among the branches of government rather than the autonomy of each.

The Council of State

The "council of state" is the constitutional agency established for the primary purpose of achieving coördination among the national organs of government.[5] All of the national functions are represented in this nineteen-man body. The council of state is composed of the president of the supreme court, who is its presiding officer; the attorney general of the nation; the comptroller general of the nation; the president of the supreme electoral tribunal; one senator, designated annually by the senate; one deputy, chosen for a one-year term by the chamber of deputies; two citizens selected annually by a joint session of congress;

---
[5] The term "council of state" has appeared in seven of Ecuador's pre-1945 constitutions, but in none of these had the same significance as in the Constitution of 1946.

one representative of the national council of economy, selected by that agency; the president of the National Institute of Social Welfare; an officer in the armed forces; and the eight members of the president's cabinet. The structure of the council of state reflects the theoretically subordinate position of the executive function in two ways: the president of the republic is not himself a member of the body; and the cabinet members, representing the executive function, may not vote in the council of state, although they may participate fully in its debates.

In a sense, the council of state, coördinating all national functions of government, operates as a defender of the constitutional system outlined in the fundamental law of 1946. The council of state investigates the constitutionality of the official acts of the national executive and legislative functions, and in general is expected to enforce a guarantee that government officials will not violate the constitution. Moreover, the council of state performs a number of the duties of the legislative function during periods in which congress is out of session. Among these latter powers of the council of state are the authority to grant or deny extraordinary powers to the president of the republic; to call special sessions of congress; to accept or reject resignations presented by senators and deputies; to receive charges of misconduct in office which might be brought against the president of the republic and other officials; to authorize the president to promote army officers to the ranks of lieutenant colonel and major; and to fill such nonjudicial vacancies as may occur. In addition to these duties which the council of state possesses while congress is out of session, the council has the exclusive authority to settle conflicts of jurisdiction among administrative agencies.

On the basis of both its constitutional powers and the record of its first two years of life, the council of state appears to be a powerful agency of government. Yet neither of these considerations permitted conclusive evaluation of the council of state at the time these lines were written. The first two years of the council were, in a sense, unusual years for Ecuador. The three presidents who held office under the Constitution of 1946 during those years were weak executives: Velasco Ibarra had been destroyed politically before the constitution was promulgated; Suárez Veintimilla held office for only fifteen days; and Arosemena represented an Ecuadoran political type, the "constitutional president," under whose administration the constitution normally functions largely as written. Thus it may well be that historical accident rather than the new constitutional system accounted for the apparent strength of the council of state in its initial years, and that the agency was yet to face the crucial tests of its effectiveness.

THE PRESIDENCY

The president of the republic is the principal officer of the executive function. This official has traditionally had a four-year term in Ecuador, although presidents remain in office an average of 2.74 years and only 23 per cent have been able to serve out the full terms for which they were elected. Under the Constitution of 1946, the president is popularly elected on the first Sunday in June of each year in which a presidential term expires, the inauguration taking place the following September 1. This constitution reflects a traditional Ecuadoran practice in prohibiting the immediate reëlection of an incumbent president. Except for García Moreno's celebrated "Black Charter" of 1869, this prohibition has been written into all fifteen of the country's constitutions. The 1946 document stipulates that a president who desires reëlection must remain out of office for at least one term. This requirement is also customary in Ecuador, three exceptions having been under the constitutions of 1883, 1897, and 1906, which made an interval of at least two presidential terms mandatory.

The president of the republic receives a salary of $362.42 per month plus a monthly expense account of $303.03, totaling $7,985.40 per annum.[6] To be eligible for the presidency under the Constitution of 1946, a person must be an "Ecuadoran by birth,"[7] in the exercise of Ecuadoran citizenship, and at least thirty-five years of age. Specifically declared to be ineligible for the presidency are the outgoing vice-president of the republic; the outgoing president, or any of his relatives; anyone who has been acting president within six months of the election; and anyone who served in the outgoing president's cabinet within six months of the election, or any of his relatives.

The president of the republic has two broad types of constitutional powers, ordinary and emergency. The ordinary powers of the president may be divided, for purposes of discussion, into five groups, as they relate to (1) national security and foreign relations; (2) commercial and fiscal operations; (3) administrative matters; (4) the legislative function; and (5) the judicial function.

1. In the matter of national security and foreign relations, the presi-

---

[6] In Ecuadoran currency, here converted at the rate of 16.50 sucres to the dollar, the figures are: salary, 6,000 sucres per month; expense account 5,000 sucres per month; total, 132,000 sucres annually.

[7] President Galo Plaza Lasso, who was born at New York, is an "Ecuadoran by birth" within the meaning of the constitution, since his parents, both Ecuadorans, were only temporarily abroad at the time of his birth. Cf. *Constitución Política de la República del Ecuador* (Quito, 1946), Art. 9.

dent is required by the constitution to safeguard the international position of the republic of Ecuador and to maintain internal order. In his capacity as commander in chief of the armed forces, he is required to place them in the service and defense of the republic, and to recommend to congress the promotion of army officers to the ranks of general and colonel. Promotions to the ranks of lieutenant colonel and major, as has been noted, are made by the president with the approval of the council of state. The conduct of Ecuadoran foreign policy lies within the province of the president, who directs all Ecuadoran negotiations with the governments of other states. The president appoints and removes the republic's diplomatic and consular officers. Further, when the security of the republic appears to demand it, the president may authorize the naturalization of foreigners as Ecuadorans, or cancel the naturalization papers of persons who are not Ecuadorans by birth.

2. The president's commercial and fiscal powers are linked with the national council of economy, an agency composed of experts whose duty it is to study the economic and financial problems of the nation and to make recommendations based thereon to the president. He is not required to act on the recommendations of this council, but he is forbidden by the constitution to take steps affecting the national economy without first at least consulting the body. When congress is in recess, the president may open and close ports on an interim basis, the approval of the council of state being necessary in each case. The president on his own authority issues navigation permits, and patents on and titles to industrial property.

3. In administrative matters, the president is required to see that the constitution and laws of the republic are enforced. He freely appoints and removes the members of his cabinet, provincial governors, and other government officials whose appointment and removal are not otherwise provided for by the constitution and the laws. The president, under the Constitution of 1946, has an especial obligation to guard public property and funds.

4. With reference to the legislative function, the president convokes regular sessions of congress, and when he deems it necessary, calls special sessions of the legislators. He is expected to advise congress, on the first day of each regular session, of the political, military, and financial state of the nation, and to recommend legislative action along such lines as he feels would improve the conduct of national affairs. Measures passed by congress may be vetoed by the president; bills which become law must be promulgated and enforced by him.

5. The judicial aspect of the president's ordinary powers is limited to the issuance of pardons and commutations of sentences of persons convicted of violating the laws of the republic. More extensive judicial authority is embodied in his emergency powers.

The emergency powers of the president may be invoked in two classes of urgent situations: (1) In a political emergency—that is, imminent threat of foreign invasion, war, or internal commotion—extraordinary powers may not be used by him without the prior consent of congress, or, if that body is not in session, the council of state. (2) If the emergency be nonpolitical—that is, conflagration, earthquake, or flood—the president may use these powers without the prior approval of congress or the council of state. In either event, the emergency powers may be used only for the specific purpose for which they were invoked, and must be directed toward reëstablishing normality or tranquillity as soon as possible. When the emergency, whether political or nonpolitical, has passed, the president immediately ceases to be in possession of the extraordinary powers. He must convoke a session of congress as soon as possible, and deliver to the legislators, within the first eight days of their session, an account of the uses to which the emergency powers were put. Congress is then required to declare its approval or disapproval of the action of the administration during the crisis. In the event of a vote of disapproval, the power of congress is limited to publishing a declaration that the executive function is solely responsible for such abuses of authority as may have occurred during the emergency.

The emergency powers of the president include the authority to place the Ecuadoran army in the field, to enlarge the armed forces by calling up reserve classes, and to appoint new and temporary military authorities. The president may declare all or a specified part of the republic to be under martial law; and if the crisis presents a physical threat to Quito, he may temporarily remove the seat of government to some safer city. He may order the arrest of persons agitating internal commotion or befriending potential foreign invaders. Such political prisoners may not be placed in the penal colony in the Galápagos Islands, and the establishment of concentration camps in the Oriente is expressly forbidden by the constitution. Moreover, Coastal residents may not be incarcerated in the Sierra, or vice versa, without their approval; and any political prisoner who requests a passport and permission to leave the country must be granted them. All persons imprisoned under these emergency powers must be freed when such powers are terminated, although they remain subject to court action. During the crisis, the president may censor the press and radio transmitters and may close the ports and frontiers of the republic.

Certain expressed prohibitions are placed upon the president by the constitution. He may not, for example, leave the country during his term of office or in the first year after its expiration without the permission of congress or the council of state. If such leave is given, it may not be for a longer period than thirty days if the president is still in office. Further, he may not interfere with the conduct of elections, the work of the courts, or the deliberations of congress, and cannot dissolve the latter body. He may not admit foreigners to the Ecuadoran army in the absence of a contract previously approved by congress, and he is to be held especially accountable for treason or conspiracy against the republic.

Ecuadoran presidents have been traditionally strong executives, and caudillos have not been noted for their adherence to the text of the written constitution. It is a curious fact that the republic had a strong president, Velasco Ibarra, under the Constitution of 1945, which provided for a weak executive; and three weak presidents under the Constitution of 1946, which allowed a stronger executive function than did the previous charter. It is to be noted that within the Ecuadoran political process caudillos are not likely to be bound by constitutional texts, whereas "constitutional presidents" tend to obey them scrupulously and faithfully.

The presidency has traditionally been the strongest institution in the government of Ecuador, regardless of such remarks to the contrary as may appear in the text of the constitution. "The presidential system," Paredes has said, "has done nothing more than consecrate a gross caudillismo.... We have seen certain men elevated to the status of idols, and later overthrown and unmercifully persecuted and insulted."[8] The distinctive characteristic of Ecuadoran government has normally been the existence of a strong executive.

It did not seem likely at the time this book was written that Ecuador would depart from this tradition under the Constitution of 1946. Although it may be unfair to condemn the republic's latest constitution on the basis of only two years' experience, it appears that much more fundamental work remains to be done before the country's statesmen who hope for a change in the nature of the Ecuadoran executive can see their hopes realized. In short, it may be said that Ecuadoran constitutional problems are not so much problems of law as problems of power.

[8] Paredes, *Naturaleza del Poder Público y del Sometimiento del Hombre a las Autoridades del País*, p. 316.

Perhaps the most generous thing that can be said of the presidency under the Constitution of 1946 is that the administration of President Galo Plaza Lasso, who was inaugurated in September, 1948, may be expected to set the pattern for the course and character of the executive function in its newest form.

THE VICE-PRESIDENCY

The office of vice-president of the republic has been provided for in nine of Ecuador's fifteen constitutions, including the 1946 charter. One-third of the country's twenty-four vice-presidents served out the full constitutional term; although thirty-three of the nation's presidents failed to complete their terms, only one was succeeded by a vice-president. The vice-presidential period has never been constitutionally less than four years, but vice-presidents have been in office an average of only 2.5 years.

Under the Constitution of 1946, the vice-president is popularly elected once every four years, his election and inauguration occurring simultaneously with those of the president. The vice-president must meet the same qualifications as the president, and his major constitutional function is to preside over the senate, voting only in the event of a tie.

Theoretically, the vice-president succeeds the president if the latter is unable to finish his term, but this has actually happened only once in the history of the republic;[9] the entire system of presidential succession set forth in the constitution—from the vice-president to the president of the chamber of deputies to the vice-president of the senate to the vice-president of the chamber of deputies—is divorced from reality. If, however, it should ever develop that the presidential office devolves upon the president of the chamber of deputies or anyone after him in the constitutional order, that official would hold office only until congress meets, when that body would designate an acting president to serve out the unexpired portion of the term.

A major political function performed by the vice-presidency is an attempt to straddle regionalism. When the Coast and the Sierra are both represented in an administration—one by the president and the other by the vice-president—the government is sometimes strong because of its ability to withstand regional rivalries. The political parties frequently endeavor to meet this problem by representing both major regions on each presidential and vice-presidential ticket.

The vice-presidency has held a singular political significance under

---

[9] Vice-President Mariano Suárez Veintimilla succeeded President José María Velasco Ibarra in 1947.

TABLE 6
VICE-PRESIDENTS OF ECUADOR, 1830–1948*

Vice-president	From	To
José Joaquín de Olmedo	1830	1831
José Modesto Larrea	1831	1835
Juan Bernardo de León	1835	1835
Marcos Espinel	1835	1839
Francisco Aguirre	1839	1843
Francisco Marcos	1843	1845
Pablo Merino	1845	1847
Manuel Ascázubi	1847	1851
No vice-presidency under constitution of 1851		
Manuel Bustamante	1854	1854
No vice-president in 1854–1858		
Jerónimo Carrión	1858	1860
Mariano Cueva	1861	1863
Antonio Borrero	1863	1864
Rafael Carvajal	1864	1867
Pedro José Arteta	1867	1869
No vice-presidency under constitutions of 1869 and 1878		
Rafael Pérez Pareja	1883	1884
General Augustín Guerrero	1884	1886
Pedro Cevallos Salvador	1886	1890
Pablo Herrera	1890	1894
Vicente Lucio Salazar	1894	1895
Manuel Benigno Cueva	1895	1899
Carlos Freile Zaldumbide	1899	1903
Alfredo Baquerizo Moreno	1903	1906
No vice-presidency under constitutions of 1906, 1929, and 1945		
Mariano Suárez Veintimilla	1947	1947
José Rafael Bustamante	1947	1948
Manuel Sotomayor y Luna	1948	

* This table is based largely on Carlos A. Rolando, "Anuario Administrativo de la República del Ecuador," *Boletín del Centro de Investigaciones Históricas* (Guayaquil, 1947), Vol. VII, Nos. 12–17, pp. 280–283.

the Constitution of 1946. It has been the major constitutional device employed on a national scale by the Conservative party in its post-1944 renaissance. Two vice-presidents under this constitution, Suárez Veintimilla and Sotomayor y Luna, have been Conservatives. The fact that the former has been the only vice-president to succeed to the presidency in the history of Ecuador is suggestive of much, as regards the realignment of political parties in recent years. Moreover, the president and vice-president have always, under the Constitution of 1946, been affiliated with opposed political organizations, a factor which has contributed to instability in the republic.

The vice-presidency could, of course, become a major stabilizing influence if it were to operate as the writers of nine of the country's constitutions had hoped. Constitutional succession to the presidency has not, however, occurred on anything like a large scale in the past. No indication that the immediate future would differ from this experience had appeared on the Ecuadoran political scene by 1950.

MINISTRIES AND CABINET

The president of the republic is assisted by a group of eight ministers through whom the powers and duties of the executive function are administered. These officials are appointed by the president and are responsible primarily to him, no legislative confirmation of their appointments being required. Each of the ministers is the chief of a ministry and is required to keep the president informed of the progress of affairs within that ministry's jurisdiction. The ministers also formulate proposed legislation, send congress any information in their possession requested by that body, and may participate without vote in congressional debates. No presidential order has the force of law unless it bears the signatures of the ministers expected to enforce it. Should the president violate the constitution, his ministers are collectively responsible with him for that act. In no other case are they collectively responsible to any other authority than the president himself.

The number of ministries is not stipulated in the constitution, but rather in the law of administrative organization of the republic of Ecuador. Under that legislation, as promulgated in 1947, there were eight ministries which according to the 1949 budget employed a total of 36,705 persons. These agencies were the ministry of government, the ministry of foreign relations, the ministry of public education, the ministry of national defense, the ministry of public works and communications, the ministry of social welfare, the ministry of national economy, and the ministry of the treasury.

The ministry of government is, in general, the agency through which the national government maintains public order and supervises the internal administration of the republic. Command of the national police force is exercised through this ministry, which is also the point of liaison between the national administration and the civil officials of the provinces and other regional and local governmental units. The ministry also achieves a species of coördination of the executive and judicial functions through its control of arresting agencies and supervision of the administration of the lowest courts in the judicial hierarchy. The government's printing office, which publishes the *Registro Oficial,* the *Gaceta Judicial,* and other official documents, is under the administrative control of this ministry.

Ecuadoran foreign policy is conducted through the ministry of foreign relations. It should be noted that certain aspects of the republic's foreign relations are set forth in the constitution. That document requires the government to abide by the norms of international law and to adhere to the principles of good neighborliness among states in the solution of international controversies by nonviolent means wherever possible. The constitution, further, proclaims Ecuador's especial solidarity with the other Latin American republics, and authorizes the formation of associations with one or more of them for the furtherance of common interests. In this connection, discussion of the restoration of Gran Colombia is frequently heard in the republic; and Ecuador has entered into various forms of economic collaboration with Colombia, Venezuela, and, occasionally, Panama. However, Dr. José Vicente Trujillo, who was Ecuadoran foreign minister in the cabinets of Presidents Velasco Ibarra, Suárez Veintimilla, and Arosemena, told the writer that it was never the Quito government's intention during his stewardship in the foreign office to reëstablish Gran Colombia on a political basis.

The government's influence over national education—"culture," as Ecuadorans say—is exercised through the ministry of public education. This agency administers anti-illiteracy campaigns and is charged with the promotion of the fine arts and the maintenance of museums, laboratories, observatories, and libraries. Curricula in public primary and secondary schools are prescribed by the ministry, which also administers Ecuador's four universities: the Central University at Quito, and the universities of Guayaquil, Cuenca, and Loja.

The ministry of national defense maintains the armed forces of the republic, exclusive of the national police force. This ministry is also charged with the construction and maintenance of military and naval installations, and the government and administration of the Galápagos Islands.

Governmental distribution of mail and regulation of telegraph, telephone, and radio are administered by the ministry of public works and communications. This agency also maintains the Quito-Guayaquil railroad and the highways of the republic, and directs irrigation projects.

The maintenance and construction of ports and other public works are under the jurisdiction of the ministry, as is the regulation of navigation.

The ministry of social welfare administers legislation and policies relating to the social problems of the nation. Special attention is devoted by this agency to the Indian question, the protection of children and expectant mothers, and the enforcement of social security legislation.

The youngest of the eight executive agencies is the ministry of national economy, which was created on August 4, 1944. This step was sponsored by President Velasco Ibarra, who felt that the previous arrangement had placed too great a work load on the desk of the chief of the old ministry of finance. Accordingly, that agency and the former ministry of agriculture were abolished in 1944, their functions being more or less equally distributed between the newly established ministries of national economy and the treasury. To the former were assigned the regulation of industries and foreign and domestic commerce, and the administration of public policies relating to mining, agriculture, and stock raising. The ministry of national economy is also charged with the development of land use and colonization projects, the issuance of patents and trademarks, and the regulation of banks and money. The compiling of such social statistics as exist is within the purview of this agency, together with the responsibility for the still-to-be-taken national census.

The ministry of the treasury collects such taxes, duties, and imposts as are susceptible of collection, and authorizes expenditures of public funds roughly in conformity with budgetary appropriations. This ministry also operates the government monopolies on tobacco, alcoholic beverages, salt, matches, and perfumes. These monopolies were expected to account for approximately 40 per cent of the public revenue in 1949.

The ministers have traditionally operated in Ecuador as a group of political advisers to the president. In this capacity they are known collectively as the "cabinet." The development of the cabinet in Ecuador has been similar to that of the analogous institution in the United States: the cabinet has taken form largely as a matter of tradition and usage. Only two of Ecuador's fifteen constitutions—the 1843 and 1929 documents—have referred textually to the cabinet function of the ministers. The emergence of the Ecuadoran cabinet has been primarily a process not written into law.

There is no definite or fixed practice with respect to the holding of cabinet meetings. The cabinet's function is merely advisory, and the extent to which it is used depends largely on each president's view of the value of this type of advice. As a general proposition, it may be said that a cabinet meeting is held whenever the administration faces a major political decision. The practice has been varied even during the short period in which the Constitution of 1946 has been in force: President Velasco Ibarra rarely held cabinet meetings; Arosemena normally called one whenever a policy decision of more than routine importance was to be made; and Plaza announced shortly after his inauguration in 1948 that he would begin his term experimenting with the practice of holding two cabinet meetings weekly, on Tuesdays and Thursdays.

The cabinet—that is, the ministers considered collectively—is responsible to the legislative function only if the president should violate the constitution. In all other cases the cabinet is responsible to the president alone. This has been the traditional constitutional practice in the republic, only two of the fifteen charters, those of 1929 and 1945, giving the legislators the authority to force the resignations of cabinets by means of votes of no confidence. Under the Constitution of 1946, however, congress may censure individual ministers. The vote of censure, in Ecuadoran law, differs from a vote of no confidence in two fundamental respects: (1) Only individual ministers, *not* the cabinet, may be subjected to censure. (2) A vote of censure is in order only when congress has declared that the minister in question was guilty of misconduct in office, and may *not* be applied when the legislative function registers disagreement with the policies pursued by a minister not declared guilty of such misconduct. Censured ministers are removed from office and may not be reappointed during the same presidential terms in which they were removed. In no case may a censured minister be reappointed within two years of his ouster. Thus, the vote of censure runs closer to removal in consequence of impeachment than to parliamentary responsibility. The law of the Constitution of 1946 preserves the presidential system despite the constitutional doctrine that the legislative is superior to the other two functions. Ecuador's only experiments with a species of parliamentary government occurred under the Constitution of 1929, and to a lesser extent under that of 1945.[10]

Ministers must be Ecuadorans by birth, in the exercise of the rights of citizenship, and at least thirty years of age. Beyond these constitutional requirements, the president is free to appoint ministers on the

---

[10] Readers interested in comparing Ecuadoran usage with parliamentary systems elsewhere in Latin America may wish to consult William S. Stokes, "Parliamentary Government in Latin America," *American Political Science Review*, Vol. XXXIX, No. 3 (June, 1945), pp. 522–536; Paul S. Reinsch, "Parliamentary Government in Chile," *American Political Science Review*, Vol. III (November, 1909), pp. 507–538; and Stokes, "The Cuban Parliamentary System in Action, 1940–1947," *Journal of Politics*, Vol. XI, No. 2 (May, 1949), pp. 335–364.

basis of any considerations he deems appropriate. Political factors normally dictate the appointments. It is frequently said that personal favoritism is the only basis of selection of ministers, but this is not true. Although no formal standards have been developed and promulgated as such, a survey of Ecuadoran cabinet appointments indicates that at least the following five elements enter into the formation of a cabinet:

1. A minister must be a person whom the president feels he can trust. Cabinet members are generally trusted confidants of the president, and the personal factor plays a large part in determining the composition of a cabinet.

2. The party affiliations of ministers are also taken into consideration. The parties represented in the cabinet at any given time reflect the general political situation in the republic. All ministers may be members of the president's party; an opposition party may be appeased by being assigned a number of cabinet posts; if the president was elected on a coalition ticket, the ministries may be divided among the components of the coalition; or the president may deem it prudent to name as ministers certain persons not affiliated with any political party. The party composition of the cabinet varies in accordance with the exigencies of the national political scene, and this factor enters into the rapidity with which cabinet resignations sometimes occur.

3. Regionalism also is involved in the formulation of a cabinet. The Coast and the Sierra are generally more or less equally represented in this body, and in this sense a political function of the cabinet is akin to one of the services performed by the vice-presidency.

4. Tradition also affects cabinet appointments somewhat. The foreign minister has traditionally been a member of the Conservative party, although occasional exceptions to this formula (for example, Foreign Minister José Vicente Trujillo, a Radical Liberal) may be noted. Similarly, the minister of social welfare generally is a Socialist, although departures from tradition are more frequent in this regard than in the case of the foreign office. When the Conservative and Socialist parties, or either of them, declare their opposition to an administration to the extent of forbidding their affiliates to accept cabinet posts, this factor is of course temporarily inoperative.

5. Last, and perhaps unfortunately least, among the considerations involved in the formation of a cabinet is the desire that a minister have some familiarity with the types of problems under the jurisdiction of his ministry.

Shortly before his inauguration as president, Galo Plaza Lasso told the writer: "I am now in the process of completing my cabinet. And in doing so, I have wished to comply with the following political formula: in the cabinet there will have to be represented the Coast and the Sierra. There will be someone who will inspire the absolute confidence of the left; someone of the center; and someone of the right. These will necessarily have to be capable, dynamic people who can work as a team with me and who are prepared for any sacrifice for the good of the country. I prefer a cabinet which will operate efficiently to one which, from the point of view of politics, would have more prestige; but it is possible to fill both requirements."

The cabinet has had a twofold political significance in Ecuador. In the first place, it is one of the few elements of government which have had a stable and orderly development throughout the history of the republic, one of the few institutions of republican life which have become deeply embedded in Ecuadoran practice. The evolution of the Ecuadoran cabinet has progressed in a manner largely independent of constitutional texts. Second, the cabinet is more directly and immediately sensitive to political conditions in the country than any other element of the executive function. Political instability in the republic is frequently dramatized by rapid cabinet changes. Twenty-seven different ministers occupied the eight posts between May 29, 1944, and August 23, 1947; and no fewer than twelve foreign ministers endeavored to conduct the country's international relations in the period between August and October of 1933. It would appear that fluidity in the composition of the cabinet is a reflection rather than a cause of political instability in Ecuador.

CHAPTER VI

THE NATIONAL LEGISLATURE

THE THEORETICAL position of the legislative function under the Constitution of 1946 dramatically illustrates the chronically unrealistic nature of Ecuador's written constitutions. The republic's legislatures have been notoriously weak despite constitutional pronouncements to the contrary, and this basic pattern has continued under the 1946 charter.

THE LEGISLATIVE FUNCTION

The Constitution of 1946 proclaims the doctrine of legislative supremacy, ignoring rather than defying the inescapable fact that the strongest element in the governmental system of the country has normally and traditionally been the executive. An analysis of legislative infirmity would involve such factors, discussed in the following paragraphs, as: (1) the nature of the Ecuadoran class system; (2) the condition of the country's electoral process; and (3) the weakness and fluidity of many of the political parties of the republic.

1. Ecuadoran government officials, regardless of the particular functions with which they happen to be affiliated, are always "whites." The same upper class, the same small stratum of Ecuadoran society, controls the legislative as well as the executive and judicial functions of government. The great majority of the nation's peoples—Indians, cholos, montuvios, and Negroes—are excluded from effective representation in congress with the same degree of thoroughness already noted in connection with other aspects of Ecuadoran government and politics. The ruling class, constituting approximately 20 per cent of the population of the republic, monopolizes control of the legislative function, in which are represented the basic instruments of power upon which the Ecuadoran political process rests. Members of congress are the landowners, officers of the armed forces, *de facto* agents of the Church,[1] and the men of letters and the liberal professions.

Since the same class interests are represented by the legislative and executive functions, significant conflicts between these two organs of government normally do not occur. Thus the national legislature tends to fall into the role of a kind of rubber stamp endorsing and ratifying the actions of the executive. Differences of economic or ideological in-

---

[1] Since a 1937 agreement with the Vatican, Church officials have—nominally, at least—been forbidden to participate directly in Ecuadoran politics.

terests rarely separate the two functions. Strained legislative-executive relationships seldom develop; and when they do occur their base is to be found primarily in regionalism or personalismo. The infrequent disagreements between the two functions merely reflect the emergence of some crisis dividing the "whites" among themselves.

2. Caudillismo and its influence on the Ecuadoran electoral process provide the instrument of adjustment rendering the legislative subservient to the executive function. Caudillismo combined with the fraudulent election has the effect of bringing legislators into office on the caudillo's coattails; and a relationship of personalismo between the president and a majority of the members of congress frequently relegates the latter to a subordinate role in the government. During times when the executive function is headed by a "constitutional president," the legislative function normally exercises greater authority in the government than during periods of caudillo rule. Should a conflict develop between the president and congress, the weapons of the former are such that he is usually able to do away with the legislature or bend it to his will. Ecuadoran constitutions have traditionally prohibited dissolution of congress, but this has not prevented presidents from taking that step nevertheless. The caudillo cannot retain power if he does not effectively control the army, and the threat of force or its actual use has frequently overcome such antiexecutive movements as occasionally arise in congress and other deliberative bodies. One form of pressure employed by President Velasco Ibarra against the constituent assembly of 1946 is a case in point. A probable majority of the members of that body had given favorable consideration to a proposal to terminate the president's period in office before the assembly adjourned. The body rapidly changed its attitude toward the proposal, however, when it was learned that a cordon of picked troops was being formed around the National Palace, the building in which the assemblymen were meeting.

3. Loose, ineffective party organization, along with the fluid, transitory nature of many of the political groups of the republic, also tends to undermine the authority of the national legislature. Lack of discipline and effective organization within the legislative body has become increasingly acute in the years since 1944. The general absence of a definite and more than fleeting political orientation on the part of the majority of the members of congress contributes to a chaotic condition within that body. The legislature tends to be a directionless, weak, and sometimes easily manipulated organ of government. Congressional effectiveness would have to be based on "the existence of organized political

parties capable of undertaking the responsibility of exercising power," Senator Jaramillo Alvarado has said; in the absence of this prerequisite, the doctrine of congressional supremacy "is almost always false, causing grave damage to the constitutional system."[2]

Yet, according to the Constitution of 1946, the legislative function theoretically stands above the executive and judicial functions. The role of the legislative function, according to Zevallos, is nothing less than to "declare the ends of the state, seeking at the same time methods adequate to achieve them."[3] Legislative methods theoretically differ from those of the judiciary in that the former are general in nature, applying to events in the future, whereas judicial methods are individual and specific, applying to cases arising out of past events. The text of the constitution attempts to implement the doctrine of legislative supremacy by conferring upon the legislative function the exclusive authority to: (1) control the public purse; (2) censure and impeach ministers, the president, and other enumerated government officials; (3) amend the constitution; and (4) decide questions of substantive unconstitutionality.

1. The national budget enacted by congress enters into force on January 1 of each year. The constitution urges but does not require the legislators to pass the annual budget bill on or before the preceding October 9. The general constitutional rule is that no officer of the executive function may effect an expenditure of public funds unless in accordance with an express provision of the budget law. The power of the purse, if substantially guaranteed, could, of course, become an essential pillar in the structure of legislative supremacy. There are, however, at least two legal methods by which the executive may wrest this function from congress. First, the president, once he has acquired emergency powers, may constitutionally divert public funds from the purposes for which they were originally appropriated. Second, the president may allow budget deficiencies to arise during the course of the fiscal year provided that he is able at the end of that period to explain the deficiencies to congress to the satisfaction of the majority of its members. No caudillo who effectively controls a majority of the legislators experiences difficulty in explaining to their satisfaction any arbitrary fiscal procedures which he may have taken. Although it may be unfair to condemn the Constitution of 1946 on the basis of such brief experience with it, it seemed in 1950 that the power over appropriations was not effectively in the hands of the legislative function.

2. The legislative power of censure is somewhat more effective than

---

[2] Jaramillo Alvarado, *El Régimen Totalitario en América*, p. 63.
[3] Zevallos, *op. cit.*, p. 236.

the authority of impeachment. No Ecuadoran president has ever been impeached under any of the fifteen constitutions, although the power of impeachment has been contained in all of them with the sole exception of the 1830 document. Ministers have on occasion been removed from office by congressional censure, although this had not yet occurred under the Constitution of 1946 at the time this book was written. The constitution specifically prohibits removal of cabinet ministers through votes of no confidence; this parliamentary practice has been permitted by only two of Ecuador's constitutions, the 1929 and 1945 charters.

3. The authority to amend the constitution has—wholly or in large part—theoretically rested with the legislature under all fifteen of the republic's charters. Considered collectively, these documents have been amended three times during the entire history of Ecuador,[4] and constitutions have been legislatively "interpreted" on seventeen occasions. The traditional Ecuadoran practice is to replace rather than to amend a constitution, a practice which removes the constituent authority from the hands of congress. The 1946 document may be amended if the proposed alteration is passed in the same form by two successive sessions of congress, an affirmative vote of a simple majority of the membership of that body being required. The power to change the constitution, were it effectively a legislative monopoly, would constitute a major aspect of a congressional claim to supremacy. Ecuadoran constitutional history, however, argues against the probability that the Constitution of 1946 will be amended in conformity with the process as outlined in its text. The statistical probability is that the change will be made by some organ of government other than the legislative function.

4. The ostensibly sole and exclusive right of the legislative function to rule with finality on questions of substantive unconstitutionality superficially appears to be a matter of some consequence. Investigation of the concept of unconstitutionality in Ecuadoran constitutional law, however, indicates that the congressional role in this area is negligible. The function of declaring public acts unconstitutional has developed in Ecuadoran law in a manner which has vitiated the legislature's voice in constitutional matters. The power to rule on the constitutionality of measures has been decentralized and apportioned among various agencies of government. The courts and the council of state perhaps play a greater part in determining issues of questioned constitutionality than does the legislative function.[5]

[4] The Constitution of 1852 was amended in 1853; the 1883 document was altered in 1887; and the 1897 charter was amended in 1905.
[5] For a systematic discussion of the concept of unconstitutionality in Ecuadoran constitutional law, see pp. 137–138, below.

The doctrine of legislative supremacy is, in summary, a grotesque fiction from several points of view.

The legislative authority, such as it is, is exercised by a bicameral congress. The Constitution of 1946 is in conformity with traditional Ecuadoran usage in providing for a two-chamber national legislature, only three of the republic's fifteen constitutions having prescribed the unicameral form. The latest constitution likewise follows traditional procedure in naming the upper chamber the "senate" and the lower house the "chamber of deputies." In 1949 there were forty-five senators and sixty-four deputies, giving congress a total membership of 109.

Regular sessions of congress open on August 10 of each year for a period of sixty days, extendable an additional thirty days. During the last decade there has developed in Ecuador an antipathy to prolonged sessions of legislatures and other deliberative bodies, with the result that legislators have developed an almost obsessive desire to dispose of the year's work within sixty days. Use of the constitutionally permitted thirty-day extension is regarded as an error to be eschewed at almost any cost. This attitude, prevalent among Ecuadoran political leaders, is perhaps unfortunate from the standpoint of the possibility of the development of more democratic procedures in the country and the emergence of effective legislative control over the executive. Periods in which legislatures and other deliberative bodies have been in session have in general been times of tension and imminent instability in Ecuador. A striking atmosphere of impending crisis appears to settle upon politically articulate sectors of the population during the week before congress meets, and rumors of impending revolts and similarily disturbing matters are normally given wide circulation during this period.

Most Ecuadoran politicians hold that, during the course of the republic's history, deliberative bodies have been in session too often and too long. As of September 1, 1950, national legislative bodies had held sixty-nine regular and thirty-nine special sessions. These figures do not seem excessive in themselves; but to them might be added the fact that no fewer than seventeen constituent assemblies, called for the purpose of adopting new constitutions, have met during the history of the country. Moreover, the belief was general in 1950 that the constituent assembly of 1944–1945, which wrote the Constitution of 1945, had seriously overstayed its welcome by remaining in session for seven months. Statements by the nation's leaders warning against frequent or lengthy sessions of deliberative bodies have not been lacking in recent years. Conservative party leader Mariano Suárez Veintimilla warned in 1946 that "the excessive prolongation of a constituent assembly or a congress always causes democratic deviations";[6] and President Carlos Mancheno asserted a year later that such bodies were "hotbeds of unrest and personal ambition."[7] It is against such a background that congress has refused to use the thirty-day extension permitted by the Constitution of 1946.

In addition to the annual regular sixty-day session, special sessions of congress may also be held. These may be convoked either by the president of the republic or by the presiding officer of the senate, the latter having this authority only when at least two-thirds of the members of congress petition for such a session. Special sessions may consider only those matters specifically cited in the convocation, and must adjourn immediately after disposition of that business.

Whether the session be regular or special, both chambers must open and adjourn on the same days, and neither may be recessed for more than three days without the consent of the other. A majority of the members of each house constitutes its quorum, and all sessions are public unless a majority of either chamber agrees that it should consider a given item of business in secret. Each house is the final judge of the election of its own members. Senators and deputies may not be sued for remarks made by them on the floors of their chambers.

THE SENATE

Members of the forty-five-man senate serve four-year terms, the entire chamber being renewed at once. Senators are indefinitely eligible for reëlection. Two *suplentes* or alternates are chosen for each incumbent senator to facilitate his replacement if he dies, resigns, or otherwise vacates his seat before the next election. Senators must be Ecuadorans by birth, in the exercise of citizenship, and at least thirty-five years of age. Persons holding Ecuadoran government contracts for the exploitation of the natural resources of the country are ineligible for election to the senate, the same prohibition applying to the agents and representatives of such persons or of foreign companies.

No consistent principle of representation underlies the apportionment of senate seats. The composition of this body rests on a curious mixture of two principles of representation, with the result that a constitutional distinction is made between the "functional" and "provincial" senators. The former represent economic, professional, and occupational groups as such; while the latter represent the provinces as such and the Galápagos Islands.

[6] *El Comercio*, Quito, July 4, 1946.
[7] *Ibid.*, August 29, 1947.

The principle of functional representation has had a development in Ecuador which seems to suggest that the practice will not be abandoned in the near future, although it was severely criticized during the life of the Constitution of 1945. Functional representation appeared upon the Ecuadoran scene with the promulgation of the Constitution of 1929, and has been retained in the two constitutions written since that time. The idea as it operated under the 1929 document produced a rather influential body of partisans of the functional principle, a result being that the practice was written with great enthusiasm into the Constitution of 1945. Whereas many had been convinced of the success of the principle in the 1929 charter, the ill-fated Constitution of 1945, providing for functional representation in a unicameral legislature, was followed by a storm of adverse criticism. This reaction, however, was not strong enough to eliminate functional representation from the 1946 document, which provides for a reduced and limited form of the practice, and that in the senate only. Twelve of the forty-five members of this body are "functional senators"; these fall into two groups, national and regional.

There are four national functional senators. These represent, respectively, public education, private education, journalism and the scientific and literary societies, and the armed forces. The eight regional functional senators are apportioned equally between the Sierra and the Coast, representing for each of these regions agriculture, commerce, labor, and industry. Functional senators are required to have been actively affiliated for at least a year prior to their election with the economic, professional, and occupational groups which they represent. Twelve electoral colleges meet once every four years, each electing a functional senator. The electoral colleges are variously organized, depending on the nature of the economic or occupational group involved. For the purpose of electing the national functional senator for public education, for example, the faculty of each of the four universities of the republic designates one of its members to serve as an elector. This four-man electoral college then meets to choose the national functional senator for public education. The electoral college for Coastal labor, to cite another example, is composed of one representative from each labor organization of the Coast; again, the landowners of the Sierra meet as the electoral college for Sierra agriculture; and each of the military and naval commands chooses one elector to serve as a member of the electoral college for the armed forces. Each of the twelve electoral colleges casts its ballots and then communicates its choice to the supreme electoral tribunal, which investigates the qualifications of the twelve nominees before officially announcing the names of the twelve functional senators-elect.

Functional representation in the senate performs two basic services within the constitutional system of Ecuador: (1) The practice adds a measure of protection to such instruments of power underlying the political process as the pattern of landownership, the armed forces, and the political role of formal education peculiar to countries like Ecuador. (2) From the standpoint of regionalism, the institution of functional representation tends to guard against catastrophic disruption of the delicate balance of power maintained between the Sierra and the Coast. Moreover, since it increases the number of senators from these two regions, functional representation has served to silence protests that concessions to the Oriente and the Galápagos Islands would result in the underrepresentation of the major regions of the republic.

Thus, functional representation under the Constitution of 1946 has operated in accordance with the realities of Ecuadoran politics, despite the illogical nature of the over-all system of senatorial apportionment. With the exception of the two functional senators for labor—this group is small, undeveloped, and essentially unorganized in Ecuador—the system has in general given realistic recognition to the major instruments of power which underlie the political system as it actually operates, and little dissatisfaction has been expressed with functional representation as provided for in the latest constitution. This situation contrasts markedly with Ecuadoran experience under the Constitution of 1945, which gave unrealistically heavy representation to labor. Moreover, during the life of that document, the two most influential newspapers of Ecuador, *El Comercio* of Quito and *El Telégrafo* of Guayaquil, were continually protesting against the functional deputy for journalism. These discrepancies did not appear under the Constitution of 1946, which was a conservative document so far as it recognized and rested upon the preëxisting instruments of power.

The remaining thirty-three senators are called "provincial senators." The designation is not strictly accurate as applied to the entire group, since one senator represents the Galápagos Islands, which do not have provincial status. For purposes of representation in the senate, all Sierra and Coastal provinces are regarded as equal, each being entitled to two senators. Each of the two Oriente provinces, assigned a species of junior status, sends only one member to the senate. A provincial senator is required to have established a domicile in the area he represents at least three years prior to his election, the term "domicile" being liberally interpreted in the case of senators "from" the Oriente and the Galápagos Islands. Thus the ten Sierra provinces are represented by twenty senators; the five Coastal provinces, by ten; the Oriente, by two; and the archipelago by one senator. The provincial senators are popularly elected once every four years. The votes in these elections are counted by the appropriate provincial electoral tribunals.

The system of senatorial representation is at once strikingly illogical and curiously effective. The singular use of what is called "functional representation" allows for realistic recognition of the power relationships which constitute the Ecuadoran pattern. Underlying the manner of selecting provincial senators is the proposition that all provinces are constitutionally equal for the purposes of senatorial apportionment; yet departures from this idea in dealing with the provinces of the Oriente take cognizance of the realities of the situation. The Oriente and the Galápagos Islands in the Ecuadoran political system are "poor relations," and are represented as such in the senate. The system of functional representation is not applied to either of these areas; and the inescapable fact that the Oriente contains second-class provinces is implicit in the apportionment of provincial senators among the regions of the republic.

Senators, provincial as well as functional, are exclusively "whites." Preponderant representation is given to the small ruling class of the republic and to the instruments of power which maintain its position. Thus, the landowners, the Church partisans, the armed forces, and—especially in the case of the Coastal delegation—the merchants constitute the majority of the senate. Men of advanced formal education, notably university professors, are also conspicuous in the body. Exceptions to the observation concerning the ruling class are the two functional senators for labor, including the Communist leader Pedro Antonio Saad, who in 1948 was the functional senator for Coastal labor. Such deviations, however, scarcely affect the comfortable preponderance of representation given in the senate to the small ruling class of Ecuador.

The vice-president of the republic is the presiding officer of the senate, and votes only in case of a tie. An officer called the "president of the senate" is elected by that body from among its own members, and presides over its sessions when the vice-president is unable to do so. For the conduct of its business, the senate has fourteen standing committees.

The constitution confers five exclusive powers upon the senate. (1) This body tries all cases of impeachment brought by the chamber of deputies. Officials who may be tried in this way, according to the constitution, include the president, vice-president, or acting president of the republic; members of the supreme court; members of the supreme electoral tribunal; senators and deputies accused of committing crimes; and members of the president's cabinet, when the executive function is charged with having violated the constitution. The president of the supreme court presides over the senate when it hears impeachment cases brought by the chamber of deputies. (2) Further, the senate has the exclusive power to demand that the president of the republic enforce the responsibilities of other employees and officials of the executive function. (3) Once each year, the senate elects one of its own number to serve as a member of the council of state. (4) The senate may also declare the innocence of persons unjustly condemned, and (5) restore Ecuadoran citizenship to certain classes of persons who may have been deprived of it.

The political composition of the senate normally demonstrates that this body responds more slowly to political developments in the republic than does the chamber of deputies. Although a major characteristic of Ecuadoran politics since 1944 has been the revival of the strength of the Conservative party, the senate was less Conservative on August 10, 1948, than the lower house was. Of the senate membership 38 per cent was Radical Liberal, 31 per cent was Conservative, 18 per cent was Socialist, 2 per cent was Communist, and 11 per cent was independent. The next senatorial election, at which time all forty-five seats would be at stake, was scheduled for the first Sunday in June of 1951.

THE CHAMBER OF DEPUTIES

The chamber of deputies is composed of sixty-four members popularly elected for two-year terms. Deputies are indefinitely eligible for re-election. They must be Ecuadorans by birth, in the exercise of the rights of citizenship, and at least twenty-five years of age. Persons holding Ecuadoran government contracts for the exploitation of the natural resources of the country may not be elected to the chamber of deputies, the same prohibition applying to the agents and representatives of such persons or of foreign companies. Each deputy is required to have established a domicile in the province he represents at least three years prior to his election.

"Each province will elect one deputy for every 50,000 inhabitants, and, if there remains an excess of 25,000 or more, it will elect another deputy," the Constitution of 1946 declares. "Every province, except the Archipelago of Columbus [Galápagos Islands],[8] will elect at least two deputies, even though it may not have 50,000 inhabitants."[9] This article of the constitution has never been put into operation, for the simple reason that no population census has ever been taken in Ecuador. Supplementary legislation has provided that, until such time as a census is at last completed, the Sierra provinces will elect forty deputies, the Coastal provinces nineteen, the Oriente provinces four, and the Galápagos Islands one, giving the chamber a total membership of sixty-four deputies.[10]

No Sierra or Coastal province sends fewer than three deputies to the chamber, and no Oriente province more than two. This distinction is of significance in determining the manner of election of deputies, which is essentially different in the Sierra and the Coast from that in the Oriente and the archipelago. It will be remembered that the constitution proclaims the principle of proportional representation, which governs all elections in which each voter casts a ballot for three or more members of the same body. The provinces of the republic are not districted for the purpose of electing deputies, as all deputies representing a given province represent it at large. The result is that deputies from the Sierra and the Coast are selected by proportional representation, while deputies representing the Oriente and the Galápagos Islands are not.

A variety of the list system of proportional representation is used. The Coastal province of Guayas, for example, is entitled to five deputies, and each Guayas voter, unable to split his ballot, votes for all five. Political organizations, singly or in combination, nominate lists of candidates for the five seats, and the voter casts his ballot for an entire list. The count is conducted by the Guayas provincial electoral tribunal, which divides the total number of valid votes cast for deputies in the province by the number of offices to be filled—five, in this case—the result of this process being known as the first quota. Any list of candidates receiving a number of votes totaling less than half of the first quota is eliminated at that point; and a second quota is arrived at by

---

[8] Strictly speaking, the islands are not a province. They are governed through the ministry of national defense.

[9] *Constitución Política de la República del Ecuador* (Quito, 1946), Art. 47.

[10] The Sierra provinces, and the number of deputies assigned to each, are as follows: Carchi, three; Imbabura, three; Pichincha, five; Cotopaxi, four; Tungurahua, four; Chimborazo, five; Bolívar, three; Cañar, three; Azuay, five; and Loja, five.

The Coastal provinces, and the number of deputies assigned to each, are as follows: Esmeraldas, three; Manabí, five; Los Ríos, three; Guayas, five; and El Oro, three.

Each of the two Oriente provinces—Napo-Pastaza and Santiago-Zamora—is entitled to two deputies.

dividing the total number of valid ballots cast for the remaining lists by the number of offices to be filled. The number of valid votes cast for each list involved in the computation of the second quota is then divided by that quota, the result for each list indicating how many of its candidates for deputy have been elected to the five-man Guayas delegation to the chamber of deputies.

The process in the Oriente provinces and in the Galápagos Islands is simpler. Each Oriente province is represented at large by two deputies, the two candidates receiving the largest number of votes in each province being declared elected. The islands are represented in the chamber of deputies by the one candidate receiving the largest number of votes for deputy.

Like the senate, the chamber of deputies essentially represents the small and controlling "white" class. Landowners, Church partisans, military men, lawyers, and professors constitute the bulk of the lower chamber's membership. Despite the fact that the chamber of deputies contained in 1948 a proportionately greater number of Conservatives than did the senate, it was nevertheless true that the former chamber also gave greater representation to commerce, industry, and the virtually nonexistent labor movement, all of these elements finding their spokesmen exclusively in the Coastal delegations. Two Communists, Enrique Gil Gilbert of the Coastal province of Guayas and Nicolás Kingman of the Oriente Province of Napo-Pastaza, were deputies in 1948, but their presence in the chamber did not alter the fact that basically the legislative function served the interests of the small ruling class within which the republic's peculiar political process operated.

The chamber is presided over by a president of the chamber of deputies, elected from among the membership of that body. A vice-president of the chamber is also elected for the purpose of officiating when the president is unable to do so. For the conduct of its business, the chamber has thirteen standing committees.

The constitution delegates these two exclusive powers to the chamber of deputies: (1) This body investigates charges brought against the president, vice-president, or acting president of the republic; members of the supreme court; members of the supreme electoral tribunal; senators and deputies accused of crimes; and members of the president's cabinet, when the executive function is charged with having violated the constitution. A decision of the chamber of deputies against an accused official is known as an impeachment. Impeachment is analogous to indictment in signifying only that, in the opinion of the chamber, the charges against the official are sufficiently grave to warrant his being tried by the senate. Officials impeached by the chamber and convicted by the senate are removed from office, any further action against them lying within the province of the judicial function. (2) The chamber of deputies also has the exclusive power to elect one of its members to a one-year term on the council of state.

The political composition of the chamber of deputies demonstrates the proposition that this body normally responds earlier than does the senate to political conditions in the republic. The rising strength of the Conservative party in recent years has found political expression in the chamber of deputies earlier than in the senate, largely because deputies have only two-year terms as compared with the senators' four-year terms. Thus, in 1948, 36 per cent of the deputies—as contrasted with 31 per cent of the senators—was Conservative; 31 per cent of the chamber of deputies—as against 38 per cent of the senate—was Radical Liberal; 14 per cent of the deputies—compared with a senatorial percentage of 18—was Socialist; 3 per cent of the deputies was Communist; and 16 per cent of the chamber's members was independent. These figures represented the political composition of congress just before the election for the chamber of deputies held on June 5, 1949.

Powers and Operation of Congress

The powers of congress are constitutionally divided into two classes: powers which may be exercised when both houses meet in joint session, and those which may be employed when the two chambers sit separately.

When meeting in joint session, congress is under the presidency of the vice-president of the republic and possesses six types of powers. A vote of two-thirds of the legislators present is necessary for an affirmative decision on the exercise of any of these powers, described below:

1. The power of congress to amend the constitution is a function of the joint session, it being required that a given amendment be passed in the same form in two successive years. Presidential approval of constitutional amendments is not required.

2. Congress meets in joint session to elect, or confirm the election of, a number of the officials of the republic. This provision applies to congressional review of the work of the supreme electoral tribunal, the legislators having the final authority to declare the president and vice-president of the republic legally elected. In this connection, the power of congress to elect the judges of the supreme and superior courts and two of the members of the legislative commission may be noted. In

addition, congress elects the superintendent of banks, the comptroller general, and the attorney general of the nation. Congress must act in joint session when accepting or rejecting the proffered resignations of any of these officials.

3. One form of the authority of congress to remove the president, vice-president, and cabinet ministers from office is exercised in joint session. The president or vice-president may be removed in this manner if, in the opinion of congress, he is either physically or mentally unable

TABLE 7
PARTY COMPOSITION OF ECUADORAN CONGRESS ON AUGUST 10, 1948

Party	Senate		Chamber of deputies		Both houses	
	Number	Per cent	Number	Per cent	Number	Per cent
Totals...............	45	100	64	100	109	100
Conservative......	14	31	23	36	37	34
Radical Liberal....	17	38	20	31	37	34
Socialist...........	8	18	9	14	17	16
Communist........	1	2	2	3	3	3
Independent[a]......	5	11	10	16	15	13

[a] Senators and deputies who had no formal party affiliation at the time of their election are listed as "independent."

to continue at his post. Removal from office in this fashion is to be distinguished from removal in consequence of impeachment, which involves charges other than physical or mental disability.

4. Acting in joint session, congress may censure individual ministers on charges of misconduct in office. This action has already been distinguished from a vote of no confidence, which is specifically prohibited by the constitution.

5. Congressional authority to enact the annual national budget is employed in joint session.

6. Certain defense powers of congress may be used only when the two chambers are sitting jointly. Included in this group are the authority to grant or deny emergency powers to the president of the republic, to declare war, and to approve treaties of peace. Authority to approve or reject promotions of army officers to the ranks of colonel and general also lies in this category.

A wide range of additional powers is employed by congress when the two chambers sit separately. Bills implementing these powers may be passed by a simple majority of the legislators present in each house, and must of course be approved in the same form by both chambers. For purposes of analysis, the powers exercised by congress when the chambers sit separately may be classified under six headings, discussed in the paragraphs that follow: (1) constituent, (2) defense and military, (3) fiscal, (4) judicial, (5) administrative, and (6) relating to public works.

1. The constituent powers of the legislative function include the authority to interpret the constitution and to rule with finality on questions of substantive unconstitutionality. A reading of the Constitution of 1946, unaccompanied by other materials, would convey the impression that this authority constitutes a power of considerable consequence. This, however, is not the case. The development of the concept of unconstitutionality in Ecuador has been such as to distribute aspects of the function of interpreting the constitution among a number of government agencies, among which the courts and the council of state figure prominently, with the result that the congressional role in this process is negligible. More real among the constitutional powers of the legislative function is the authority to create, change, and abolish provinces and cantons. An important phase of the Ecuadoran constitutional system is the unitary nature of the internal organization of the republic; and the extent of congressional authority to influence this organization is significant.

2. The power of the legislative function in defense and military matters includes the determination of the peacetime strength of the armed forces. Further, congress may grant or deny permission to foreign powers to send their troops through Ecuadoran territory, or to station their warships in the territorial waters of the republic for a longer time than is normally required by international practices. Similar legislative authority relates to the landing of foreign warplanes on Ecuadoran soil, although forced landings are excepted. It is to be noted that the voice of the legislative function is controlling in defense and military matters only in peaceful times; it is displaced by the emergency powers of the president in urgent situations.

3. The fiscal authority of congress includes the power to establish uniform systems of weights, measures, and currency. For most purposes of measurement, Ecuador has adopted the metric system. The monetary unit is the sucre, valued in 1949 at 12.50 to the United States dollar, official rate. This rate was effective almost exclusively in intergovernmental transactions, most business being conducted at the free rate,

which hovered in the neighborhood of 16.50 sucres to the dollar. The legislative function possesses the authority to establish taxes and other revenue measures, and to authorize the executive to borrow money on the credit of the republic of Ecuador. Congress is required to receive a periodic accounting of public funds and to make provisions for the servicing of the country's public debt. The authority to open and close ports—the only port of major consequence is at the Coastal city of Guayaquil—also lies within the jurisdiction of the legislative function.

4. Foremost among the judicial powers of congress is the authority to enact legal codes governing the operation of the judicial function. The principal codes establish Ecuadoran civil, penal, commercial, and labor law. Congress may also grant amnesties and pardons, the constitution stipulating that this is the sole instance in which the legislators may interfere with the work of the courts.

5. The administrative powers of congress include the organization of all government agencies and offices. The legislators may also require the appropriate authorities to make more effective the responsibilities of public employees.

6. Congress may at any time declare a given sphere of activity to be within the public interest. Such a declaration has the effect of authorizing public works projects within that sphere, and is accordingly a matter of some significance as a constitutional vehicle for the expansion of governmental power.

The constitutional distinction between the types of authority exercised by congress in joint session and the types exercised when the chambers sit separately is of prime importance in providing an insight into the actual operation of congress. Bills dealing with most measures to be considered in joint session are prepared by an agency known as the legislative commission. The joint session as such does little more than ratify the work of the commission. Up to the time this book was written, no revolt against the proposals of the commission had ever occurred in a joint session under the Constitution of 1946.

Within the constitutional system of Ecuador, the legislative commission performs a service somewhat analogous to that already noted for the council of state. Since 1944, emphasis has been placed on the coördination of functions as a reaction against the earlier doctrine of the separation of powers. Reflecting this change of emphasis, the legislative commission acts as an agency of interfunctional coöperation in the preparation of bills of major importance. This five-man body is composed of one senator, chosen by the senate; one deputy, selected by the chamber of deputies; one representative of the executive function, named by the president of the republic; one representative of the judicial function, designated by the supreme court; and the dean of the faculty of jurisprudence at the Central University at Quito, who is an ex officio member of the commission. Members of the body must meet the constitutional qualifications of a senator; that is, they must be Ecuadorans by birth, in the exercise of the rights of citizenship, and at least thirty-five years of age.

Bills formulated by the legislative commission and presented to a joint session of congress are not submitted to any of the standing committees of either chamber before being subjected to action on the floor. The five members of the presidium-like legislative commission thus play a crucial role in the formulation of legislative policy. Weakened party organization has generally resulted in a lack of congressional leadership which might conceivably develop a floor revolt against the commission's bills, and their removal from the committee machinery reduces the probability of their amendment or rejection by the joint session. Once passed by the two chambers meeting jointly, a measure is sent to the president for signature and promulgation. All affirmative decisions of the joint session, it will be remembered, require the approval of two-thirds of the legislators present; and measures of this kind cannot be vetoed by the executive.

The case is quite different in the exercise of powers employed when the two chambers sit separately. In such circumstances, legislative initiative is transferred from the legislative commission and is generally seized by party leaders in congress and key members of the various standing committees of the chambers. In general, committee work and floor debates tend to add merely institutional ratification to decisions already made elsewhere on an informal basis. Most legislative decisions are actually made at house parties held in the homes of the more influential political leaders; and where matters of exceptional moment are decided upon, these gatherings are generally attended by members of the legislative commission as well as by other key political figures. Informal meetings held during the legislative day may determine the progress of measures before congress. The bar of the Hotel Majestic—near the National Palace at Quito, in which congress meets—is a favored site for many of these informal gatherings.

These meetings, whether at house parties or over cool glasses at the Hotel Majestic, constitute the essence of the extralegal machinery of the legislative body. They are normally attended by the leaders of the major groups and blocs in Congress, and provide an atmosphere of relatively easy informality in which major policy decisions are made. The foreign observer experiences difficulty in gaining access to such meetings, and can usually do little more than guess at what takes place. Party leaders are reluctant to discuss such matters with outsiders. The writer was, however, impressed by the fact that he could be told immediately before a legislative session such things as (1) who would make what motions, (2) who would speak against them, (3) how long the floor debate on a given issue would last, (4) what aspects of the issue would not be raised during the debate because they were "delicate" or "inconvenient," and (5) what the final vote on the matter was likely to be. These were usually fairly accurate predictions if they came from a congressman who had attended an important informal gathering a night or two previously, or who had come from the bar of the Hotel Majestic just before he took his place on the floor of the chamber of which he was a member.

Under the constitution a bill may be introduced in congress if it has the support of at least three qualified members of the legislative, executive, or judicial functions. Any senator or deputy may qualify for this role on behalf of the legislative function; the task may be performed for the executive by any cabinet minister; and any member of the supreme court may represent the judicial function for this purpose. The task of introducing measures in joint sessions is generally performed by the legislative commission.

When the chambers sit separately, each introduced bill is assigned to the appropriate standing committee of the chamber receiving the measure. Committees have the power to bury a bill in a fashion similar to that enjoyed by the committees of the Congress of the United States. Committees may also amend bills under their care; and once a bill is in the form approved by the committee, the measure is reported out to the full chamber. A committee which does not wish to report out a bill may be forced to discharge the measure by a majority vote of the chamber. A bill which has emerged from committee treatment is debated on the floor of the chamber, at which time the measure may be passed in its original form as received from the committee, amended, or rejected. A bill rejected after floor debate in the chamber of its origin may not again be considered until the next regular session of congress, unless it is reintroduced in substantially altered form. Whether or not the revamping is sufficient is normally a routine question decided by the secretary of the chamber in which the reintroduction takes place.

His ruling may be reversed by the presiding officer of that house, whose decision may in turn be overruled by a simple majority of the members of the chamber who are present.

Bills approved by a majority vote in the chamber of their origin are transmitted to the other house, where they are again assigned to committees and subjected to floor debate. The power of the second chamber over a bill is essentially the same as that of the chamber of origin. The measure approved by the first chamber and rejected by the second dies at that point; bills further amended by the second chamber must again be considered in a joint session, at which time two-thirds of the legislators present must agree on the same form of the measures if they are to continue on their course toward promulgation as law.

Bills approved in the same form by both chambers are sent to the president of the republic, who must approve or object to the measures within ten days of their receipt by his office. A bill which has not been acted upon by the executive at the expiration of the ten-day period automatically becomes law if congress is still in session; if congress has adjourned before the ten days expire, the president may pursue either of these two alternatives: (1) He may cause the bill to be published in the *Registro Oficial* within twenty days after the adjournment of congress, in which case the measure—if it is to avoid extinction—must be reintroduced in congress during the first three days of its next regular session. (2) He may deny the measure publication in the *Registro Oficial* within the stipulated twenty-day period, in which case the bill—with or without the president's signature—becomes law thirty days after the adjournment of congress and must be published in the *Registro Oficial* at that time. No measure may become law unless it is published in that organ. All laws enter into force as of the date of their publication in the *Registro Oficial,* unless a later date is specified in the text of a given measure.

Under the constitution, the president may veto a bill on either or both of two grounds: he may object to the measure because he feels it to be politically unwise, or because he believes that it is unconstitutional. In either case he must return a vetoed bill to the chamber of its origin together with a statement of his objections to the project. If the veto message does not raise questions of constitutionality, the chambers may then meet in joint session to reconsider the matter. If two-thirds of the legislators present insist on the passage of the bill, it then becomes law over the president's objections. If, on the other hand, the veto message raises a point of constitutionality, the measure is transmitted to the supreme court, which is required to deliver an advisory opinion within eight days. If, in the opinion of the supreme court, the bill would violate the constitution, the measure dies at that point; if the court advises otherwise, the final decision on the bill rests with the joint session of congress.

As in the United States, the veto power of the president depends for its effectiveness on the state of the relations at any given time between the executive and congress. In Ecuador the executive is normally strong politically, and for most purposes the constitutionally supreme position of the legislative function is fictitious. In any basic struggle between the president and congress, the former is likely to emerge as victor, textual declarations in the constitution to the contrary notwithstanding. Legislative revolts against presidential vetoes normally do not get far if the executive regards the issues at stake as vital. The history of the republic is replete with instances of presidential decrees quite unconstitutionally dissolving or otherwise destroying the legislature. President Velasco Ibarra, for example, did so in 1935. Executive-legislative conflicts have, in fact, occasionally resulted in the suspension of Ecuadoran constitutions. It is to be stressed, however, that such conflicts do not occur frequently, since both the executive and legislative functions represent essentially the same small sector of the republic's class system. The great majority of the people of the country—Indians, cholos, montuvios, and Negroes—are normally not directly affected by this phase of the constitutional system of Ecuador.

CHAPTER VII

THE NATIONAL JUDICIARY

IT IS A curious fact that the Constitution of 1946 discusses the judicial function in brief and general terms, in marked contrast with the lengthy and detailed provisions dealing with the other two functions. Whereas the document has thirty-two articles on the executive function and fifty-five articles on the legislative, the section on the judiciary is confined within the brief space of eleven articles in which details are significantly absent. Only the broad outlines of the judicial function are sketched in the constitution—reference to specific types of courts is limited to the supreme and superior courts—and most of the detailed arrangements dealing with the structure and powers of the courts are left to supplementary legislation.

STRUCTURE OF THE JUDICIAL SYSTEM

In practice, Ecuadoran executives have tended to dominate the scene, and legislatures have generally been weak and ineffective. Constitution writers have, as a rule, deplored this situation, and felt that a remedy lay in lengthy and detailed textual provisions designed to impose detailed restraints upon the executive and to strengthen the legislative body by the sheer force of verbiage. But experience has demonstrated that, regardless of the number of articles consumed in the process, the mere declaration in a constitution that the executive is to be chastened and the power of congress expanded is not enough.

Thus, many of the constitutional provisions dealing with the executive and legislative functions are remedial in nature; but this is not true of the constitution's treatment of the court system. Indeed, there was no need for the constitution writers of 1946 to devote therapeutic attention to the judiciary. It had functioned relatively successfully for generations, and during a century of gradually evolving customs and usages there had developed a body of Ecuadoran law which withstood the storms that struck down presidents and legislatures. Like the functioning of the cabinet, the republic's judicial practices have not been written into the constitution and appear only peripherally in legislation.

The structure of the judicial function, which was assigned only 1.98 per cent of the 1949 budget, rests on the organic law of the judicial power[1] of 1938, as amended thirteen times during the subsequent decade.

---
[1] This law was promulgated before the term "function" was substituted for "power" in Ecuadoran constitutional law.

As elaborated by this legislation, the Ecuadoran court hierarchy contains four levels of tribunals. On these levels are to be found (1) the supreme court, (2) eight superior courts, (3) fifteen provincial courts, and (4) seventy-seven cantonal courts. If each recorded case heard by each court were regarded as a unit of litigation,[2] figures for 1946 would indicate that the supreme court handled 2 per cent of that year's litigation, the superior courts 11 per cent, the provincial courts 42 per cent, and the cantonal courts 45 per cent. All these courts are located in the Sierra or the Coast, no branch of the judicial function existing in the Oriente or the Galápagos Islands.

THE SUPREME COURT

The supreme court of Ecuador consists of fifteen judges elected for six-year terms by congress meeting in joint session. To be eligible for election to the supreme court, a person must be an Ecuadoran by birth, in the exercise of the rights of citizenship, and at least forty years of age. Moreover, supreme court judges are required to have served as members of lower courts or to have been lawyers for at least twelve years before their election to the highest court. A political factor entering into the selection of supreme court members is the careful balance generally maintained in giving the Sierra and the Coast more or less equal representation on the tribunal. Judges, whether of the supreme or inferior courts, are forbidden to exercise their professions on a private basis or to vote while serving as officials of the judicial function.

The supreme court is really three courts in the sense that it is divided into three chambers of five judges each. The chambers are assigned their own groups of cases and for many purposes function relatively independently of each other. In this regard, Ecuadoran practice is not essentially different from that to be found in many Latin American republics. The supreme courts of Mexico and Cuba, for example, are likewise divided into a number of chambers which operate simultaneously, each handling its own group of cases. In one respect, however, the Ecuadoran chamber system is unique: the three divisions of the supreme court do not specialize in types of law or cases, all three chambers handling all types of cases coming before the court. The only principle is the principle of chance. This arrangement is in striking contrast to the situations in Mexico and Cuba, where a given chamber specializes in the sense that it receives all supreme court cases dealing with, for example, labor or maritime problems.

---

[2] For example, a case originally heard by a provincial court, reviewed by a superior court, and carried to the supreme court would be calculated as three units of litigation.

The principle of chance, operating in this fashion, has been developed in Ecuadoran law as an element of justice. It has been held that the impersonal and objective nature of adjudication is enhanced by the absence of any prior method of determining which chamber of the supreme court will consider a given case if it is carried to that tribunal. It is argued that the classical concept of "blind justice" is refined when the principle of chance adds a measure of clouding to the vision. Moreover—and this is held to be a distinctly secondary advantage of the principle of chance—this method of assigning cases to chambers assures an equal apportionment of the burden of litigation among the three divisions. Under this system no chamber is ever overburdened with cases while the other two have relatively light dockets.

In recent years there has arisen a body of opinion within the Ecuadoran legal profession in favor of the development of specialization in each of the three chambers of the supreme court. It is increasingly felt that the principle of chance might well be foregone and a three-way specialization be introduced within the supreme court. This movement was gaining momentum in 1949, at which time many influential lawyers and judges were proposing that a bill to this effect be introduced in congress. It thus appeared not unlikely that the principle of chance might in the near future slip from the cluster of factors constituting justice as administered by the supreme court.

Generally speaking, the cases handled by the supreme court may be divided into two broad classes: those over which the court may exercise either original or appellate jurisdiction, and those involving the court's appellate jurisdiction only. The overwhelming majority of supreme court cases are in the latter category.

The supreme court may exercise either original or appellate jurisdiction with regard to six types of cases. These include, first, any further action brought against government officials who have already been removed from office in consequence of impeachment or censure. Subject to this type of action are removed presidents or vice-presidents of the republic, cabinet ministers, attorneys general, comptrollers general, and members of the supreme court itself. Second, it may hear in either the first or second instance[3] any cases involving charges brought against provincial governors or against commanders of the armed forces, the latter being subjected to this type of action when accused of abuses during times of peace. Third, suits involving Ecuadoran diplomatic and

---

[3] In Ecuadoran usage, a case tried for the first time is heard in the "first instance," a case appealed once is heard in the "second instance," and a case appealed twice is heard in the "third instance." No case may be heard in more than three instances.

consular officials may be tried before the supreme court on either an original or appellate basis. Fourth, it may exercise the same types of jurisdiction in cases permitted by international law involving the diplomatic or consular officers of foreign states. Fifth, it may hear any case in maritime law in either the first or the second instance. Sixth, it may exercise original or appellate jurisdiction with regard to cases arising out of contracts entered into by the executive function.

The supreme court may exercise exclusively appellate jurisdiction over any case coming before it during the normal course of litigation originating in the lower courts. The sole restriction on its authority in this connection lies in the constitutional proviso that no case may be appealed more than twice. The great bulk of litigation which it handles is made up of matters over which that tribunal exercises exclusively appellate jurisdiction.

In addition to the duty of deciding cases, the supreme court performs two categories of services which may be designated as constitutional and administrative. One of its constitutional duties is the resolution of any doubts which the lower courts may formally express with regard to the interpretation or meaning of a given law. Ecuadoran practices in interpretation of the laws are considered at length later in this chapter, and further comment on this function is deferred until that point. A second constitutional duty of the supreme court is to serve as an agency of liaison between the judicial function on the one hand and the other two functions on the other. This obligation involves such activities as guarding the province of the judiciary against encroachment by the legislative and executive functions and submitting to the congress an annual report on the problems and policies of the courts.

Five administrative duties are performed by the supreme court: First, it exercises general supervisory powers over the superior and inferior courts with a view to preserving the quality of the work done by the judicial function. Second, it keeps an annual statistical record of all cases handled by all of the courts of the republic. Third, it establishes standards and qualifications which lawyers practicing before it must meet, and may disbar any supreme court attorneys who in the opinion of the tribunal fail to meet these standards and qualifications. Fourth, it appoints and removes its own employees. Fifth, it establishes the rules and by-laws governing its internal administration and operation.

SUPERIOR COURTS

Immediately below the supreme court in the judicial hierarchy stand the eight superior courts.[4] The territory of the republic of Ecuador has been divided into eight judicial districts, each superior court exercising jurisdiction in one of them.[5] The judges of these tribunals are elected for four-year terms by congress meeting in joint session. They are required to be Ecuadorans by birth, in the exercise of the rights of citizenship, and at least thirty-five years of age. Further, superior court judges must have served as lawyers or members of lower courts for at least eight years prior to their election.

As in the supreme court, suits coming before the superior courts may be divided into two broad classes, the distinction being between matters over which the superior courts may exercise either original or appellate jurisdiction, and cases in which their authority is exclusively appellate. These tribunals are similar to the supreme court in the additional sense that the great majority of the cases coming before them have already been heard by inferior courts.

The superior courts may exercise either original or appellate jurisdiction over all cases arising in their respective districts involving charges brought against the political chiefs of cantons, provincial officials other than governors, port administrators, provincial or local custodians of public funds, judges of provincial and cantonal courts, police officials, and cantonal councilors. In all other matters coming before them, the superior courts possess exclusively appellate jurisdiction. Should it develop that any case heard by a superior court points to the probability that government funds or property have been abused, the

---

[4] Superior courts are composed of either one chamber of three judges or two chambers of three judges each. The tribunals at Ibarra, Ambato, Riobamba, Loja, and Portoviejo fall in the former category; the superior courts at Quito, Cuenca, and Guayaquil fall in the latter.

[5] The district of the superior court at Ibarra contains the Sierra provinces of Carchi and Imbabura; the Quito court's jurisdiction embraces the Sierra provinces of Pichincha and Cotopaxi; the district of the superior court at Ambato covers the Sierra province of Tungurahua and the Oriente province of Napo-Pastaza; the territory of the Riobamba court includes the Sierra provinces of Chimborazo and Bolívar; the Cuenca court's district embraces the Sierra provinces of Cañar and Azuay, and the following cantons of the Oriente province of Santiago-Zamora: Macas, Morona, and Santiago; the jurisdiction of the superior court at Loja extends throughout the Sierra province of Loja and the following cantons of the Oriente province of Santiago-Zamora: Zaruma, Zamora, and Chinchipe; the territory of the court at Guayaquil covers the Coastal provinces of Guayas and Los Ríos, the Galápagos Islands, and the following cantons of the Oriente province of Santiago-Zamora: Machala, Santa Rosa, and Pasaje; and the district of the Portoviejo court embraces the Coastal provinces of Manabí and Esmeraldas.

tribunal is required to abstain from handing down a decision. Superior courts must certify all such cases directly to the supreme court for final action.

The work of the superior courts is not limited to hearing and deciding cases, as these bodies possess additional functions which may be classified as (a) constitutional and (b) appointive and administrative. The constitutional duties relate exclusively to questions raised by judges concerning the meaning or interpretation of laws. Where these questions are brought by members of the superior courts themselves, the queries are communicated by these tribunals to the supreme court. Where the questions are raised by provincial or cantonal court judges, the members of these inferior tribunals transmit the queries to the appropriate superior courts. In such instances the superior courts are forbidden to use their own judgment or discretion, as they must transmit the questions to the supreme court for action. Thus, the superior courts serve as a species of relay station, dispatching to the highest tribunal any inquiries received from the provincial and cantonal courts regarding the interpretation of the laws.

Each of the eight superior courts has been assigned certain appointive and administrative tasks. It appoints all provincial and cantonal court judges and all other judicial personnel operating within its district. It supervises the work of the lower tribunals in its territory and keeps records of all cases handled within its territory. It is, further, charged with the responsibility of seeing that all the prisons and other places of involuntary confinement within its territory are properly administered.

PROVINCIAL COURTS

The third level in the judicial pyramid is occupied by the provincial courts. There are, in all, fifteen of these bodies, with thirty-eight provincial court judges. One provincial court has been organized in each of the Sierra and Coastal provinces, but none exists in either of the two provinces of the Oriente. Provincial courts employ courtrooms presided over by single judges. This practice differs from the supreme court, where five judges sit together in each chamber, and from the superior courts, where three judges sit together in each chamber. Although provincial court judges preside singly, a given province may have more than one provincial court judge, which means simply that more than one courtroom is used by a decentralized provincial court. Thus, five judges are to be found on this level in the Sierra province of Pichincha, signifying that five courtrooms are simultaneously in use by the provincial court of Pichincha. The judges of the provincial courts are appointed by the appropriate superior courts.

The provincial courts have original jurisdiction in the majority of cases coming before them. With the exceptions already noted, all criminal cases are heard in the first instance by these courts, as are all civil and commercial suits involving sums in excess of about sixty dollars.[6] These tribunals submit monthly reports to the appropriate superior courts summarizing the activities of the provincial courts.

CANTONAL COURTS

The lowest court of record in the Ecuadoran judicial hierarchy is the cantonal court. One tribunal exists on this level in each of the seventy-seven cantons of the Sierra and the Coast, no cantonal court being in operation in the Oriente or the Galápagos Islands. Like the provincial courts, judges of the cantonal courts are appointed by the appropriate superior courts. Cantonal court judges sit singly. There may be as many as nine or ten such officials—that is, courtrooms—in a given canton, depending on the size, social complexity, and patronage situation of the area. The jurisdiction of the cantonal courts is exclusively original, dealing in the main with civil and commercial suits involving sums between $6.60 and $66.00.

Although the political lieutenant, the chief officer of civil government in the Ecuadoran parish, is not, strictly speaking, an official of the judicial function, mention might be made of him at this point since he performs a number of judicial duties. In the parishes of the Sierra and the Coast, the political lieutenant, normally unschooled in law and not employing procedures used in the courts of record, decides civil and commercial controversies which arise in his parish and involve sums of money under $6.60. In the Oriente, where provincial and cantonal courts are absent, the political lieutenant performs many of the duties assigned to those courts in the two major regions of the republic, although the more important cases are transmitted directly to the appropriate superior court. The political lieutenant is essentially an official of the executive function and is controlled through the ministry of government.

Minor cases arising in the Galápagos Islands, which are governed through the ministry of national defense, are handled by the military and naval authorities. Major controversies developing in the archipelago are submitted for adjudication to the superior court at Guayaquil.

---

[6] In Ecuadoran currency, the figure is 1,000 sucres, here converted at the rate of 16.50 sucres to the dollar.

Some Ecuadoran Judicial Practices

Much of what has been written on the subject has conveyed the impression that a sharp contrast exists between common law, as developed in the United States and the United Kingdom, and Roman law, as practiced in the Latin American republics. This distinction, insofar as Ecuador is concerned, is for the most part artificial and false. The similarities between Ecuadoran and United States judicial practices are striking. In both countries many decisions are based on precedents established by earlier cases; members of courts write opinions in handing down their decisions; and judges who do not agree with the majority of their colleagues write dissenting opinions (*votos salvados*). "The law" in Ecuador is unwritten law in the same sense as that normally applied to the common law. The similarities are especially striking in view of the circumstance that there is little evidence of the direct borrowing of one system's usages by the other. It may well be that the very nature of the judicial process—the individual and specific application to concrete cases of norms arising out of past events—compels a relatively uniform approach in its development.

Although it is true that Ecuadoran law is code law in the sense that codes have been formulated in connection with a number of matters coming before the courts, this practice does not constitute as fundamental and thoroughgoing a contrast with common-law procedures as some writers have suggested. The principal codes in Ecuador, enacted by the legislative function, deal with civil, commercial, labor, and criminal law. Each code is a relatively comprehensive statement of the law of the subject with which it deals. While the codes are lengthy, they are not even theoretically complete treatments of their subjects, and are employed by the courts in conjunction with other statutes, previous court decisions on other matters, and the constitution. The judge is in theory a passive agent in that he is expected to do little more than apply the law. But applying the law means interpreting it, and an Ecuadoran judge exercises as much leeway and independence of judgment in interpreting the law as does a common-law judge. An Ecuadoran lawyer must be familiar not only with the four major codes, but also with other legislation in civil, commercial, labor, and criminal matters, and with interpretations of these statutes as made by the courts.

The legal circumstances under which a case may be carried from one court to another have been gradually developed during the last century of Ecuadoran usage. Each court level on which a given case is tried is known as an "instance." The rule that no case may be heard in more than three instances—that is, no case may be appealed more than twice—had been settled "unwritten" usage in Ecuador for years before it found its way into the text of the Constitution of 1946. For the purpose of determining the conditions under which a case may move from one instance to another, Ecuadoran practice divides litigation into three classes: (1) "political" cases; (2) matters involving administrative errors made by lower courts; and (3) cases appealed by one or more of the litigants.

1. No "political" case may ever be appealed. Political questions defy precise legal definition in Ecuador with the same alacrity as in the United States. For all practical purposes, a political question in Ecuador is one which in the opinion of the judicial function lies principally within the province of the executive or congress. Broadly speaking, the major difference between the Ecuadoran and United States judicial approaches to political questions is that in Ecuador the courts will hear such a case in one instance only. No appeal may be lodged against the original decision so far as the higher courts are concerned. In this connection it is to be noted that the chief use to which the power of the Ecuadoran congress to grant amnesties and pardons has been put has related to political cases. In the United States the courts generally do not decide a case in any instance if it is held to rest on a political question.[7]

2. The administrative powers of the supreme and superior courts of Ecuador are of controlling importance in cases where administrative errors have been made by inferior courts. The higher courts exercise general administrative supervision of the tribunals beneath them in the judicial pyramid, and by virtue of this power possess the authority to rectify such administrative errors as the lower bodies may make. The term "administrative error," like the term "political case," is exceedingly flexible and difficult to define with precision. In practice the administrative powers of the higher courts are employed for purposes of review whenever those tribunals declare that inferior courts have proceeded improperly in the handling of cases. In such circumstances, the cases are brought before the higher court, on that court's exclusive initiative, for purposes of rectification. This practice differs from appeal in that litigants involved in a case are forbidden to petition for, or otherwise exercise initiative in obtaining, administrative rectification by the higher

---

[7] For representative expressions of the positions taken on political questions by the Supreme Court of the United States, see the opinions in *Luther v. Borden*, 7 Howard 1 (1849); *Mississippi v. Johnson*, 4 Wallace 475 (1867); *Georgia v. Stanton*, 6 Wallace 50 (1868); *Neely v. Henkel*, 180 U. S. 109 (1901); and *Oetjen v. Central Leather Co.*, 246 U. S. 297 (1918).

court. Rectification of administrative errors is distinguished in law from reversal of decisions made by the lower courts in that the higher tribunals, in exercising their administrative powers, are theoretically concerned with the procedures of the lower courts rather than with their interpretation or application of the laws. Ecuadoran practice tends to fortify this distinction between the procedural and substantive bases of review by prohibiting the higher courts from exercising their administrative powers to substantively reverse the decisions of the inferior tribunals.

3. Appeals may be taken to the higher courts on the initiative of one or more of the litigants in a case, provided that the appellant holds that the lower court has misapplied or substantively misinterpreted the laws. There is no recourse to appeal where the higher court feels that the matter is political or that it involves an administrative error of the lower court; and the appellant must refrain from holding that either of these conditions is involved in his case. It is difficult to maintain in practice the sharp theoretical distinctions established among the three types of cases. In general, the determination of whether a matter is political, involves an administrative error of a lower court, or is properly subject to appeal depends largely on the attitude toward each case adopted by the higher courts. In actual practice in dealing with appealed cases, the higher courts usually support the decisions made below them in the judicial hierarchy. In thirty cases appealed to the supreme court in 1946, that tribunal confirmed the earlier rulings in twenty of them; "modified"—that is, substantially confirmed, but altered in a minor respect—the previous decisions in nine cases; and revoked the earlier ruling in only one case.

In making their decisions, all courts are required to write out their opinions, giving full reasons for their rulings. This practice became general during the 1890's, and was thus a part of the "unwritten" law of Ecuador for approximately half a century before it was written into the Constitution of 1946. A reading of the opinions of the supreme and superior courts reveals that in making decisions these bodies tend to rely on the precedents established by rulings in earlier cases as well as upon the texts of the codes and other legislation. Thus, to cite a single illustration, the superior court at Portoviejo declared in a 1940 case that its decision was based upon its reasoning from the constitution then in force, and that, "moreover, law to this effect exists in many decisions of the supreme court, among them the one herein cited."[8]

---

[8] Action against Germán Cevallos, for Injuring a Cow, VI *Gaceta Judicial*, No. 2 (February, 1940), p. 207.

Despite the striking success of the judiciary in establishing a relatively stable body of law, it is a curious fact that very little has been published in Ecuador on judicial practices or constitutional law. This is all the more surprising since the legal profession is probably overpopulated, and the heavy concern of the country's intelligentsia with legalistic approaches to public problems has long been an object of caricature. It is jokingly said, for example, that 100 per cent of the population of Cuenca ("the Athens of the south") are lawyers. "If you desire advice on any legal question," the writer was told at Quito, "go to Cuenca and ask any shoeshine boy." The best professional schools in the republic's four universities are law schools.

Yet the literature on Ecuadoran constitutional law is sterile. Such textbooks as exist—the standard works are Rodrigo Jácome Moscoso's *Derecho Constitucional Ecuatoriano* and Francisco Zevallos Reyre's *Lecciones de Derecho Constitucional*—are either histories of the constitutions or compilations of their texts, or both. The sole commentary on the laws of Ecuador is embodied in Francisco Ochoa Ortiz's *Ley Orgánica del Poder Judicial*, which, published in 1932, was somewhat out of date in 1949. No magazine or periodical is devoted to the law as such, although articles on legal matters occasionally find their way into journals devoted primarily to other subjects. A feeble attempt was made in 1948 to establish a legal periodical. Its editors called it the *Boletín Judicial*, and announced that they were "pleased to place it at the service of the judicial function, the lawyers, the law students, and the public in general, to diffuse the immutable principles of the law and justice."[9] The *Boletín Judicial* was projected as a weekly publication; its first, and unpromising, issue appeared on August 23, 1948, and contained four pages. The second issue had not appeared by the end of the year.

Government publications dealing with problems of the judiciary are also rare. Only one court, the supreme court, maintains a publication. This journal, the *Gaceta Judicial*, was founded in 1895, and attempts have been made since then to publish a new issue each month. Publication was, as usual, behind schedule in 1948: the most recent copy available in the library of the supreme court at Quito in August of that year was dated January, 1946. Persons may keep reasonably well informed, albeit tardily, on the activities and decisions of the supreme court by reading the *Gaceta Judicial*. If they are interested in the activities of any other court, they must travel to that tribunal itself, where they may examine its unpublished papers.

---

[9] *Boletín Judicial*, Vol. I, No. 1 (Quito, August 23, 1948), p. 1.

Each issue of the *Gaceta Judicial* contains three types of information regarding the supreme court's activities during the period covered by that issue: (1) All cases decided by the court during that time are contained in the publication. A section of the *Gaceta Judicial* is devoted for this purpose to each of the three chambers of the highest court. The information made available for each case includes the name of the case, a summary of its handling in each of the instances before it reached the supreme court, and a record of its disposition as made by the supreme court itself. These data include the texts of the opinions written by all courts involved in all instances of the case, and a brief summary of the arguments advanced by the litigants. (2) Each issue of the *Gaceta Judicial* also contains a summary of the interpretations of Ecuadoran law embodied in the decisions made by the supreme court during the period reviewed by the publication. (3) The *Gaceta Judicial* also contains the texts of such resolutions as the supreme court has made during the period. These resolutions consist largely of expressions of sorrow occasioned by the deaths of variously notable persons.

The system of naming cases is somewhat similar in Ecuador to that adopted in the United States. If the suit is civil or commercial, the title of the case will include the names of the parties together with an indication of the objective sought by the plaintiff. Representative case names of this type include the following: "Ladislao Hunyadi against Aurelio Andino, for the Performance of a Contract"; "Luis Alberto Llerena against Dr. Rodrigo Puig Mir y Bonín, for Money"; "Luis D. Cardozo against María Mercedes Suárez, for Divorce"; "Manuel Roberto Valencia *et al.* against Honorio Polo, for the Demarcation of a Boundary"; and "Guayaquil Branch of the Central Bank of Ecuador against Carlos, Otto, and José Icaza Overweg, for Money." If the suit involves criminal action, the name of the case contains the defendant's name together with an indication of the crime of which he is accused. Typical case names in this group are: "Action against Manuel Mesías Migüez, for Theft of Cattle"; "Action against Julio Verdezoto, for Theft of Money"; and "Action against Germán Cevallos, for Injuring a Cow."

CASE OF CARDOZO V. SUÁREZ

Some insight into Ecuadoran judicial practices may be gained from a detailed examination of a representative case decided by the supreme court. The case selected for this purpose is typical of a suit for which appearance before the supreme court constituted its third instance.

On October 21, 1905, Luis D. Cardozo and María Mercedes Suárez were married at the city of Riobamba in the Sierra province of Chimborazo. Their ensuing twenty-six years of married life produced four children and, as was later affirmed, a minimum of bliss. The mounting friction and strife in their household at length reached its climax on the night of December 4, 1931, when Cardozo deserted his wife and children and established a separate residence.

The marriage was thus terminated in fact in 1931, although no legal action was taken until 1944, when Cardozo instituted a divorce action in the provincial court of Chimborazo. The suit was based on the Law of Civil Matrimony of 1935—the "three-year law"—Article 5 of which stipulated that, should a separation or desertion endure for more than three years, the "injured party" was entitled to bring court action for divorce. It was, of course, obvious to Cardozo that he was the "injured party." His complaint, as summarized in the *Gaceta Judicial*, asserted "that, during conjugal life, there had not existed the slightest relationship of cordiality; on the contrary, there were domestic disturbances and scandals ... provoked by his aforementioned wife, María Mercedes Suárez.... Their conjugal relations have been broken since 1931, by reason of the absolute separation at that time of the spouses, the husband being the injured party."[10]

María Mercedes Suárez, for her part, agreed that "the lack of harmony in the matrimonial life of the aforementioned parties has been proved," but pointed out that "the action which [Cardozo] seeks is prohibited"[11] by the divorce law of 1940. This legislation had provided that "it is an indispensable prerequisite [of divorce] that the parents must provide for the economic situation of minor children."[12] Lucio Vicente Cardozo, the youngest of the four children, was eighteen years of age at the time the divorce action was instituted in 1944.

Judge Jorge Argüello of the provincial court of Chimborazo, after hearing the case in the first instance, ruled on June 26, 1944, that "in view of the separation of the parties with a rupture of conjugal relations for more than three years ... the matrimonial bond contracted by Luis D. Cardozo and María Mercedes Suárez ... is declared dissolved."[13] Judge Argüello felt that the demands of the 1940 law were met by his stipulation that "a board will be convoked in due time to decide the situation of the minor Lucio Vicente Cardozo."[14]

---

[10] VII *Gaceta Judicial*, No. 1 (December, 1945), p. 37.
[11] *Ibid.*, pp. 37–38.
[12] *Registro Oficial*, October 18, 1940.
[13] VII *Gaceta Judicial*, No. 1 (December, 1945), p. 38.
[14] *Ibid.*, p. 38.

This board, however, failed to devise a workable formula for the care of the minor. María Mercedes Suárez accordingly appealed the decision of the provincial court of Chimborazo on the ground that it violated the 1940 law since no provision had been made for the son Lucio. Hearing the case in the second instance, the superior court at Riobamba was in substantial agreement with the basis of the appeal. It declared on June 13, 1945, that the decision of the court of first instance, made without adequate economic arrangements for Lucio Vicente Cardozo, was "illegal and premature. . . . Accordingly, the said decision is revoked."[15]

Luis D. Cardozo thereupon appealed this ruling, and the case was reviewed in the third instance by the first chamber of the supreme court. As this body saw the matter, the major question to be decided was whether or not Cardozo had been within his rights in instituting the original divorce action. Under the "three-year law" the "injured party" could sue for divorce if the desertion were of more than three years' duration. It had been assumed in the provincial and superior courts that Cardozo was the "injured party," a claim which had not been contested by María Mercedes Suárez.

The supreme court, however, did not agree that this was the case, and pointed out that, "on the contrary, it was Luis Cardozo who abandoned the home, according to the testimony of the witnesses. . . . Whatever may have been the cause . . . which determined the separation or the desertion of the home on the part of Luis Cardozo, it is certain that the act [of desertion] was committed by him, and that the injured party is therefore his wife; for nobody can be injured by his own act."[16] The supreme court, finding that Cardozo "is not entitled to bring this action for divorce because he is not the injured party," accordingly ruled that the "decisions of the first and second instances are revoked, and the request [for divorce] is denied."[17]

Thus was justice done: Luis D. Cardozo and María Mercedes Suárez continued to live apart; the rigid mores of the Sierra branded them anew as sinful folk; and Lucio Vicente Cardozo lived out the remaining years of his minority in economic insecurity. More significantly, perhaps, the case illustrated the role of the judicial function in defending the ruling class's instruments of power: the Roman Catholic Church had again beaten down the feeble threat, represented by the institution of divorce, to its hold on the Sierra.

[15] *Ibid.*, p. 38.
[16] *Ibid.*, p. 39.
[17] *Ibid.*, p. 40. Cf. Gordon Ireland and Jesús Galíndez Suárez, *Divorce in the Americas* (Buffalo, 1947).

Luis D. Cardozo's suit for divorce against María Mercedes Suárez may illuminate a number of Ecuadoran judicial practices if viewed in the light of the four questions explored in the following paragraphs:

Did either of the lower courts commit an administrative error in handling the case? It will be remembered that the 1940 divorce law provided that "it is an indispensable prerequisite [of divorce] that the parents must provide for the economic situation of minor children," and that the court of first instance endeavored to apply this law by granting the divorce with the proviso that arrangements would later be made for the support of the minor Lucio Vicente Cardozo. In the opinion of the court of second instance, this had been an improper application of the 1940 statute. The superior court at Riobamba read that law to mean that the arrangement must *first* be made for the support of the minor, and that the divorce might be granted *later*. The reverse procedure, the court of second instance said, was "illegal and premature." But was it an administrative error? If it was, the case would not be subject to appeal; if it was not, the superior court could legally entertain the appeal brought by María Mercedes Suárez. In agreeing to entertain the appeal, the court of second instance implicitly ruled that the decision below had *not* been an administrative error. It is important to point out, however, that the superior court's action in this regard does not serve as a legal basis for holding that the court of first instance did not err administratively, since the finding of the superior court was revoked by the supreme court. The legal basis for this view lies in the final court's ruling that the courts below had substantively misapplied and misconstrued the term "injured party" as it appeared in the "three-year law."

In the opinions of several Ecuadoran lawyers with whom the writer discussed the Cardozo-Suárez case, the superior court might well have held the action of the court of first instance to have been an administrative error. The logical dichotomy between procedural and substantive misapplications fails of precise clarity in actual practice; and for many purposes it may be said that an administrative error is whatever the courts say it is. Ecuadoran lawyers must therefore be familiar not only with the dichotomy itself but with interpretations of it made by the courts; and in this sense the precedents established by court decisions are as integral a part of Ecuadoran law as the legal codes.

What types of questions may be examined by the reviewing courts? In this area, Ecuadoran law establishes a distinction, familiar to lawyers in the United States, between questions of fact and questions of law.

In general, the facts as found by the court of first instance are final in the sense that they may not be reëxamined by the reviewing tribunals in the absence of administrative error on the part of the court of first instance. The reviewing courts are thus limited to pursuing questions of law in appealed cases, being required to abstain from questions of fact. Here again there arises a logical distinction which tends to disintegrate in actual practice. If a question of law be regarded as a matter which establishes the existence or nonexistence of the rights of the litigants, then wherein lies the question of law upon which the final decision in the Cardozo-Suárez case turned? The question of whether or not Luis D. Cardozo deserted his wife and family on the night of December 4, 1931, is a question of fact; the issue of who the "injured party" was, within the meaning of the "three-year law," is a question of law. Yet the supreme court has held that for the purposes of that statute the deserted spouse is by definition the "injured party." Thus, in inquiring into the events of the night of December 4, 1931—even to the point of pursuing the "testimony of the witnesses"—the supreme court was examining a question of law rather than a question of fact.

What role in the case was played by the principle of chance? This principle determined which of the three chambers of the supreme court would hear the Cardozo appeal. It is probably true that the assignment of the case to the first chamber of the supreme court foredoomed Cardozo's cause to failure, whereas the result might have been otherwise in either of the other chambers. The five-man first chamber was dominated by one of its members, Dr. Manuel Elicio Flor, long an outstanding member of the Conservative party and politically supported by the Church. At the time of the Cardozo case, Flor was the president of the supreme court, where his record so enhanced his standing with the Church that he won the Conservative nomination for the presidency of the republic in 1948. The rise of Flor's political star depended in large part upon his acceptability to the Church. His acceptability was greatly enhanced during the period of his membership in the supreme court through decisions such as that rendered in the case of Luis D. Cardozo against María Mercedes Suárez, for divorce. The singular nature of the mores of the Sierra, combined with the strong hold of the Church on that region, has resulted in the emergence of the question of divorce as an issue of some political importance in Ecuador. The Church and the Conservative party have resolutely taken their stand against divorce. Flor and Belisario Ponce, also of the Conservative party, gave the first chamber of the supreme court its political course and character, the other three judges not being affiliated with any political party. It would be difficult to imagine a more decisive effect of the principle of chance than the writing of the supreme court's unanimous opinion in the Cardozo-Suárez case by Dr. Manuel Elicio Flor, president of the supreme court, defender of the Faith, and future Conservative candidate for the post of president of the republic of Ecuador.

Do court decisions serve as precedents in the development of Ecuadoran law? The legal circumstances under which a divorce could be obtained in the republic were substantially different after the Cardozo-Suárez ruling from what they had been before. For the definitive significance of the term "injured party" as it appears in the text of the "three-year law," lawyers must look to the decision of the supreme court in the case of Cardozo against Suárez. Since 1945 it has been impossible to obtain a divorce in Ecuador under the "three-year law" unless one has been deserted by his spouse, the separation having endured for more than three years; and the initiative lies exclusively with the spouse who was left. The fact that this is the law as applied by the courts stems fully as much from the precedent established by the suit of Luis D. Cardozo against María Mercedes Suárez for divorce as it does from the statutes of 1935 and 1940.

INTERPRETATION OF THE LAWS

Largely in consequence of their gradual development through the years, Ecuadoran practices in interpreting the constitution and the laws are complex. The task of giving interpretation to the laws does not lie exclusively with the courts, the judicial function sharing this authority with the council of state and with congress. For the purposes of the present discussion, laws or projected laws undergoing interpretation may be divided into the three groups discussed in the numbered paragraphs that follow:

1. Laws questioned by the superior or lower courts in connection with cases before them must be forwarded by these tribunals to the supreme court for disposition. The superior courts play a twofold role in this area in that they may either direct their own questions to the supreme court or relay to that tribunal queries raised by the lower courts functioning in their districts. When the question is originally raised by the superior court itself, that tribunal is required to submit its own opinion on the law together with the question to the supreme court. On the other hand, when the question is raised by a cantonal or provincial court in its district, the superior court serves merely as a relay station. It is forbidden

in such cases to express its own opinion on the query or otherwise exercise its own judgment, being required to relay the question immediately and without comment to the supreme court.

Where the questioned law is not believed by the supreme court to be unconstitutional, that tribunal has full authority to act. In such cases, the supreme court formulates its interpretation of the questioned measure. This interpretation is final in that the court which originally raised the question must then proceed with the case and is bound to accept the supreme court's interpretation as the law. Moreover, if such a case is appealed, the supreme court's interpretation is likewise binding on the reviewing tribunal unless that body be the supreme court itself.

If the supreme court believes the questioned law to be unconstitutional, it may declare the measure null and void only if it is held that the procedures involved in enacting the law had been in violation of the constitution in force at that time. Should it be held that unconstitutionality stems from some other consideration, the supreme court may not invalidate the measure, but must instead refer it to congress for further action. The case before the questioning court is not suspended in such an instance, as suspension of proceedings is authorized only when the final authority to dispose of a delaying query lies entirely within the domain of the judicial function.

2. Bills in congress which have been objected to on constitutional grounds by the president of the republic are referred to the supreme court if at least two-thirds of the members of congress meeting in joint session believe that the measure would not violate the constitution. If, in the opinion of the supreme court, the measure would not be in violation of the basic law, the joint session is then free to pass the bill over the president's objections. If, conversely, the supreme court agrees with the president that the law would be unconstitutional, the court's opinion is final and the bill may not be enacted. This procedure is somewhat similar to the Canadian advisory opinion, the major difference being that in Ecuador recourse to it may be had only when at least two-thirds of the members of congress disagree with the president on the constitutionality of a bill.

3. The concept of "double unconstitutionality" has been developed in Ecuadoran constitutional law to distinguish between (a) those laws which either the supreme court or congress may invalidate; and (b) those which may be nullified only by congress, the two houses sitting separately. Ecuadoran practice recognizes two types of unconstitutionality, procedural (*inconstitucionalidad de forma*) and substantive

(*inconstitucionalidad de fondo*). A law may be held to be procedurally unconstitutional if the appropriate procedures were not observed in its enactment or promulgation—for example, if the presiding officer of either house of congress neglected to sign the bill, if it was not correctly dated, if it was not properly published in the *Registro Oficial*, etc. In contrast, a law may be held to be substantively unconstitutional if the proper procedures were followed in its enactment and promulgation but the content of the measure conflicts with the letter or spirit—as defined by the interpreting body—of the constitution. A law may be declared procedurally unconstitutional by either the supreme court or congress; but congress alone has the authority to find a measure substantively unconstitutional.

Statutes are virtually never declared substantively unconstitutional, since they are enacted by the same body which possesses the exclusive authority to invalidate them. Where congress feels that a given statute has substantively conflicted with the constitution, the remedy normally lies in repeal of the statute. For most intents and purposes a congressional declaration of substantive unconstitutionality is practically indistinguishable from repeal. Thus, some Ecuadoran constitutional lawyers hold that congress does not actually have the power to declare a law unconstitutional, despite the fact that this legislative authority is proclaimed in the text of the Constitution of 1946. At any rate, the stipulation in that document that the legislative function has the sole and exclusive authority to declare laws substantively unconstitutional does have the effect of limiting the invalidating power of the supreme court to declarations of procedural unconstitutionality only.

The council of state also plays a part in the interpretation of the laws. This agency serves not only as an instrument of the coördination of functions, but also as a watchdog in defense of the constitution. Should an unconstitutional act be committed by either the executive or the legislative function, it is the duty of the council of state to call this condition to the attention of invalidating authorities. The term "unconstitutional act" as used here refers to any action by the executive or by congress which the council deems unconstitutional. Should the warning of the council of state go unheeded, it is the duty of that agency to give the fullest publicity to the act in question. Thus the council of state plays a role in the interpretation of the laws, although its constitutional opinions do not have the force of law unless ratified by the supreme court or congress, depending on the nature of the allegedly unconstitutional act.

Is an unconstitutional statute invalid *ab initio?* This is a question on which Ecuadoran lawyers enjoyed exercising their powers of logic until it was answered by fiat in the text of the Constitution of 1946. Under that document, no nullified law is invalid *ab initio*. Those who formerly supported the reverse position held that if the properly constituted authority ruled that a law was unconstitutional, the measure became invalid as of the time it entered into conflict with the constitution rather than at the time the ruling was made, the conflict beginning as soon as both the constitution and the statute were on the books.

This is an issue which is familiar to students of constitutional law in the United States. The question has especial significance in Ecuador, however, in view of the fact that written constitutions are normally short-lived in that republic. What was the legal position in 1948 of a law passed under the Constitution of 1929, assuming that the statute in question did not violate the charters of 1929 and 1945, but was in conflict with the Constitution of 1946? What is the status in law of a statute valid under an outgoing constitution but violating its successor?

The practice in Ecuadoran law has been to assume that all previously existing legislation in conflict with a new constitution "automatically" goes out of force at the moment that document is promulgated. This is a general rule which is simple enough to state but does not serve in concrete practice. In everyday judicial usage, a statute is valid from the time it is enacted and promulgated until it is either specifically repealed by congress or is declared unconstitutional by that body or the supreme court. The number of constitutions intervening between the two events has no effect on the matter in practice, and the writers of the Constitution of 1946 have done little more than submit to the logic of the situation in providing that no court decision may have retroactive effect.[18] It would likewise seem to follow that the judge's decision "makes" rather than "discovers" the law, but this is a proposition which many Ecuadoran constitutional lawyers resist with varying degrees of vehemence.

Perhaps the most effective index to the role of the judicial function within the Ecuadoran constitutional system can be found in the attitude toward law prevalent in the country. Velasco Ibarra once declared that in the republic "everywhere there is a tendency to ridicule the

---

[18] The net effect of Ecuadoran practice in this area curiously parallels a number of the ideas advanced by Hans Kelsen. Cf., for example, his *General Theory of Law and State* (Cambridge, 1945), pp. 146–152. Josef L. Kunz has observed with much truth that "the greatest influence on Latin-American theory of law is presently being exercised by Hans Kelsen." Association of American Law Schools (ed.), *Latin-American Legal Philosophy* (Cambridge, 1948), p. xxi.

laws";[19] and the observer who has spent any length of time in Ecuador would probably agree that this is true to an appreciable extent. The laws ridiculed and ignored, however, are not so much the laws applied by the courts as they are the rules proclaimed by the executive and legislative functions in broad and general terms. These pronouncements have no meaning as law to a large sector of the Ecuadoran people if they are not specifically enforced in individual cases, and the primary organ of specificity in the laws is the judicial function.

"Law exists," Max Weber has said, "when there is a probability that an order will be upheld by a specific staff of men who will use physical or psychic compulsion with the intention of obtaining conformity with the order."[20] The courts in Ecuador have been the basic agency of specific application of the laws. It may well be that in the nature of the judicial approach, that is, application of the law through individual, concrete instances—the *case* method, some notions of Roman law to the contrary notwithstanding—lies the enduring strength of the judicial function in the constitutional system of Ecuador.[21]

---

[19] Velasco Ibarra, *Conciencia o Barbarie*, p. 67.

[20] Weber, *op. cit.*, p. 180.

[21] Readers desiring to compare Ecuadoran judicial practices with those to be found in the republics of Guatemala and Colombia may wish to consult the following articles by J. A. C. Grant: "Due Process for Ex-Dictators: A Study of Judicial Control of Legislation in Guatemala," *American Political Science Review*, Vol. XLI, No. 3 (June, 1947), pp. 463–469; and "'Contract Clause' Litigation in Colombia: A Comparative Study in Judicial Review," *American Political Science Review*, Vol. XLII, No. 6 (December, 1948), pp. 1103–1126.

CHAPTER VIII

PROVINCIAL AND LOCAL GOVERNMENT

I told him I was a foreigner. He said he had heard of France. Not France, the United States, I said. He said, was that in Peru?

José Manuel's idea of the world was a valley in which he lived, an outer world consisting of Cuenca, Oña, Quito, Loja, and Saraguro, and, beyond them, France on the one side and Peru on the other.

France was the country to which wealthy owners of large pieces of land sent their sons for an education. Peru was the country of great wealth which lay to the south. It developed, as I pursued the line of questioning... that his political ideas were fully as vague. He had not heard of any of the last three Presidents of Ecuador. It was not clear to me whether he thought of himself as an Ecuadorian or not.[1]

IT IS IN a sense unfair to ask the Ecuadoran Indian to name any of the presidents of his country. If he lives in the rural sections of the southern Sierra, he is doing well if he can name the Republic of Ecuador. These words refer to some vague, distant, and abstract concept which he has probably overheard "whites" discussing. The republic as a living reality does not normally enter into the day-to-day lives of the great mass of the Ecuadoran people—the Indians and cholos of the Sierra, the montuvios and Negroes of the Coast. The republic belongs to the ruling class, to the "whites"; let *them* name the presidents and explain what congress is. If they are obsessively interested in government and politics, they may even know which constitution is now in force.

This does not mean that the Ecuadoran Indian is not familiar with government. He knows government well. Government is the political lieutenant of his parish. The political lieutenant is the man who apologetically explains why a tax ought to be paid, or why the Indian must go to jail if he has drunk too much chicha and gotten into trouble, or why he is required to work on the roads four days out of every year if he cannot buy his way out. Sometimes the Indian hates the political lieutenant, but more often he sympathetically realizes that this official is himself only doing the bidding of a higher authority, the political chief of the canton. If the Indian is exceptionally understanding, he realizes that the blame lies even higher than that: the final tyrant is the provincial governor. Beyond him? "France on the one side and Peru on the other."

Government on the national level in Ecuador is essentially removed from the overwhelming majority of the people, who play no direct part

[1] Franklin, *op. cit.*, pp. 200–201.

in the formation or execution of public policy. Such terms as "executive function" or "legislative function" are alien to these people and to their lives. The Indian knows about the judicial function if he or his friends have ever been haled into court. The judiciary is where "the law" is; the courts dispense justice. "Justice" is a word which means that the Indian always loses.

The case is quite different, however, in the matter of provincial and local government. These are the only real levels of government so far as the bulk of the people of Ecuador is concerned. These people know their parishes and their cantons and normally have a deep and abiding love for them, if not for the officials thereof. These units of government, together with the provinces, are the most fundamental and real expressions of the political organization of the Ecuadoran nation. It has been guessed that 400,000 of the republic's estimated 3,383,655 people are "whites." For the other 2,983,655 Ecuadorans—if these figures are anywhere near the truth—government is almost exclusively provincial and local. Moreover, government of this type is hard and actual; it is not a fiction, it is not divorced from reality.

ECUADOR AS A UNITARY STATE

As every university student in the United States knows, if he has not cut the opening lecture in his first course in political science, governments may be internally organized in any one of three theoretically possible ways. The national or central government may have unlimited legal power over all territory within the state, in which case it is said that the organization is unitary; political authority may be divided by the constitution between self-governing parts and the central whole, when the state is designated as federal; or legal power may belong to parts which are loosely associated through a weak central organ, in which case the arrangement is called confederate. Ecuador is a unitary state. All the republic's fifteen constitutions, with one exception, have provided for the unitary form.

Under the system of centralization of authority as it operates in Ecuador, the continental territory of the republic is divided into seventeen provinces. Each province is itself divided into a number of cantons; and each canton is divided into a number of parishes. These provincial and local units of government serve in actual fact as well as in constitutional theory as the regional agents of the central government at Quito. As such, they execute within their respective jurisdictions the laws and policies developed by national authorities. Provinces, cantons, and parishes represent the interests of the national government rather than those of the people residing in their areas; and provincial, cantonal, and parish officials are employees of the national government.

The central authorities virtually exercise the power of life and death over the provinces and their subdivisions. The functions performed by these units are determined by national officials at Quito; the operation of the units is under constant national supervision; and the legislative function, as an organ of national government, may at any time change the number of provinces and subdivisions, alter their boundaries,[2] and add to or subtract from the authority delegated to them. The constitution places only four limitations on the power of the national government over the provincial and smaller entities. These restrictions deal with: one, nomenclature; two, form of government; three, the "relative autonomy" of the provinces; and four, the right of municipalities to revenue derived from taxes on urban property.

The system of naming the regional and local units of government is established in the constitution, and congress may not alter the nomenclature unless the fundamental charter is changed. Thus, the primary political divisions of the republic must be called "provinces," the secondary units "cantons," and the smallest "parishes."

The constitution stipulates that "there will be a governor in each province, a political chief in each canton, and a political lieutenant in each parish." Further, the charter asserts that "there will be, in each capital of a province...a provincial council."[3] This basic general outline of the form of provincial and local government may not be altered by national officials unless the constitution is also changed.

The constitution declares that "the state guarantees the relative autonomy of the provinces."[4] What does the term "relative autonomy" mean? The writer was privileged to attend a meeting of the council of state when this section of the constitution was debated. The members of that national agency were in general agreement that "relative autonomy" was primarily a literary phrase, although a motion to regard it as devoid of the force of law was defeated. It was felt that the writers of the constitution must have intended the provinces to have *something* of autonomy. At length the council of state decided by a vote of seven to four that the term "relative autonomy" as it appears in the

---

[2] One phase of this power is essentially academic. No geographic survey has yet been completed in Ecuador, with the result that the locations of provincial and cantonal boundaries have not been definitely established. This is one factor which has contributed to the difficulty of census taking in the republic.
[3] *Constitución Política de la República del Ecuador* (Quito, 1946), Art. 125.
[4] *Ibid.*, Art. 126.

constitution means that the provinces may make purchases involving more than $1,818.18[5] without submitting the transactions to national authorities for approval. How much more than $1,818.18 is involved in "relative autonomy" remained undecided early in 1949.

The constitution provides that "no later law may deprive municipalities, in whole or in part, of the right they have to the revenue from the tax on urban property." The purpose of this article is to prevent municipal budgets from being upset by national authorities. The latter may make fiscal demands upon the municipalities, but they must take such measures *before* the municipal budget enters into force or wait until the municipalities' next fiscal period. The municipality—an entity apart from provinces, cantons, and parishes—enjoys a special position in the Ecuadoran constitutional system, and is discussed at length later in this chapter.

Within the limits established by the four restrictions just discussed, the national government exercises complete control over provincial, cantonal, and parish governments. "The essential point is that the power of policy-determination rests in the central government," García has explained. "The subordinate organs do not have autonomous power to proceed independently in acts and decisions.... The delegation [of authority] to such organs means that they are the media or the merely mechanical vehicles of such acts or decisions."[6] The provinces, cantons, and parishes are the creatures and the servants of the national government.

Ecuadoran authorities on the internal organization of their republic generally advance the following five arguments in defense of the proposition that the unitary arrangement is better suited than any other to Ecuadoran needs.

1. It is said that the unitary system insures administrative uniformity throughout the country. Such uniformity as is obtained by the arrangement, it should be pointed out, is largely in the realm of legalistic fiction. The three continental regions of Ecuador differ basically from one another in their social and political characteristics and problems, and a case may be made for the recognition in law of these regional differences. The constitutional assumption that the Sierra, the Coast, and the Oriente are so similar that they might be governed in the same way simply adds another instance to the long catalogue of blindness to reality which is so peculiarly characteristic of the Ecuadoran constitutional system. The governmental problems of the Coastal province of

---
[5] That is, 30,000 sucres.
[6] Aurelio García, *op. cit.*, Vol. II, 303.

Guayas are about as identical to those of the Oriente province of Santiago-Zamora as the problems of the state of New York are to those of the island of Guam. "In an attempt to achieve an administrative assimilation, the Oriente provinces have been given an organization similar to that of the other parts of the republic," *El Comercio* has observed editorially. "In our concept this is a huge though well-intentioned error, because organizations and structures do not arise as a product of a law but rather of the particular conformation of peoples. Our Oriente does not have the conditions which can use in their fullness such institutions as exist and function in the other regions."[7] Juridical uniformity among the three continental regions of the republic is little more than a legalistic façade.

2. A further argument in defense of the unitary system for Ecuador is that the arrangement strengthens the national government by helping to combat regionalism. This appears to be a consideration of some merit. So far as the unitary form is effective, it does tend to ease the centrifugal relationship between the Sierra and the Coast. Ecuadorans may be right when they say that a federal or confederate arrangement might have resulted in the substitution of at least two republics for the present one.

3. It is said that the centralization makes for more efficient administration. It is difficult to imagine greater inefficiency than that encountered in many areas of government in Ecuador, but it may be that only poverty of imagination stands in the way of full appreciation of this argument. In Ecuadoran government and administration, "channels" is the word given to those huge dark caverns into which many items of public business disappear forever. And it may be that the suppression of the unitary system would mean the creation of more "channels." The republic already possesses more than its share of these.

4. An additional defense of centralization of authority in Ecuador lies in the contention that under the unitary system the national government "can settle administrative questions with greater equality and justice."[8] "Justice," of course, defies objectification, even if "equality" does not. What is meant by this argument is probably that a greater perspective is forced upon the deciding authority if its jurisdiction is nationwide in scope. The ability to decide—or necessity for deciding—a Sierra problem within the context of responsibility for the entire republic is doubtlessly sobering in its effects; and the results are probably beneficial for the republic of Ecuador.

[7] *El Comercio*, Quito, May 4, 1948.
[8] Aurelio García, *op. cit.*, Vol. II, 306.

5. Lastly, it is held that the unitary form of organization facilitates the maintenance of order in the country. Again, it may simply be lack of imagination that frustrates the picturing of a more disorderly national history than Ecuador's. The achievements of unitary organization have not only been unspectacular in the matter of curbing revolutions, but they have also been conducive to authoritarianism and to the limited nature of political freedom in the republic. The system has discouraged local initiative in the handling of public affairs and has contributed to the appalling retardation of the political consciousness of the mass of the people of Ecuador. It is not a matter for wonder that the Indian may not be able to name any of the presidents of the country. Such a feat would be to little purpose, since the final tyrant is the provincial governor.

PROVINCES, CANTONS, AND PARISHES

PROVINCES

The continental territory of the republic of Ecuador is divided into seventeen provinces. Ten of these are in the Sierra, five in the Coast, and two in the Oriente. As the primary legal division of the country, the province is of significance in giving course and character to the smaller units of government.

The chief officer of civil government in the province is the governor. He is appointed by the president of the republic and holds office so long as he enjoys the confidence of the president. National control and supervision of the governor are exercised through the ministry of government. The governor of each province is required to be in possession of the rights of citizenship and at least twenty-five years of age. These are the sole legal requirements a governor must meet; and within them the executive is free to base the selection on any factors he deems fit.

It is frequently said that political favoritism is the exclusive basis upon which provincial governors are chosen. This overstates the case: favoritism certainly enters into the selections, but a study of the appointing process reveals a pattern of factors entering into the choice of provincial governors. At least these four factors seem to be involved:

1. A provincial governor must be a man whom both the president of the republic and the minister of government agree that they can trust. The governor is, it must be remembered, the major agent of the executive function within the province.

2. The provincial governor is in every case a member of the ruling class, a "white." This is in a sense a legal requirement in that "posses-

sion of the rights of citizenship" means that the governor must, among other things, be able to read and write Spanish, a faculty largely monopolized by the "whites."

3. The political party affiliation of the governor is of some importance. Most governors belong to the president's party, although it rarely happens that all of them do. The party affiliations of the governors normally reflect the political composition of the president's cabinet. Governors of Sierra provinces are frequently Conservatives, those of Coastal provinces are normally Radical Liberals, and those of Oriente provinces are generally members of the president's party. On occasion—depending on the political exigencies of the moment—it may be necessary to appoint governors who have no party affiliations at all.

4. Normally, the governor must be familiar with the peculiar problems of the province to which he is assigned. He is usually but not necessarily a native of that province. In the event that a serious political cleavage should exist within a given province, the governor may well be an outsider who is not associated with either faction. Under such circumstances, it may happen—and be considered politically expedient—that the governor is largely unfamiliar with the particular problems of the province which he administers.

The provincial governor, within the republic's constitutional system, acts as the agent and representative of national rather than provincial interests, and the executive is legally free to make gubernatorial appointments in defiance of the wishes of the politically articulate inhabitants of the provinces. The governor is usually loyal to national rather than to provincial political elements. Frequently, governors tend after a period of time to become identified with provincial instead of national interest groups; and when this occurs such governors are usually dismissed. This aspect of the unitary arrangement was well illustrated by President Velasco Ibarra's attitude toward a protest raised in 1944 by a group of citizens in the Coastal province of Manabí when the executive dismissed their governor. "You have absolutely no right to protest because the government has decided to change the governor of Manabí," the president asserted. "I do not accept impertinent impositions from anybody."[9] This position was constitutionally correct; its political wisdom was another—and, for the present purpose, unrelated—matter.

The powers and duties of the provincial governor are not to be found in the text of the constitution. They are determined by the legislative function, which may at any time add to or subtract from the responsi-

---

[9] *El Comercio*, Quito, September 13, 1944.

bilities of the governor. The sole restriction upon the legislators in this connection is that congress may not abolish the office of governor in any of the provinces without a change in the constitution. The legal position of the governors at the time this book was written rested largely on the

TABLE 8
THE PROVINCES OF ECUADOR: SELECTED DATA*

Regions and provinces	Provincial capital	Number of members of provincial council	Number of cantons	Number of parishes
Totals................................	....	..	86	651
Sierra				
Carchi.......................	Tulcán	5	3	22
Imbabura....................	Ibarra	5	4	42
Pichincha....................	Quito	9	5	71
Cotopaxi.....................	Latacunga	7	5	34
Tungurahua..................	Ambato	7	4	41
Chimborazo..................	Riobamba	7	6	51
Bolívar.......................	Guaranda	5	3	24
Cañar........................	Azogues	5	3	27
Azuay.......................	Cuenca	9	6	61
Loja.........................	Loja	7	8	55
Coast				
Esmeraldas...................	Esmeraldas	5	2	23
Manabí......................	Portoviejo	9	10	53
Los Ríos.....................	Babahoyo	5	6	21
Guayas......................	Guayaquil	9	7	52
El Oro.......................	Machala	5	5	24
Oriente				
Napo-Pastaza.................	Tena	5	4	24
Santiago-Zamora..............	Macas	5	5	26

* This table is based on Ministerio de Gobierno, *División Territorial de la República del Ecuador* (Quito, 1947); and *Ley de Elecciones* (*Registro Oficial*, February 24, 1947), Art. 114.

Law of Administrative Organization of the Republic of Ecuador, which entered into force on April 26, 1947. The duties of the governors under this instrument may be divided into six groups: (1) relating to security and defense, (2) executive and supervisory, (3) developmental, (4) fiscal, (5) advisory, and (6) reportorial.

1. In general, each governor is required to preserve tranquillity and public order in his province. Normally, the governor is the commander

of units of the armed forces stationed within his jurisdiction. He enforces the military conscription laws in his province. He must endeavor to prevent social conflicts from arising in his territory. Should he be unsuccessful in this endeavor, or should public disorder occur for any other reason, he may be given broad authority to restore normal conditions. The emergency powers of the president may be delegated to the governor for use within his province in urgent circumstances; and the governor may appoint additional personnel to the police force on an emergency and temporary basis. In times of crisis he may use provincial funds, originally set aside for other purposes, to restore order.

2. The executive and supervisory duties of the governor are directed toward guaranteeing that all national laws are enforced within his province. As the agent of the national government, he assists various national agencies of government in the performance of their functions. Thus, the governor assists the supreme electoral tribunal by coöperating with the provincial electoral tribunal established in his territory for the conduct of elections. Governors' roles in this connection have frequently added to charges of electoral fraud, an outstanding case in point being the political position of the governors as tools of the Arroyo del Río regime in the aborted election scheduled for June of 1944. The governor's authority to issue passports to residents of his province who intend to travel abroad is a further instance of his position as the agent on the provincial level of national government institutions—in this case, the ministry of foreign relations. The governor is the chief executive officer of provincial administration: he directs and disciplines provincial employees, and is required to make their responsibilities effective. During his time in office, the governor must visit all cantons and parishes in his province for the purpose of familiarizing himself with the status of government and administration throughout its territory.

3. The governor is expected to encourage the development within his province of agriculture, industry, and commerce. He is, further, required to stimulate the growth of culture and the fine arts.

4. Foremost among the fiscal responsibilities of the governor is the preparation of the province's annual budget estimate. In the more developed provinces—for example, Pichincha in the Sierra, or Guayas in the Coast—this is a function of major significance in the over-all economy of the nation, and is watched with considerable interest by the press and the politically articulate sectors of the population. The governor is also under especial obligation to safeguard such public funds as may be located in his province.

5. In his advisory capacity, the governor plays a role of some significance in the development of the policies executed by the national ministry of government. The governor is expected to suggest to the executive function, through this ministry, policies which would aid his province; and many domestic measures are formulated on the national level in consequence of compilations of suggestions and advice received from the provincial governors. These officials also recommend to the executive function possible candidates for the posts of superintendents of police, political chiefs of cantons, and political lieutenants of parishes. It should be remembered that these latter functionaries are appointed by the executive, usually on the recommendations of the appropriate governors; but once these lesser officials are named, they are under the supervision of the governors.

6. A considerable amount of paper work falls to the provincial governor. In the first place, he must submit to the minister of government an annual report on the problems of his province and the progress of government and administration therein. Moreover, the governor is expected to gather statistical data on various aspects of provincial life. These data are sent to the ministry of national economy.

The legally prescribed duties outlined above constitute one grand fiction insofar as they convey the impression that the seventeen governors play anything like equal parts in the development of Ecuadoran government and politics. Discounting for the moment such rapidly changing imponderables as political exigencies and the personalities of the individuals involved, such long-range factors as regional, economic, and social differences among the provinces can have no other effect than to brand as unrealistic fiction any proposition of gubernatorial uniformity. The governor of the Coastal province of Guayas must of necessity be considered a different political factor than the governor of the Oriente province of Santiago-Zamora. It should not be assumed that the governor of the Sierra province of Pichincha and the governor of the Coastal province of El Oro exercise equal influence on the Ecuadoran system.

The size, social complexity, economic development, and location of each province actually play a greater part in determining the powers and duties of its governor than does the Law of Administrative Organization of the Republic of Ecuador. A curiously inverse correlation normally exists between the power which a governor exercises within his province and his influence on the national political scene. The governors of the Oriente provinces of Napo-Pastaza and Santiago-Zamora are lords and masters within their domains, but they are the presiding officers of an almost uninhabited and a politically inarticulate jungle, carrying negligible weight in national affairs. The governors of the Sierra province of Pichincha (which contains Quito) and the Coastal province of Guayas (which contains Guayaquil) are, on the other hand, relatively powerless within their provinces but are major figures in national politics. These two governors are frequently hamstrung by strong and determined provincial councils, a hostile and hawklike press, and a body of public opinion such as exists nowhere else in Ecuador. Pichincha and Guayas, which are the nerve centers of the republic and for many purposes *are* Ecuador, contain an estimated twenty-four per cent of the nation's population and probably three-fourths of Ecuador's "whites." If one were to name the six offices of greatest potential political power in Ecuador, he would undoubtedly cite the presidency of the republic, the mayoralty of Quito, the mayoralty of Guayaquil, the ministership of government, the governorship of Pichincha, and the governorship of Guayas, probably in that order.

Each of the seventeen governors is aided—or harassed, as the case may be—by a provincial council. This is a relatively new development in Ecuadoran constitutional organization, having been provided for only in the constitutions of 1929, 1945, and 1946. The provincial councils are small, ranging from five to nine members. The members of these bodies are popularly elected by proportional representation for two-year terms, the elections taking place in all provinces on the first Sunday in November of each odd-numbered year. Provincial councilors must be Ecuadorans by birth, in the exercise of the rights of citizenship, and at least twenty-five years of age. The councils serve as constitutional watchdogs against the governors, reporting allegedly unconstitutional acts of these officials to the minister of government. These bodies also authorize public works projects, impose provincial taxes, and supervise the fiscal operations of the municipalities under their jurisdiction.

As in the case of the governors, it is difficult to generalize on the actual positions of the provincial councils. Each of the seventeen provinces presents a unique situation. In some the councils are effective checks against the governors, in others they merely rubber-stamp decisions. The councils in the Oriente are normally subservient bodies; elsewhere the position of the councils varies with numerous political developments. The councils of Pichincha and Guayas, like their governors, are exceedingly sensitive to national political developments and are of greater significance in the over-all Ecuadoran context than are the councils of any of the other fifteen provinces.

CANTONS

For purposes of its internal administration, each province is divided into a number of cantons. The largest number of cantons (ten) is to be found in the Coastal province of Manabí; the smallest number (two) in the Coastal province of Esmeraldas; and the average number of cantons per province is five. The number of cantons in a province normally depends on the latter's size, social complexity, patronage situation, and local traditions. A province which is predominantly rural and has a large Indian population generally develops local traditions and loyalties in terms of cantons, with the result that it is frequently more difficult to alter the number or names of these units than it is to change the provinces.

The canton occupies an anomalous position in the Ecuadoran constitutional system. A canton may be either rural or urban. If it is rural—and most Ecuadoran cantons are—it is normally a highly significant entity in the life of its people, especially in the Sierra. If, on the other hand, the canton is urban, it is territorially coterminous with a municipality, and becomes lost so far as the consciousnesses of the urban dwellers are concerned. For these city folk the municipality is an ever present and all-important reality, and they usually do not know about the canton unless they have had some legal or political training. The urban canton is discussed in a later section of this chapter; its rural counterpart is, from a constitutional point of view, primarily an administrative subdivision of a province. The rural canton bears a relationship to the province which is somewhat like that between a rural county and the state in the United States.

The nature of the rural cantons differs according to regions. In the Oriente, rural cantons are lines on a map and little more; and it must be admitted that the lines are in different places on different maps. This is also true, but to a lesser degree, of the rural cantons in the northern Coastal provinces. One is tempted to say that it is necessary to be a Sierra Indian to understand and appreciate fully the true nature of the rural canton. The Sierra Indian is tied to the land; his attitude toward the earth involves a sentiment of somewhat mystical religiosity toward the soil. It is not *any* land that possesses this incalculable value, the Indian avers; his deep, abiding harmony with the earth is exclusively with *his* land. It is not "his" land in the sense that he has title to it, for the "whites" normally hold the papers. It is the Indian's land in the sense that it is his universe: it sets the style and color of his clothes, the manner of his speech, the extent of his community. Mapmakers cannot agree as to the precise boundaries of rural cantons, for surveyors' instruments cannot *feel* the end of a friendly and beloved world and the beginning of a strange and sometimes hostile universe as the Sierra Indian feels it. The "white" mapmaker, despite his instruments, is forced to admit that he has crossed a cantonal line when the color of the Indian women's headgear turns from orange to red or to dark blue, and he draws his map accordingly. His chart cannot be as accurate and unfailing as the map in the heart of the Sierra Indian.

The rural canton is one of the Sierra Indian's basic points of contact with government. It is a secondary contact, to be sure; for the political chief—the canton's principal officer of government—is far removed from the Indian, who knows him primarily as the taskmaster above the political lieutenant of his parish. The political chief is appointed by the president of the republic on the recommendation of the appropriate provincial governor, and is supervised through the ministry of government. He sees that the constitution and the laws are obeyed in his canton and carries out instructions received from the governor. The political chief preserves public order in the canton, is the commander of the armed forces stationed therein, and sees to it that the military conscription laws are obeyed in his territory. He presents a periodic report on his work to the governor.

PARISHES

For purposes of its internal administration, each canton—rural or urban—is divided into a number of parishes. The average number of parishes per canton is eight; the largest number—forty-seven—is in the canton of Quito in the Sierra province of Pichincha; and the smallest number—one—is in the canton of Baños in the Sierra province of Tungurahua. The number of parishes in a canton normally depends on the latter's size, social complexity, patronage situation, and local traditions.

Parishes, like cantons, fall into two legal classes: rural and urban. The urban parish lies within an urban canton, becoming a species of neighborhood or *barrio* within the municipality. Usually the city dweller knows how many parishes there are in his municipality if he knows how many polling places operate in the city on election day. The urban parishes perform functions which are unknown as such to most city folk, for example, enforcing the compulsory voting laws—when they are enforced—and providing the basis for the organization tables of the local police and fire-fighting forces.

The rural parish is essentially dissimilar to its urban counterpart. Like cantons, parishes differ from region to region. In the Oriente, rural parishes are actually nonexistent in most areas, although the ministry of government claims that fifty parishes lie beyond the eastern cordillera. The rural parish of the Coast contrasts with its Sierra equivalent in a highly important respect. The montuvios, the lower class of the Coast, are not cut off from the "national life" in the same sense in which the Sierra Indians are. Some political consciousness and activity, for the most part organized around rural parishes, are to be found among the montuvios. The long-range significance of the Coastal rural parish perhaps lies in its operation as a vehicle for the incorporation of the montuvios in the "national life"; the rural parish has failed to accomplish this for the Sierra Indian, and the political ramifications of this circumstance lay bare a significant aspect of the governmental system of Ecuador.

So far as the overwhelming majority of the people of the republic are concerned, the fundamental officer of government is the political lieutenant, the principal official of the rural parish. He is appointed by the executive function and holds office during its pleasure. The political lieutenant, whose task is to carry out all instructions received from the appropriate political chief, is generally what the Sierra Indian means when he talks about "the government."

The political lieutenant, the Indians' and the cholos' primary point of contact with the state, is the "government" in a sense which is difficult for people of English-speaking countries to appreciate: he is, for the Sierra Indian, the state personified. "He performs the functions of sheriff, judge, state's attorney, manager of the general store, chief moneylender—he is the Pooh-Bah of each town, though the larger the town, the less absolute his power," Franklin has written. "He is the person of the national government in his bailiwick and need fear no man on earth except the priest."[10]

The extent to which the Sierra Indian is removed from the "national life" is well illustrated by the failure of the parish council as an institution. This three-man body was designed to aid the political lieutenant, and is theoretically composed of members of the local community. The Indian, however, normally refuses to serve on the council, for to do so generally results in ostracism by his people. From the Indian's viewpoint, the honor of serving on the parish council is to be avoided at all costs. The situation is somewhat reminiscent of the scalawag of the

---

[10] Franklin, *op. cit.*, pp. 137–138.

United States, who, after being tarred, feathered, and run out of a Midwestern town on a rail, observed: "If it weren't for the honor of the thing, I would rather walk." The Ecuadoran Indians doomed to service on the parish council "receive no salary: they serve 'patriotically,'" Buitrón and Collier have noted in their study of Indian life in the Sierra province of Imbabura.

> Their actual obligations ... consist of going from house to house naming workers needed by the political lieutenant or some other public authority for public work or private. The Indians thus recruited may clean a public plaza, a street or road, or a private garden, orchard, or corral without receiving pay. ... Every year in each community the political lieutenant sponsors what in Ecuador are called free elections, at which he appoints an Indian committee composed of president, vice-president, and secretary. ... The Indians do not understand these names and call all the members of the committee "mayors." Very few Indians care to have these positions. Many refuse to accept them upon being appointed, first because they lose time in the constant walking about from house to house, and second because the jobs will gain them enemies and the disapproval of other members of the community.[11]

It is incontestably true, as Moisés Sáenz has discovered, that "the Indians do not really have their own [formal] local authorities."[12] Typically, the Indian has no positive or active part in government on any level, be it parish, cantonal, provincial, or national. With rare exceptions, the Indian does not vote. Consider a few representative parishes of the Sierra: "In the parish of Ilumán, there are ... 250 'whites' and 650 Indians, totaling 180 voters. ... In the parish of Flores, there are 11,500 Indians and 500 'whites'; the voters total 133. ... In Espejo, there are about 250 'whites' and approximately 3,700 Indians. The voters total ninety-eight..."[13]

What is government? The sophisticated of other lands, the folk who will answer in terms of kings and presidents, constitutions and legislators, may think the Ecuadoran Indian naïve and uninformed when he says that government is the parish and the political lieutenant. Yet the Indian knows a great truth. The presidents and the legislatures, the constitutions and the ambassadors—paraphernalia which are here today and gone tomorrow—are they government? Or are they a superficial coating—a weak superstructure struck down by the first breath of crisis? Can that which is so transitory and is so far removed from the overwhelming majority of the people of the nation be called government? Government is the parish and the political lieutenant.

---
[11] Aníbal Buitrón and John Collier, "Taita Imbabura" (MS, 1948), pp. 34–35; published as *The Awakening Valley* (Chicago, 1950).
[12] Sáenz, *Sobre el Indio Ecuatoriano*, p. 131.
[13] *Ibid.*, p. 128.

What is government? Government is the destruction of the Indian. "The political consolidation of the country, that is, the creation of political entities, parishes . . . is a process which affects adversely the community and the personality of the Indian," said Sáenz. "The establishment of a rural parish in Indian territory means that there has been founded a center of 'white' and cholo population within this territory, a center which becomes the governing and ruling nucleus. The authorities who govern the new entity are 'whites' and cholos. . . ."[14] Government—the parish and the political lieutenant—destroys the Indian, but it is to be stressed that this destruction is more social and cultural than biological, that the terms "Indian," "cholo," and "white" do not rest on physical factors. The destroyed Indian is a man who has changed his way of life, his manner of dress, the language in which he speaks. The cholo is a liquidated Indian.

Government is the continuing conquest of the Indian. Francisco Pizarro lay dead in 1541, but his work has not yet ceased. His mantle has fallen upon the political lieutenant. Who is this Pooh-Bah, this sheriff, judge, and state's attorney, this manager of the general store and chief moneylender? He is nothing less than the conquistador in twentieth-century dress. He is government as no president ever was. The work of the political lieutenant is done when the Indian community no longer exists, when the "whites" and the cholos have displaced the Indian and deprived him of his land, his society, and his heritage.

The Ecuadoran Municipality

Municipalities are legally defined in Ecuador as "associations of persons residing in those territorial units which the constitution establishes as cantons."[15] Every Ecuadoran municipality is territorially coterminous with a canton. Not all cantons, however, coexist with municipalities; and in this circumstance is to be found the legal distinction between rural and urban cantons.

A canton must meet certain qualifications before a municipality may be erected within it. These qualifications as stated in the law differ markedly from the qualifications established by practical politics, the distinction presenting an additional instance in which the written laws of the republic depart from reality. According to the law, a canton may become urban (that is, entitled to embrace a municipality) when it (1)

---
[14] *Ibid.*, p. 133.
[15] *Ley de Régimen Municipal* (Quito, 1945), Title I, Art. 1. Cf. also Eduardo Riofrio Villagómez, *Gobierno y Finanzas Municipales* (Quito, 1945), pp. 459 ff.; and *Constitución Política de la República del Ecuador* (Quito, 1946), Art. 127.

contains a population of 20,000 or more persons; (2) has a definitely delimited territory; and (3) possesses the economic ability to perform municipal services. To the non-Ecuadoran observer, at least two of these qualifications may appear to lend themselves readily to objective determination; but this appearance is deceptive. It is to be remembered that no national population census has ever been taken in Ecuador: by early 1949, an official census had been taken only in the canton of Quito. Moreover, the republic remains to be mapped. Cantonal, and even provincial, lines on maps of Ecuador represent little more than the cartographers' guesses, and no two maps of the republic agree on cantonal, provincial, or even national boundaries.

In actual practice, municipalities are created—that is, rural cantons become urban—when a sufficiently large nucleus of "whites" has been established in the canton to displace or dominate on a local scale the Indians, cholos, or montuvios. When the local area is safely in the hands of the "whites," the canton becomes urban and its form of government changes, a cantonal or municipal council[16] being created.

The organization of municipal government is fairly uniform throughout the republic. Each cantonal or municipal council contains seven, nine, or eleven members. Every municipality which is not a Sierra or Coastal provincial capital has a seven-man council and no mayor, the ceremonial head of the municipality—called interchangeably the "cantonal president" or the "municipal president"—being the presiding officer of the council. In twelve of the fifteen Sierra and Coastal provincial capitals there are nine-man councils and separately elected mayors (alcaldes) who are not members of the councils. Each of the three largest cities of the republic—Guayaquil, the nation's chief port; Quito, the national capital; and Cuenca, the "Athens of the South"—has an eleven-man council and a separately elected mayor who may not participate or vote in meetings of the council. The members of all municipal councils are popularly elected by proportional representation for two-year terms. Nationwide municipal elections are held on the first Sunday of November of every odd-numbered year. The fifteen mayors have two-year terms and are popularly elected at the same time as the councils.

The cantonal council in each municipality is in general charged with the responsibility of directing the process of government within the urban canton. In some respects the council is the agent of the national government, being required, for example, to see that the municipality

---

[16] In Ecuadoran usage—legal and otherwise—the terms "cantonal council" and "municipal council" are synonymous and interchangeable.

lives in conformity with the constitution and the laws of the republic. The powers of the council lie principally in the field of public works. The councilors determine the building and construction projects to be undertaken in the municipality, and direct the maintenance of parks, streets, and such lighting as exists. They endeavor, usually unsuccessfully, to make electricity and potable water available in the canton, and sponsor various health and sanitation projects. They are required to foster the progress of education and "culture" in the municipality. Some economic powers are lodged with the council. It is authorized, for instance, to institute price control over commodities of prime necessity, and to see that stores and other agencies of distribution of needed materials exist in the canton.

The success with which the councils are able to perform the foregoing functions varies in accordance with many factors, among which the resources of the urban cantons are prominent. With the exception of Quito and Guayaquil, most municipalities in Ecuador are economically unable to perform these services on a scale which observers with North American standards would regard as adequate. Since most municipalities are without water that is safe to drink, their people normally use a gaseous mineral water, bottled soft drinks, beer, and chicha for thirst-quenching purposes. Outside of Quito and Guayaquil, electrical services are for the most part an exotic luxury which only the very wealthy can afford. Health and sanitation remain major problems in the urban as well as the rural cantons of the republic, and sewers and similar facilities are exceedingly rare. Streets in almost all urban cantons are dirt or cobblestone roads. Virtually every Ecuadoran municipality boasts a park, or plaza. The plaza performs a significant function in the political life of the municipality, as the citizens generally gather there in times of revolution or other crisis; and most holidays are observed by fitting ceremonies held in the plaza. Some plazas (those at Quito, Ambato, and Latacunga, for example) are carefully tended and lush in colorful vegetation. But the plaza is generally little more than a clearing or barren open space in the center of town.

The mayor of each of the fifteen provincial capitals already mentioned, in addition to being the ceremonial representative of the urban canton, advises the council and may veto any of its measures, although his veto may be overridden by a simple majority of the council. The mayor prepares the annual budget requests of the municipality—the council possesses the power of appropriation—and supervises municipal administration. The mayor appoints and removes most municipal employees.

These functions, in the municipalities which do not have mayors, are performed by the members of the seven-man councils in a fashion somewhat similar to practices in those cities of the United States which use the commission form of government.

The constitutional and political position of the Ecuadoran municipality is anomalous. In terms of the unitary organization of the republic, the municipality is in a sense an agent or tool of the national government; yet a considerable degree of autonomy rests with the municipality. Municipal autonomy is a more fundamental and real concept than the "relative autonomy" of the provinces. The roots of municipal autonomy are deeply embedded in the history of Ecuador and have become interwoven with problems of regionalism and particularism.

As contrasted with provincial authority, municipal autonomy in Ecuador dates from the sixteenth century and has been a major factor in the history, government, and politics of the republic. Without defining Ecuadoran democracy, the country's historians have said that its cradle was to be found in the colonial *cabildo*, the agency of town government established by the conquistadors. Royal decrees in the wake of the Spanish conquest established cabildos for the purpose of tending "to matters touching the service of God and His Majesty, and the common welfare of the people and inhabitants of the city."[17] During the bulk of the colonial period, a "salutary neglect" on the part of the major officials of the Spanish empire gave the cabildos a considerable measure of self-government. This power was in large part acquired through default: a *de facto* distribution of powers emerged within a *de jure* unitary empire. "There was introduced into America a centralized system which left a marked autonomy to the cabildos. . . . So long as the king or the viceroy or the governor took no steps to the contrary, the cabildos governed without consulting the central power, and without seeking its approval or authorization."[18]

On the eve of political separation from Spain, the cabildos were the major organs of government in what is now Ecuador. The calendar of national holidays reveals that Ecuador does not have one independence day, but rather two: independence was declared on August 10, 1809, by the cabildo at Quito, and on October 9, 1820, by the cabildo at Guayaquil. As these entities played the leading role in the struggle for independence from Spain, so their political heirs—the municipalities—have been the major units around which the regionalism of the twentieth century has developed. The recognition by the constitution of municipal

---

[17] Riofrio Villagómez, *op. cit.*, p. 179.
[18] *Ibid.*, p. 183.

autonomy is merely the acknowledgment of a basic fact in Ecuadoran politics: regionalism, in large measure based on municipalities, has meant the distribution of political influence between the Sierra and the Coast. The municipal council at Quito often provides the political leadership of the former, while the council at Guayaquil frequently performs a similar service for the Coast. The autonomy of Quito and Guayaquil is especially obvious and is not enjoyed on a comparable scale by the other municipalities of the republic. In general, it may be said that a number of the older and larger cities of the Sierra—Cuenca, Ambato, Riobamba, and Latacunga—enjoy something of political autonomy, but to a lesser degree than do Quito and Guayaquil. Thus, municipal autonomy is a hard fact of history and politics as well as a number of phrases in a constitution.

Yet Ecuador is a unitary state, and the anomalous position of the municipality is thus cast in terms of a peculiar dualism. Leaving aside the constitution and the laws for the moment, it may be said that the position of the Ecuadoran municipality rests on a balancing of forces, a precarious equilibrium established between autonomy or decentralization on the one hand and centralization on the other. The historical role of the municipal cabildo, the overbalancing position of Quito and Guayaquil in the Ecuadoran pattern, and the extreme variety of regionalism in the republic combine to produce a type of municipal autonomy which probably no quantity of legal verbiage could obviate. However, centralizing factors have likewise been powerful: the absence of self-government in the Spanish tradition, the influence of the French Revolution on administrative organization, and the constant danger that regionalism might result in the disruption of the republic have frequently combined to motivate vigorous measures directed toward greater centralization of government. The Ecuadoran municipality is caught in the crossfire of centralizing and decentralizing tendencies; its life is dualistic; it is the Dr. Jekyll and Mr. Hyde of Ecuadoran government and politics.

Under the constitution, the basic theory of the municipality fits into the unitary scheme of internal organization by holding that municipal officials, even though they are elected by the voters of the city, are agents of the national government. These officials are supervised and controlled in their functions through the national ministry of government; the structure of municipal government rests on the controlling concept of uniformity; the canton, whether rural or urban, is an administrative subdivision of the province; and most administrative services in the cities are provided by the national government. Ecuador is a unitary state, though there are times when the constitutional provision to this effect must be reread to the members of the eleven-man councils at Quito and Guayaquil.

QUITO AND GUAYAQUIL

For most foreign visitors, the story of Ecuador is a tale of two cities. The country is dominated by the Sierra and the Coast, the government of the republic resting on an uneasy equilibrium between these two major regions. Quito, the capital, dominates the Sierra; Guayaquil, the chief port and biggest city, is the "capital" of the Coast. It has been noted that the Conservatives are the party of the Sierra, and that the Radical Liberals are the party of the Coast. Quito is the Conservatives' stronghold, while Guayaquil is the headquarters of the Radical Liberal party.

QUITO

San Francisco de Quito was founded by Sebastián de Benalcázar in August of 1534, the historians say; but nobody knows how old Quito really is. The Quitus, the Caras, and the Incas established centers of civilization there long before the arrival of the Spaniards. Quito is ageless and looks it; the *quiteños* were not alone in looking askance at a 1945 resolution of the cantonal council to "modernize" the city within the ensuing fifty-five years. This picturesque and colorful capital, with its narrow, winding cobblestone avenues, with its streets whose names are constantly changing, is called the "City of Light" by those who wish it to be remembered that the cabildo at Quito was the first in all of Hispanic America to declare independence of Spain. And Quito is called the "City of Eternal Spring" by those who wish that the "winter"—the rainy season—once ended, would never return.

Until 1948 nobody knew what the population of Quito was. In that year the quiteños were still vividly describing the chaotic "Census Day" in August, 1947, when the city was thoroughly paralyzed by orders that everybody stay home and be counted. Persons discovered on the streets on that day were taken to the prisons, where they remained until the tally was completed. When the number of people in the houses was added to the number in jail and the number of the census takers, a four-hundred-year-old mystery was at last cleared up. The capital of the republic was officially declared to contain 94,825 males and 105,360 females, totaling 200,185 persons. Quiteños could point out with pride that theirs was the only canton in the entire republic in which a population census had been taken. The imposingly aged government buildings surrounding the Plaza de la Independencia proclaim that this Andean city is the capital of the republic. That Quito is the nucleus of the literate and "cultured" folk of the Sierra is attested by its press, which embraces two-thirds of the newspapers of the Sierra. Quito supports six newspapers: *El Comercio* (founded in 1905), *El Día* (1913), *El Debate* (1937), *Ultimas Notícias* (1938), *La Patria* (1942), and *La Tierra* (1945). The newsboys like to explain that government officials read *El Comercio*, Church people read *La Patria*, and Socialists read *La Tierra*.

In the years since the revolution of 1944, the Radical Liberal party has rapidly declined in strength and prestige, and the Conservative party's fortunes have perhaps been better than they have been at any other time since 1895. This is a nationwide characteristic of Ecuadoran politics since 1944, and the developments at Quito have done little more than mirror this trend.

The Conservative renaissance which followed the 1944 upheaval became apparent at Quito earlier than elsewhere in the republic. In the municipal elections of November, 1945, Conservative victories were reported in many areas of the republic, but that at Quito was most striking. The post of mayor of the capital city was won by Dr. Jacinto Jijón y Caamaño, leader and chief mentor of the Conservative party. The post-1945 composition of the eleven-man cantonal council likewise represented great Conservative strength. This body contained eight Conservatives, two Socialists, and one Communist. The Radical Liberals, in power almost uninterruptedly from 1895 to 1944, were not able to capture a single seat on the municipal council of the canton of Quito in the election of 1945. The Conservatives stood resolutely against all challengers as the nationwide municipal elections of 1947 approached.

The rout of the Radical Liberals had been a matter of considerable concern to all anti-Conservative elements as early as the end of 1946, and the M.C.D.N. appeared on the scene in the following year with the avowed purpose of forestalling the Conservatives' return to national power. The broken and demoralized Radical Liberals announced through their provincial junta for Pichincha, the province in which Quito is situated, that they would not support any municipal candidates in the province for the elections of November, 1947, a move which led the M.C.D.N. to attempt to corral all anti-Conservative elements in a drive to oust that party from the mayoralty and council of Quito. The M.C.D.N. was, however, unsuccessful in uniting the non-Conservative groups, as many dissident Radical Liberal elements, desiring to preserve their separate identity, formed a rival anti-Conservative coalition known as the Independent Popular Movement (M.P.I.), which nominated its own candidate for mayor and a separate list of eleven candidates for the council.

Meanwhile, the Conservatives embarked upon a tactic somewhat similar to that of the M.C.D.N., but carried off with better success. In an effort to secure the support of rightist elements not formally associated with the Conservative party, the latter organization's cantonal directorate for the canton of Quito announced the formation of a coalition—called the Concentration of Rightists (*Concentración de Derechas*)—to which all anti-M.C.D.N. and anti-M.P.I. elements were invited to adhere. This maneuver won support from the cantonal units of such rightist "ad hoc" organizations as the Ecuadoran Nationalist Revolutionary Union (U.N.R.E.) and the Ecuadoran Nationalist Revolutionary Association (A.R.N.E.), with the result that rightist strength was to a large extent united in the Concentration of Rightists. On the other hand, anti-Conservative strength was divided between the rival M.C.D.N. and M.P.I.

The result seemed a foregone conclusion when the voters went to the polls on November 2, although the official results were not announced until eighteen days later. The mayoralty was won by the Concentration of Rightists, Alfonso Pérez Pallares, a Conservative, being installed for a two-year term ending late in 1949. Under the system of proportional representation in use, the Concentration of Rightists won five seats on the eleven-man council; the M.C.D.N., three; and the M.P.I., three. Thus, the Conservatives retained the mayoralty, but lost three seats on the council. In the months after the election, the U.N.R.E. and the A.R.N.E. slipped away from their agreement with the Conservatives, weakening that party's position somewhat; and the M.P.I. dissolved, many of its affiliates joining the M.C.D.N. The Conservatives thus remained the most powerful organized political group in the canton of Quito, but their position was by no means secure. Mayor Pérez Pallares offered to resign after the M.C.D.N. won the presidential election of June 6, 1948; but it appeared likely that he would remain in office until his term expired late in 1949.

M.C.D.N. affiliates were hopeful at the outset of that year that they had not yet lost everything to the Conservatives in the Sierra. The struggle, however, remained close, and the results of the 1949 contest would in part depend on the ability of the M.C.D.N. to consolidate its gains in the wake of the presidential contest of 1948.

GUAYAQUIL

It is generally agreed that Santiago de Guayaquil, nerve center of the Coast and Ecuador's chief port, is the republic's largest city, although no census has yet been taken there. Estimates usually place the city's population at somewhere between 275,000 and 300,000. Guayaquil was founded on July 25, 1538, by Francisco de Orellana, who is remembered principally for his amazing and epoch-making voyage down the length of the Amazon River. Although the official date of Guayaquil's founding is only four years later than Quito's, the port city is new and modern in appearance. It is situated along the Guayas River, which flows into the Gulf of Guayaquil and the Pacific Ocean. In appearance the city is reminiscent of several cities in the southern part of the United States. Indeed, Guayaquil strikes the foreign observer as a kind of architectural cross between New Orleans, Louisiana, and Havana, Cuba. Ecuador's major port and biggest city is served by three newspapers: *El Telégrafo* (founded in 1884), *El Universo* (1921), and *La Prensa* (1923).

The sharp physical contrast between Guayaquil and the infinitely older-appearing Quito is explained in part by Guayaquil's history. This has been to a considerable extent a history of catastrophe and calamity, causing the city to be rebuilt totally on a number of occasions. Pirates—"ocean statesmen," the British called them—completely burned down Guayaquil no fewer than three times during a period of eighty-three years. These fires were the work of the Dutch buccaneer Jacob Heremite Clerk, in 1624; of the British pirate Edward David, in 1687; and of the fabulous William Dampier, in 1707. Moreover, until the early years of the twentieth century, tropical and other diseases ran rampant at Guayaquil, earning for the port the designation of the "Pesthole of the Pacific." Throughout most of its history Guayaquil was notorious as a center of yellow fever, malaria, bubonic plague, dysentery, and typhoid fever.

The port was frequently quarantined in the nineteenth and early twentieth centuries during particularly severe epidemics of yellow fever and malaria. The fatalities caused at Guayaquil by these diseases were legion. Among the more celebrated victims was Thomas Nast, sometimes regarded in the United States as the inventor of the political cartoon, who spent the closing years of his life as the United States consul at Guayaquil. "We have no mail from the United States, because the quarantine keeps it away from the port," he wrote during the disastrous yellow fever epidemic of 1902. "The ships do not stop here, but continue south with the mail on board, and we can have our mail in a month, when the ships return.... A ship is outside the port now, but ... it is not permitted to dock. Oh, I need my mail!"[19] Nast died at Guayaquil—"succumbed to the climate," the record says—in 1902.

Following its acquisition of the Panama Canal Zone in 1903, the government of the United States began to take an active interest in health and sanitation problems at Ecuador's major port. "Guayaquil is in direct and constant communication with Panama, and is now one of the few ports in the world where yellow fever exists," the War Department declared in a message to the Department of State in 1909. "The failure to stamp out this disease ... is a constant menace to the Canal Zone.... In the face of these conditions, the remedy of quarantine is costly, unsatisfactory, and ineffective; the only effective method is the eradication of the source of the disease.... So long as this step is not taken, the health of the inhabitants of the Canal Zone, and consequently of the inhabitants of the coasts of [North] America, will be in constant danger."[20]

A series of health and sanitation agreements subsequently entered into by the governments of the United States and Ecuador has resulted in the cleansing of the port city, which is today no more dangerous from the standpoint of disease than most other South American ports. Early in the 1920's, the view was taken that Guayaquil's disease problems were questions in engineering rather than medicine, and the sanitation of the port city has accordingly been reflected in public works projects directed toward the clearing of swamps, the paving of streets, and the removal of disease-ridden houses. Physically, Guayaquil is a new city. Yellow fever was stamped out early in the 1920's; typhoid fever has been controlled, although a small epidemic followed the bursting of a water main in 1942; and no case of the bubonic plague has been reported since 1939. In conformity with the standards established in the Pan American Sanitary Code, Guayaquil has been rated as a Class A-1 port since 1930. The "Pesthole of the Pacific" has become the "Pearl of the Pacific."

Guayaquil is the center of Ecuador's commerce and industry, in contrast to Quito's role as the heart of the agricultural economy of the Sierra. In 1946 no less than 96 per cent of Ecuador's legal imports and

---
[19] Quoted in Lois F. Parks and Gustave A. Nuermberger, "El Saneamiento de Guayaquil," *Boletín del Centro de Investigaciones Históricas,* Vol. VII, Nos. 12–17 (Guayaquil, 1947), pp. 162–163.
[20] Quoted in *ibid.,* p. 167.

80 per cent of its legal exports cleared through the port at Guayaquil. This economic consideration has in part underlain the anti-Conservative nature of the politics of the Coast: the Conservatives, as the party of the Church and the large landholders, were never very powerful at Guayaquil. The Radical Liberals, whose interest in commerce and contact with other nations of the world found ready response in the Coast, have had their stronghold there since the 1880's.

In terms of Coastal politics, the overthrow of the Radical Liberal party in 1944 has probably resulted in a temporary disintegration of the party system. In the Sierra, as has been noted, the vacuum created by the failure of the Radical Liberals has been in large part filled by the renascent Conservative party. In the Coast, the pattern has differed. The Radical Liberal rout has divided and confused the anti-Conservative parties, but the Coast's traditional liberalism has prevented the Conservatives from making as large inroads in this region as they have in the Sierra. The politics of Guayaquil since 1944 illustrates a typical Coastal situation: the Radical Liberals have been demoralized and disorganized, yet the Conservatives have been unable to benefit greatly from their opponents' condition.

Chaos probably describes better than any other word the Guayaquil municipal election of November 2, 1947. The Radical Liberals, impotent, and quarreling among themselves, were unable to agree on candidates; the M.C.D.N. was not yet accepted by a large proportion of the voters; and the Coast continued to reject the Conservatives. The result was a disastrous splintering of the political parties: no fewer than seven candidates ran for mayor, and eight lists of aspirants for seats on the cantonal council were presented to the bewildered voters.

The first organization to enter candidates in the 1947 race for Guayaquil municipal posts was the Conservative party. This group announced on July 18 the mayoral candidacy of Colonel Aurelio Carrera Calvo (until then chief of the fire department of the canton of Guayaquil) together with a list ("List A") of eleven candidates for the municipal council. No further nominations were made until October, when a general rush into the field was begun by Dr. Rafael Mendoza Avilés of the faculty of the University of Guayaquil, supported for mayor by a university group which also announced eleven candidates ("List B") for the council. Bitter strife among the Radical Liberals of Guayas was aggravated on October 7 by the announcement of Carlos Enrique Hurtado Flor (accompanied by "List 2") as the party's candidate for mayor. Dissident Radical Liberals expressed their disaffection with the nominations by placing a renegade candidate, Rafael Guerrero Valenzuela (and "List D") in the field. The M.C.D.N. remained to be heard from: it nominated Enrique Boloña Rodríguez (and "List F") on October 11. Some Communists and Socialists—both groups defying their formal leaderships—banded together to form the Popular Alliance, nominating Alfredo Vera for mayor (and "List C" for the council). The regular Socialist organization persuaded Dr. Abel A. Gilbert,

TABLE 9
OFFICIAL RESULTS OF THE GUAYAQUIL MUNICIPAL ELECTION
OF NOVEMBER 2, 1947*

Party	Mayoralty		Cantonal council		
	Candidate	Votes	List	Votes	Council seats won
Totals.................	....	*28,281*		*25,947*	*11*
Conservative............	Carrera	4,894	A	5,084	3
Radical Liberal (Dissident).................	Guerrero	6,085	D	5,042	3
Popular Alliance........	Vera	4,150	C	4,244	2
Independent............	Mendoza	5,227	B	3,985	1
Socialist...............	Gilbert	2,149	3	2,661	1
M.C.D.N.ᵃ.............	Boloña	3,620	F	2,370	1
Independent............	....	......	E	524	0
Radical Liberal (Regular)	Hurtado	2,156	2	2,037	0

* This table is based on a mimeographed statement of the Guayas Provincial Electoral Tribunal, released on November 15, 1947.
ᵃ National Civic Democratic Movement (*Movimiento Cívico Democrático Nacional*).

noted physician and professor at the University of Guayaquil, to run as its candidate for mayor (accompanied by "List 3"). And a citizens' group, dissatisfied with all seven lists for the council, placed "List E" in nomination for that body, using admirable restraint in declining to name an eighth candidate for mayor. "We have a list for every conceivable taste," *El Telégrafo* observed editorially, but did not seem to be happy about it.[21]

The wide and confused range of candidates contributed to political apathy. A little more than half of the registered voters went to the polls, casting a total of 28,281 valid ballots for mayor and 25,947 for the lists of councilors. Although the balloting took place on November 2, the official results were not announced until the fifteenth of the month; and

[21] *El Telégrafo*, Guayaquil, October 21, 1947.

during the intervening two weeks, few were willing to bet on the outcome. The Guayas provincial electoral tribunal at length revealed that the dissident Radical Liberal candidate, Rafael Guerrero Valenzuela, had been elected mayor by virtue of his 6,085 votes. Under the system of proportional representation in use for the eleven-man council, the Conservatives were assigned three seats; the dissident Radical Liberals, three; the Popular Alliance, two; and the university group, the regular Socialists, and the M.C.D.N., one apiece.

It was an unusual election, and it produced an unusual mayor. Rafael Guerrero Valenzuela was not a professional politician, although his father—Alberto Guerrero Martínez—had been president of the republic for three months during 1932. Guerrero Valenzuela was better known to *guayaquileños* as a radio announcer than as a mayor. The robust sense of humor of this personable sports announcer and his vivid descriptions of bullfights had kept many a guayaquileño glued to his radio in the years before 1947, and the Guerrero Valenzuela broadcasts were among the very few which originated at Guayaquil and were also transmitted by Quito stations. Although he took his position as mayor of Ecuador's largest city quite seriously, Rafael Guerrero Valenzuela confided to the writer in 1948 that he hoped to return as an ex-mayor to his ringside seat at the bullfights.

CHAPTER IX

THE ECUADORAN SYSTEM: A RECAPITULATION

Of all human inequalities none is as important in its effects or has greater need of logical justification than that established by power. Except for certain rare enough individuals, one man is as good as another; why, then, do some men have the right to command and others the duty to obey?[1]

ON MAY 13, 1830, "the last day of despotism and the first day of the same thing," the separate national existence of the sovereign republic of Ecuador was proclaimed to be a fact. Teachers of history find this datum helpful: it is a convenient point at which to terminate a pedagogical unit of understanding, administer an examination, and begin another unit. The government of Ecuador since 1830, however, has been strikingly similar to its predecessor. The institution of divine-right monarchy was modified but not abolished. "Kings with the name of presidents" succeeded kings with the name of kings. The principal "republican" reforms centered around the abolition of the hereditary method of selecting successors to defunct monarchs. The government in Ecuador since 1830 has been something less than monarchy in the sense that no formalized vehicle of succession has effectively replaced the hereditary principle underlying the stable legitimacy of the older monarchy. The resultant chaos is known as political instability, and the monarch in republican dress answers to the name of caudillo.

MONARCHY IN REPUBLICAN DRESS

The "national life" of Ecuador has continued to be dominated by a small ruling class. These "whites" constitute approximately 20 per cent of the population of the republic. The Ecuadoran political process rests on a brand of anarchy or chaos within the ruling class. This condition is occasionally referred to by Ecuadorans as "democracy in the Greek sense": a considerable degree of liberty and equality has developed within the "white" group so far as intra-class behavior is concerned. The nation's rigid class system imposes an impressively strong barrier between the "whites" and the overwhelming mass of the people of the country.

Ecuador's "democracy in the Greek sense" has meant a chaotic intra-class struggle conducted by the "whites," an anarchical contest in which

[1] Guglielmo Ferrero, *The Principles of Power* (New York, 1942), p. 22.

the lower classes do not participate and in which they normally exhibit little or no interest. The battle of the "whites" among themselves frequently crystallizes along personal and regional lines, ideological differences usually being a distinctly minor factor. Victory in the contest is typically brief, and the victors preside over unstable and uncertain governments.

This political system, like the dominant position of the "whites," rests upon seven instruments of power which exclude the lower classes from active participation in what Ecuadorans call the "national life." These instruments are: (1) the pattern of landownership; (2) the Roman Catholic Church; (3) armed force; (4) the class distribution of literacy; (5) the status system, which confers marked prestige upon the "whites"; (6) the division of labor which bestows upon the "whites" a monopoly on positions of power and influence; and (7) the constitution and other laws of the republic. The last of these instruments of power is generally less effective than the other six.

In Ecuador, caudillismo—the political process which has replaced the hereditary principle in selecting essentially authoritarian rulers—requires the existence of a written constitution. The relationship between caudillismo and the document is twofold. In the first place, the constitution adds a measure of protection to the instruments of power which underlie the country's political system. A second phase of the relationship stems from the unpredictability of the "caudillist" process. There are occasions upon which no caudillo appears on the national scene and the organization of an interregnum is necessary. In such cases, the written constitution provides the rules for the interim government. The regent has been designated in the foregoing pages as the "constitutional president": he normally obeys the constitution scrupulously throughout the interregnum.

Since 1830, Ecuador has had fifteen written constitutions. It may be said, for the purposes of this analysis, that it is theoretically possible for an Ecuadoran constitution, depending on its relationship to the seven instruments of power, to fall into any one of six classes: (1) The constitution may textually ignore the instruments of power, in which case it may be designated as a "paper" constitution. (2) It may recognize these instruments and rest on or protect them; such a charter may be styled a "conservative" constitution. (3) It may combine the qualities of the preceding two, and could thus be dubbed a "paper-conservative" instrument. (4) It may recognize and endeavor to alter the instruments of power, in which case it may be called a "revolutionary" constitution.

(5) It may combine the characteristics of a "paper" constitution and a "revolutionary" one, and be referred to as a "paper-revolutionary" document. (6) A "revolutionary-conservative" combination is also possible.

Ecuadoran constitutions have traditionally leaned heavily in the "paper" direction, with or without combination. No trend away from this tradition has been evident in recent years, and Ecuadorans have not been without reason in saying that the "paper-revolutionary" Constitution of 1945 and the "paper-conservative" Constitution of 1946 have been divorced from reality. The normally wide divergence between the "real" and the written constitutions of Ecuador has found partial expression in the frequency with which governments have changed in ways which were independent of—and in violation of—the texts of the written constitutions. These changes, accomplished with or without violence, have been known as "revolutions," and have been an integral part of the Ecuadoran political process. The lower classes of the republic have not participated in the country's revolutions: these occurrences are but one phase of the "whites'" intra-class struggle.

The nation's party system reflects this basic pattern of the Ecuadoran political process. Only the ruling class—a small portion of it—is active in the country's political parties. The primary function of these organizations is to coördinate the activities of the "whites" as they relate to government. The parties serve this purpose by attempting to unite the "whites" of the two leading regions of the republic and by establishing a measure of harmony among the instruments of power. The failure of the parties to bridge the regionalist abyss is mirrored by the geographic orientation of the two major political organizations: the Conservatives are essentially the party of the Sierra and the Radical Liberals are basically the party of the Coast. Moreover, the nature of the party system reflects the fluid and unstable characteristics of the political process so far as the "ad hoc" organizations are an integral part of the system. These fluid parties are continually appearing and disappearing, combining and recombining, and living and dying on the basis of highly transitory factors.

Ecuadoran presidents have traditionally been strong executives, although most of the republic's constitutions have endeavored to curb their powers. These attempts for the most part have been spectacularly unsuccessful. The law of the Constitution of 1946 is especially divorced from reality on this point, continuing a practice begun in 1945 in retaining the presidential system but departing from the doctrine of the separation of powers as it had appeared traditionally in Ecuadoran constitutions. Under the newer doctrine of "coördination of functions," the three branches of government are no longer held to be constitutionally equal, the emphasis being upon coördination and harmony among the branches rather than upon their separation and autonomy, as had previously been the case. This change in a sense represents a concession to the realities of Ecuadoran politics, which have rarely if ever lent themselves to an effective three-way separation of powers. The law of the Constitution of 1946 is strikingly unrealistic, on the other hand, in holding that the executive is subordinate to the legislative function.

The legislature, theoretically supreme, is actually weak and ineffective vis-à-vis the executive. No essential conflict of interests normally arises between the two, as both functions represent the same small ruling class. In constitutional terms, the intra-class struggle involved in the "caudillist" process is a contest for control of the executive function. One index to the extent to which the president is able to consolidate his victory is the effectiveness with which he dominates the legislators. Caudillismo and the nature of the electoral process tend to render the legislative body subservient to the executive; and the unstable condition of the political parties normally contributes to the weak and directionless character of congress.

Of the three national functions, the judiciary has operated most effectively. The law of the Constitution of 1946 takes account of reality in assigning a subordinate role to the judicial function. Moreover, the law as administered by the courts has had a relatively stable and orderly development. As the primary agency of specificity in the laws, the judiciary has been effective so far as its approach has been cast largely in terms of application of legal norms to specific and individual cases arising out of past events. A considerable measure of fiction is involved in the theoretical distinction erected between Roman and common law; but, essentially, this fiction is not of Ecuadorans' making. The nature of the judicial process—leaning toward specific application in individual cases—exerts a strong influence producing marked similarities between the judicial practices of Ecuador and the United States.

Provincial and local government constitutes the major aspect of the Ecuadoran system so far as it impinges upon and affects the mass of the people of the country. The unitary arrangement as it operates in the republic continues the conquest of the Indian by depriving him of voice in government and destroying his community by planting within it nuclei of "whites" and cholos through whom local administration is conducted. So far as the formal structure of the republic is concerned, the Indian does not have his own local officials: for him "government" is the representative of the "whites" stationed in his territory. Local government in Ecuador constitutes both the continuing destruction of the Indian community and the point of liaison between the cholos and the montuvios on the one hand and the "national life" on the other. Municipal government well illustrates Ecuador's "democracy in the Greek sense." When the "whites" have effectively dominated a given canton, they may elect their own local officers and exercise a measure of municipal self-government within the urban canton. Municipal government has been the nerve center of local initiative and autonomy—for the "whites"—since the early days of the Spanish colony. In rural areas, however, the unitary arrangement has been a major instrument of authoritarianism, discouragement of local initiative in the handling of public problems, and retardation of the development of political consciousness in the overwhelming majority of the people of Ecuador.

POLITICAL ILLS AND REMEDIES

The Señora Hipatia Cárdenas de Bustamante, a patriotic lady deeply concerned with the political problems of her country, felt like many another Ecuadoran that the progress of government and politics in her republic left much to be desired. Primarily moved by her love for what she understood the welfare of her nation to be, she addressed a question—"What should Ecuador do to free herself from dictatorship?"—to more than two hundred people whom she believed to be the political, social, and cultural leaders of the country. The 108 answers which she published in book form provide valuable insight into the political thought of the "whites" of Ecuador.

Few agreed with onetime Conservative presidential candidate Neptalí Bonifaz that "nothing can be done ... other than abolishing ... the executive power, the legislative power, and the army" ;[2] with the nationalist leader L. A. Guzmán that "dictatorships ... when they are directed toward ... the aggrandizement of the fatherland, far from being undesirable, are beneficial, as Germany and Italy have shown us" ;[3] or with José M. Plaza L., of the Socialist party, that the republic simply needed still another written constitution, "and the sole and exclusive cause of these dictatorships will disappear."[4] Some concurred with Conservative party leader Mariano Suárez Veintimilla that the problem was essen-

[2] Hipatia Cárdenas de Bustamante, *Encuesta* (Quito, 1939), p. 9.
[3] *Ibid.*, p. 26.
[4] *Ibid.*, p. 34.

tially moral in nature, and that "we must restore . . . the spiritual factors: honor, patriotism, impartiality, and integrity."[5] Many, like Rafael Terán Coronel, felt that the answer lay in education: "Ecuador . . . ought to be inculcated with the most strict respect for the liberties, especially for the right to vote."[6] Still others agreed that the nature of the political parties held the key to the matter, G. Ormaza E. feeling that the question should be rephrased to read, "How can we give more efficient direction to the political parties of Ecuador?"[7] Another group, represented by J. A. Echeverría, believed that the query was essentially a problem in militarism: "Ecuador should revitalize and reorganize the army, because the militia ought to be an obedient and nondeliberative class."[8]

Ecuadoran constitutional problems are not so much questions of written laws as they are problems in power. Neither stability nor democracy is to be achieved simply by writing another constitution, whether it be of the "paper," "paper-conservative," or "paper-revolutionary" kind. These documents have said many sincere and well-intentioned things, but a fundamental change in the republic's political system is not to be had merely by writing it into another constitution. Such a remedy, Ecuadorans have discovered, is divorced from reality.

They have also begun in recent years to agree that, as *El Comercio* put it, "the first reform must take place in the mentality of the governing class."[9] It may well be, as Ferrero has affirmed, that "the beginnings of monarchy and democracy are the same: in each case they are organized from above."[10] Progress has already been made: many of the educated "whites" realize that it is they who must accomplish any change for the better. Yet the "whites" would be required to annihilate themselves as a class if they were to inaugurate a genuine change in the Ecuadoran constitutional system. A "white" is a person who is maintained in his position by a group of instruments of power. To change the Ecuadoran pattern of government, it would be necessary to alter these instruments, to do nothing less than destroy the republic's class system.

Fundamental reform would involve a far-reaching change in the pattern of landownership, the reduction of the large haciendas, the destruction of the present landowning class, and the introduction of a

---
[5] *Ibid.*, p. 67. For a further indication of Suárez Veintimilla's views on dictatorship, see p. 78, above.
[6] Cárdenas de Bustamante, *op. cit.*, p. 11.
[7] *Ibid.*, p. 25.
[8] *Ibid.*, p. 9.
[9] *El Comercio*, Quito, May 12, 1948.
[10] Ferrero, *op. cit.*, pp. 169–170.

new group of small individual holders of land. It would mean the reduction of the Church as an instrument of power, its disestablishment, and its removal from national politics. It would demand a radical alteration in the present class distribution of literacy, a termination of the ruling class's virtual monopoly on formal education. It would call for an attitude which would permit "gentlemen" to work with their hands without losing caste, it would demand an alteration in the hierarchy of social classes. And the army would be required to defend the frontiers instead of the class structure of the republic. If the "whites" desire political and constitutional stability, they must themselves undertake a sweeping program which would run essentially counter to their own short-range vital interests. Faced with a choice, most of the "whites" would undoubtedly prefer to retain their present class position—and with it political instability.

Fundamental reform, moreover, cannot be achieved overnight, as many a disillusioned Ecuadoran revolutionist knows. Institutions must take root and grow in the peculiar environment in which they are to live. As the republic's present political system is rooted deep in the character of the nation, so must another be if the system is to change. Development in Ecuador, as elsewhere, moves slowly if it is to have lasting effects. This is indicated within the republic's governmental system by the growth of the president's cabinet and the courts. These institutions have become essentially successful organs of government; and it is highly significant that neither has been treated at length in the texts of the written constitutions. They have emerged from Ecuadoran practice, not from the written word.

It has been said that Ecuador is a country "with more fundamental problems still unsolved than most countries fifty times her size."[11] Among the more crucial of these problems are those concerned with regionalism, the Oriente, and the Indian. Conscious attempts to meet these problems have been more nearly successful in the case of regionalism than in the other two instances. Political parties have failed to become national by taking effective root on both sides of the western cordillera, but an agglomeration of semieffective constitutional devices has occasionally mitigated the struggle between the Sierra and the Coast. One of these devices has been the vice-presidency, which together with the presidency permits both major regions to be represented in the same administration. A second device has been the cabinet, in which the Sierra and the Coast are normally equally represented. A third has been the illogical

---

[11] Franklin, *op. cit.*, p. v.

system of representation in congress, designed to preserve a precarious balance between the two chief regions. The regional distribution of the fifteen members of the supreme court has been a fourth device serving to ease regional tension. A fifth device developed to combat regionalism has been the unitary arrangement. Municipal autonomy, however, continues to threaten the republic with disruption; the delicate equilibrium at times seems to rest on an uneasy truce between Quito and Guayaquil.

The Oriente is at once a baffling problem and a part of Ecuador's hope for a more propitious future. If the nation does not colonize and otherwise develop it, this jungle region will eventually be lost, probably to Peru, as frontier controversies have made clear to Ecuadorans. The Oriente is largely unsurveyed, although most students of the region believe that once it is developed its resources will be a tremendous asset to the state exercising jurisdiction over it. Ecuador can still be that state. Properly developed, the Oriente may well become the nation's economic salvation. To many Ecuadorans, bringing the Oriente under control seems a vast and hopeless task. To date, colonization and development of the region have proceeded at a critically slow pace, and a large and potentially rich territory has remained virtually useless.

It has been argued concerning other countries that if reform did not come from above, revolution would come from below. The Ecuadoran ruling class, however, is under no such immediate compulsion. It need not fear revolution from below: numerous generations would have to pass before the lower classes would be able and disposed to rebel. The Indians are Ecuador's "good people": they continue their obedience to the "whites'" world with a complex philosophy fundamentally related to their survival. It has been said of the Indian that "his personal relations are with vast unchangeable values: mountains, rain, sun, and wind. His contact with these forces means far more to him than the socially conscious motivations that pattern the 'white' world. Should the Indian find his mountains desecrated, his sacred lake destroyed, his ancestral earth removed from him, he would swiftly perish. But give him his ancient pattern of plowing and harvesting, leave him access to his land and his primitive mysteries, and he can shoulder the heaviest yoke."[12]

Government in Ecuador has meant that the Indian must die. It is only in a cultural sense that he must disappear, although that is serious enough; in other terms, the Indian will live on for centuries. As Moisés Sáenz has pointed out, "in order to be fair to the Indian, it is not necessary to stick feathers in our hair or wield a war club."[13] In cultural

---

[12] Buitrón and Collier, *op. cit.*, p. 33.
[13] Sáenz, *The Indian, Citizen of America*, p. 1.

terms, the passing of the Indian means the changing of his way of life: the learning of a new language, the alteration of his style of dress, the emergence of a new community—in short, the expansion of the cholo in Ecuadoran life. As a liquidated Indian, the cholo holds the future of the republic in his hands. The cholo, a fusion of cultures, is inevitably replacing the Ecuadoran Indian. Unlike the Indian, the cholo is *not* cut off from "the national life": as a limited participant in the culture of the "whites," he is sensitive as the Indian is not to his exclusion from a fuller part in national government and politics. When the cholo replaces the Indian as the typical member of Ecuador's lower class, then—but not before—will the ruling class be under compulsion to institute reforms. Rebellion cannot be launched by the Indian; it can and probably will be carried forward by the cholo, the Ecuadoran of the future.

The process by which government in Ecuador is overcoming the Indian culture is not merely dismal, but tragic:

> The Indian ... has retreated as far as possible from organized society. He has climbed to altitudes so high and terrains so barren that "white" exploiters have found it unprofitable to follow. He has also retreated into himself and his deep mind set toward the environment and "white" society has made him well-nigh impervious to outer influences.[14]

The retreat can be little more than a delaying action. The Indian may hold his beloved if barren snow-capped peaks for a time, but his eventual destruction cannot be avoided. Then, but not before, it will probably be true that rebellion will come from below if reform does not come from above.

---

[14] Rycroft, *et al., op. cit.,* p. 81.

BIBLIOGRAPHY

ECUADORAN GOVERNMENT PUBLICATIONS (QUITO)

Constitución Política de la República del Ecuador, 1830.
Constitución Política de la República del Ecuador, 1835.
Constitución Política de la República del Ecuador, 1843.
Constitución Política de la República del Ecuador, 1845.
Constitución Política de la República del Ecuador, 1850.
Constitución Política de la República del Ecuador, 1852.
Constitución Política de la República del Ecuador, 1861.
Constitución Política de la República del Ecuador, 1869.
Constitución Política de la República del Ecuador, 1878.
Constitución Política de la República del Ecuador, 1883.
Constitución Política de la República del Ecuador, 1897.
Constitución Política de la República del Ecuador, 1906.
Constitución Política de la República del Ecuador, 1929.
Constitución Política de la República del Ecuador, 1945.
Constitución Política de la República del Ecuador (*Registro Oficial*, December 31, 1946).
Ecuador en Cifras, 1944.
El 28 de Mayo, 1946.
Gaceta Judicial, January, 1940, to January, 1946.
Ley de División Territorial, 1916.
Ley de División Territorial, 1926.
Ley de Elecciones (*Registro Oficial*, February 24, 1947).
Ley de Extranjería, Extradición, y Naturalización, 1938.
Ley de Régimen Administrativo de la República del Ecuador (*Registro Oficial*, April 26, 1947).
Ley de Régimen Administrativo Interior, 1910.
Ley de Régimen Administrativo Interior, 1915.
Ley de Régimen Administrativo Interior, 1919.
Ley de Régimen Municipal, 1922.
Ley de Régimen Municipal, 1929.
Ley de Régimen Municipal, 1934.
Ley de Régimen Municipal, 1945.
Ley Orgánica del Poder Judicial, 1938.
Mensaje Presentado a la Honorable Asamblea Nacional Constituyente por el Excmo. Señor Presidente de la República, Dr. don José María Velasco Ibarra, 6 de Febrero de 1945, 1945.
Mensaje Presentado a la Honorable Asamblea Nacional Constituyente por el Excmo. Señor Presidente de la República, Dr. don José María Velasco Ibarra, 10 de Agosto de 1946, 1946.
MINISTERIO DE GOBIERNO. *División Territorial de la República del Ecuador*, 1947.
MINISTRO DE DEFENSA NACIONAL. *Informe*, 1948.
MINISTRO DE ECONOMÍA NACIONAL. *Informe*, 1948.
MINISTRO DE EDUCACIÓN PÚBLICA. *Informe*, 1948.
MINISTRO DE GOBIERNO. *Informe*, 1948.

MINISTRO DEL TESORO. *Informe*, 1948.
MINISTRO DE OBRAS PÚBLICAS Y COMUNICACIONES. *Informe*, 1948.
MINISTRO DE PREVISIÓN SOCIAL. *Informe*, 1948.
MINISTRO DE RELACIONES EXTERIORES. *Informe*, 1948.
Recopilación de Leyes y Reglamentos Tributarios, 1945.
Reformas a la Ley de Régimen Municipal, 1921.
Registro Oficial:
  April 18, 1938.
  July 28, 1938.
  October 18, 1940.
  November 21, 1940.
  December 4, 1940.
  October 7, 1941.
  June 1, 1944, to September 1, 1948, inclusive.

BOOKS AND PAMPHLETS IN ENGLISH

ARISTOTLE (JOWETT, BENJAMIN, tr.). *Politics*. London: Oxford University Press, 1920.
ASSOCIATION OF AMERICAN LAW SCHOOLS (ed.). *Latin-American Legal Philosophy*. Cambridge: Harvard University Press, 1948.
BEEBE, WILLIAM, et al. *Galápagos: World's End*. New York: G. P. Putnam's Sons, 1924.
BELAUNDE, VÍCTOR ANDRÉS. *Bolívar and the Political Thought of the Spanish American Revolution*. Baltimore: The Johns Hopkins Press, 1938.
BENNETT, WENDELL C. *The Andean Highlands: An Introduction*. Washington: Government Printing Office, 1946.
BOAS, FRANZ. *Race and Democratic Society*. New York: J. J. Augustin, 1945.
BROWNING, WEBSTER E. *The Republic of Ecuador*. New York: Committee on Cooperation in Latin America, 1920.
CLAGGETT, HELEN. *Guide to the Law and Legal Literature of Ecuador*. Washington: Library of Congress, 1947.
CRAWFORD, WILLIAM REX. *A Century of Latin American Thought*. Cambridge: Harvard University Press, 1944.
DIFFIE, BAILEY W. *Latin-American Civilization*. Harrisburg: Stackpole Sons, 1945.
ENOCK, C. REGINALD. *Ecuador*. London: T. Fisher Unwin, Ltd., 1914.
FERRERO, GUGLIELMO (JAECKEL, THEODORE R., tr.). *The Principles of Power*. New York: G. P. Putnam's Sons, 1942.
FITZGIBBON, RUSSELL H., et al. *The Constitutions of the Americas*. Chicago: University of Chicago Press, 1948.
FRANKLIN, ALBERT B. *Ecuador: Portrait of a People*. New York: Doubleday, Doran and Company, Inc., 1944.
FRIEDRICH, CARL J. *Constitutional Government and Democracy*. New York: Ginn and Company, 1946.
GRUBB, KENNETH G. *The Northern Republics of South America*. London: World Dominion Press, 1931.
HEYE, GEORGE G. *Contributions to South American Archaeology*. New York: Irving Press, 1907, 1910. Two volumes.
IRELAND, GORDON, and GALÍNDEZ SUÁREZ, JESÚS. *Divorce in the Americas*. Buffalo: Dennis and Company, 1947.

KELSEN, HANS. *General Theory of Law and State.* Cambridge: Harvard University Press, 1945.

LASSO, RAFAEL V. *The Wonderland Ecuador.* New York: Alpha-Ecuador Publications, 1944.

MACKAY, JANET. *Interlude in Ecuador.* London: Duckworth and Co., 1934.

MANN, ALEX. *Yachting on the Pacific.* London: Duckworth and Co., 1909.

MEANS, PHILIP AINSWORTH. *Ancient Civilizations of the Andes.* New York: Charles Scribner's Sons, 1931.

MELVILLE, HERMAN. *Piazza Tales.* New York: Farrar Straus, 1948.

MULLER, RICHARD. *Land Forms of Ecuador.* Guayaquil: Editorial Jouvín, 1938.

OFFICE OF INTER-AMERICAN AFFAIRS. *Ecuador: Snow on the Equator.* Washington: Government Printing Office, 1943.

PHELPS, ELIZABETH (ed.). *Statistical Activities of the American Nations.* Washington: Inter-American Statistical Institute, 1941.

PRESCOTT, WILLIAM H. *History of the Conquest of Peru.* New York: Hurst and Co., 1890. Two volumes.

RYCROFT, W. STANLEY (ed.). *Indians of the High Andes.* New York: Committee on Co-operation in Latin America, 1946.

SÁENZ, MOISÉS. *The Indian, Citizen of America.* Washington: Pan American Union, 1946.

STIRLING, M. W. *Historical and Ethnographical Material on the Jivaro Indians.* Washington: Government Printing Office, 1938.

UNITED STATES, BUREAU OF THE CENSUS. *Ecuador: Summary of Biostatistics.* Washington: Government Printing Office, 1944.

———, DEPARTMENT OF COMMERCE. *Ecuador.* Washington: Government Printing Office, 1947.

———, DEPARTMENT OF LABOR. *Labor Legislation in Ecuador.* Washington: Government Printing Office, 1931.

———, TARIFF COMMISSION. *Mining and Manufacturing Industries in Ecuador.* Washington: Government Printing Office, 1945.

VIOLICH, FRANCIS. *Cities of Latin America.* New York: Reinhold Publishing Corp., 1944.

WEBER, MAX (GERTH, H. H., and MILLS, C. WRIGHT, tr.). *From Max Weber: Essays in Sociology.* New York: Oxford University Press, 1946.

WYTHE, GEORGE. *Industry in Latin America.* New York: Columbia University Press, 1945.

BOOKS AND PAMPHLETS IN SPANISH

AGRAMONTE Y PICHARDO, ROBERTO. *Biografía del Dictador García Moreno.* La Habana: Cultural, S. A., 1935.

AGUILERA MALTA, D., GIL GILBERT, ENRIQUE, and GALLEGOS LARA, J. *Los Que Se Van.* Guayaquil: Zea y Paladines, 1930.

ALARCÓN E., RUPERTO. *Breve Compaña a los Socialistas.* Riobamba: Imprenta Moderna, 1928.

ALOMÍA, ANTONIO. *La Defensa del Oriente Ecuatoriano.* Quito: Talleres Gráficos Nacionales, 1936.

ALSEDO Y HERRERA, DIONISIO DE. *Compendio Histórico de la Provincia de Guayaquil.* Guayaquil: Imprenta Gutenberg de Elicio A. Uzcátegui, 1938.

ALVARADO, RAFAEL. *Demarcación de Fronteras.* Quito: Talleres Gráficos Nacionales, 1942.

ANDRADE, CÉSAR D. *Aspectos de la Economía Ecuatoriana.* Quito: Talleres Gráficos del Ministerio de Hacienda, 1940.
ANDRADE, MANUEL JESÚS. *Ecuador: Proceres de la Independencia.* Quito: Tipografía y Encuadernación de la Escuela de Artes y Oficios, 1909.
ANDRADE, ROBERTO. *Historia del Ecuador.* Guayaquil: Reed y Reed, 1937.
———. *Patriotismo.* Lima: C. Prince, 1914.
———. *Vida y Muerte de Eloy Alfaro.* New York: York Printing Co., 1936.
ANDRADE COELLO, ALEJANDRO. *La Ley del Progreso: El Ecuador en los Ultimos Quince Años.* Quito: J. J. Gálvez, 1910.
ANON. *La Doctrina Social de la Iglesia.* Quito: Imprenta del Clero, 1939.
ANON. *Manifiesto No. 6.* Lima, 1844.
ARREGUI, VÍCTOR MANUEL. *Cuestiones Políticas.* Quito: Imprenta Nacional, 1908.
ARROYO, CÉSAR EMILIO. *Asamblea de Sombras.* Quito: Editorial Artes Gráficas, 1931.
ARROYO DEL RÍO, CARLOS ALBERTO. *Bajo el Imperio del Odio.* Bogotá: Editorial El Gráfico, 1946.
———. *En Plena Vorágine.* Bogotá: Editorial El Gráfico, 1948.
———. *Intereses Políticos.* Guayaquil: Imprenta Janer, 1936.
BARRERA B., JAIME, et al. *Realidades Ecuatorianas.* Quito: Imprenta de la Universidad Central, 1938.
BELALCÁZAR, SEBASTIÁN DE (JERVES, ALFONSO A., ed.). *Testamento del Señor Capitán don Sebastián de Belalcázar.* Quito: Talleres Tipográficos Municipales, 1935.
BORJA, LUIS A. *La Huella de la Historia.* Guayaquil: Editorial Jouvín, 1935.
BOSSANO, LUIS. *Apuntes Acerca del Regionalismo en el Ecuador.* Quito: Tipografía de la Prensa Católica, 1930.
———. *El Campesino Ecuatoriano.* Buenos Aires: Edición de la Revista Americana, 1937.
BRUNO, G. M. *Compendio de la Historia del Ecuador.* Quito: Librería La Salle, 1932.
———. *Geografía de la República del Ecuador.* Quito: Librería La Salle, 1935.
BUITRÓN, ANÍBAL, and BUITRÓN, BARBARA. *El Campesino de la Provincia de Pichincha.* Quito: Caja de Seguro, 1947.
CABRERA, LUIS. *El General don Leónidas Plaza Gutiérrez.* Santiago: Imprenta de la Ley, 1904.
CAICEDO, FEDERICO A. *Regiones Ecuatorianas.* Guayaquil: Empresa de Publicidad, 1924.
CÁRDENAS DE BUSTAMANTE, HIPATIA. *Encuesta.* Quito: Litografía e Imprenta Romero, 1939.
CARRERA ANDRADE, JORGE. *Mirador Terrestre.* Forest Hills: Las Americas Publishing Co., 1943.
CARRIÓN, BENJAMÍN. *Atahuallpa.* Guayaquil: Editora Noticia, 1939.
CEVALLOS, GABRIEL. *Entonces Fué el Ecuador.* Cuenca: Editorial Austral, 1942.
CEVALLOS, PEDRO FERMÍN. *Compendio de la Historia del Ecuador.* Guayaquil: Uzcátegui y Cia., 1913.
———. *Resumen de la Historia del Ecuador Desde su Origen Hasta 1845.* Guayaquil: Imprenta de la Nación, 1886.
CHIRIBOGA NAVARRO, ANGEL ISAAC. *Bolívar en el Ecuador.* Quito: Talleres Gráficos de Educación Pública, 1942.
CIEZA DE LEÓN, PEDRO. *Crónicas del Perú.* Madrid: Espasa Calpe, 1932.
CONCHA ENRÍQUEZ, PEDRO. *Realidad.* Quito: Imprenta Fernández, 1940.

CÓRDOVA M., WILSON. *La Nacionalidad Ecuatoriana.* Santiago: Imprenta Universidad, 1941.
CREMIEUX, ROBERT F. *Geografía Económica del Ecuador.* Guayaquil: Imprenta de la Universidad de Guayaquil, 1946. Two volumes.
DESTRUGE, CAMILIO. *La Expedición Flores.* Guayaquil: Imprenta de *El Tiempo*, 1906.
DÍAZ DOIN, GUILLERMO. *Diccionario Político de Nuestro Tiempo.* Buenos Aires: Editorial Mundo Atlántico, 1943.
ENDARA, CARLOS H. *Desde el Mirador de América.* Quito: Talleres Gráficos Nacionales, 1936.
ERMEL DE LA CRUZ, CARLOS (ed.). *Quito al Día.* Quito: Gráficas Cedig, 1947.
ESPINOSA TAMAYO, ALFREDO. *Psicología y Sociología del Pueblo Ecuatoriano.* Guayaquil: Imprenta Municipal, 1918.
FLORES, CARLOS ALBERTO. *Panoramas y Otros Tópicos.* Guayaquil: Imprenta y Talleres Municipales, 1939.
FRUGONI, EMILIO. *Las Tres Dimensiones de la Democracia.* Buenos Aires: Editorial Claridad, 1944.
GALLEGOS, LUIS GERARDO. *Cuestiones Económicas y Sociales Ecuatorianas.* Riobamba: Maldonado, 1935.
GÁLVEZ, MANUEL. *Vida de don Gabriel García Moreno.* Buenos Aires: Editorial Difusión, 1942.
GARCÉS, MIGUEL GABRIEL. *Consideraciones Filosóficas Sobre la Iglesia Ecuatoriana y la Administración de Veintimilla.* Quito: M. Ribadeneira, undated.
GARCÍA, AURELIO. *Ciencia del Estado.* Quito: Imprenta de la Universidad Central, 1947, 2 vols.
———. *La Autonomía Municipal.* Quito: Imprenta de la Universidad Central, 1941.
GARCÍA, CARLOS T. *Ecuador.* Quito: Talleres Gráficos de Educación, 1937.
GARCÍA KOHLY, MARIO. *El Problema Constitucional de las Democracias Americanas.* La Habana: Cultural, 1931.
GARCÍA ORTIZ, HUMBERTO. *La Forma Nacional.* Quito: Imprenta de la Universidad Central, 1942.
GIRÓN, SERGIO ENRIQUE. *La Revolución de Mayo.* Quito: Editorial Atahualpa, 1945.
GONZÁLEZ A., JOSÉ LUIS. *Nuestra Gran Realidad.* Quito: Editorial Labor, 1936.
GONZÁLEZ CALDERÓN, JUAN A. *Curso de Derecho Constitucional.* Buenos Aires: Editorial Guillermo Kraft, 1943.
GONZÁLEZ PÁEZ, M. A. *Memorias Históricas.* Quito: Editorial Ecuatoriana, 1934.
GONZÁLEZ SUÁREZ, FEDERICO. *Historia Eclesiástica del Ecuador.* Quito: I. Miranda, 1881.
———. *Historia General de la República del Ecuador.* Quito: Imprenta del Clero, 1890 ff. 7 vols.
———. *Los Aborígenes de Imbabura y Carchi.* Quito: Tipografía Silesiana, 1908.
———. *Notas Arqueológicas.* Quito: Imprenta del Clero, 1915.
HEIMAN, HANNS. *Inmigrantes en el Ecuador.* Quito: Casa Editora Liebman, 1942.
HIDALGO, DANIEL B. *El Militarismo: Sus Causas y Remedios.* Quito: R. Racines C., 1913.
———. *Evolución Política.* Quito: Tipografía de la Escuela de Artes y Oficios, 1917.
HIDALGO GONZÁLEZ, PEDRO. *Monografía Sintética de Guayaquil.* Guayaquil: Consejo Municipal, 1939.

HIERRO, RICARDO. *Estudio Sobre el Jurado en el Ecuador*. Quito: Imprenta de la Universidad Central, 1934.

ICAZA, JORGE. *Cholos*. Quito: Litografía e Imprenta Romero, 1938.

INSUA RODRÍGUEZ, RAMÓN. *Estudios de Economía Ecuatoriana*. Guayaquil: Imprenta de la Universidad de Guayaquil, 1942.

JÁCOME MOSCOSO, RODRIGO. *Derecho Constitucional Ecuatoriano*. Quito: Imprenta de la Universidad Central, 1931.

JARAMILLO ALVARADO, PÍO. *El Indio Ecuatoriano*. Quito: Talleres Gráficos del Estado, 1936.

———. *El Régimen Totalitario en América*. Guayaquil: Editora Noticia, 1940.

———. *Estudios Históricos*. Quito: Editorial Artes Gráficas, 1934.

———. *La Nación Quiteña*. Quito: Imprenta Fernández, 1947.

———. *La Presidencia de Quito*. Quito: Editorial El Comercio, 1939.

———, et al. *Cuestiones Indígenas del Ecuador*. Quito: Casa de la Cultura Ecuatoriana, 1946.

JIJÓN Y CAAMAÑO, JACINTO. *Política Conservadora*. Riobamba: La Buena Prensa del Chimborazo, 1934. 2 vols.

———. *Quito y la Independencia de América*. Quito: Imprenta de la Universidad Central, 1922.

———. *Sebastián de Benalcázar*. Quito: Imprenta del Clero, 1936.

JIMÉNEZ, NICOLÁS. *Biografía del Ilustrísimo Federico González Suárez*. Quito: Talleres Tipográficos Nacionales, 1936.

LARREA ALBA, LUIS. *Criterios Sobre la Constitución y el Funcionamiento de los Organos Directivos del Ejército*. Quito: Tipografía L. I. Fernández, 1934.

———, (ed.). *Estatutos, Principios Políticos, y Plan de Acción de Vanguardia Revolucionaria del Socialismo Ecuatoriano*. Quito: Tipografía Fernández, 1936.

LASO, LUIS EDUARDO. *Estudios Económicos*. Quito: Imprenta de la Universidad Central, 1942.

LECUNA, VICENTE. *Cartas del Libertador*. New York: The Colonial Press, Inc. Vol. XI.

LEGOHUIR RODAS, JOSÉ. *Glorias Ecuatorianas*. Quito: La Prensa Católica, 1945.

———. *Historia de la República del Ecuador*. Quito: Imprenta del Clero, 1938. 3 vols.

MALDONADO ESTRADA, LUIS. *Bases del Partido Socialista Ecuatoriano*. Quito: Ediciones "Antorcha," 1938.

———. *Socialismo Ecuatoriano*. Guayaquil: Páginas Selectas, 1935.

MARIÁTEGUI, JOSÉ CARLOS. *Siete Ensayos de Interpretación de la Realidad Peruana*. Lima: Editorial Librería Peruana, 1934.

MARTÍNEZ MORAN, LUIS. *Un Dictador y una Dictadura bajo la Lente Periodística*. Quito: Imprenta de Educación, 1937.

MATA, GONZALO HUMBERTO. *Ecuador y el Hombre*. Cuenca: Biblioteca Cenit, 1943.

MENDOZA MOREIRA, LUIS AUGUSTO. *Geografía del Ecuador*. Guayaquil: Reed y Reed, 1946.

MERA, JUAN LEÓN. *Catecismo Explicado de la Constitución de la República del Ecuador*. Quito: Imprenta del Clero, 1894.

———. *La Dictadura y la Restauración en la República del Ecuador*. Quito: Editorial Ecuatoriana, 1932.

MIÑO, ERNESTO. *El Ecuador ante las Revoluciones Proletarias*. Ambato: Imprenta del Colegio Bolívar, 1935.

MONCAYO, PEDRO. *El Ecuador de 1825 a 1875.* Quito: Imprenta Nacional, 1906.
MONSALVE POZO, LUIS. *El Indio.* Cuenca: Editorial Austral, 1943.
MORA BOWEN, ALFONSO. *El Liberalismo Radical y su Trayectoria Histórica.* Quito: Litografía y Imprenta Romero, 1940.
———. *Eloy Alfaro en la Democracia Ecuatoriana.* Quito: Talleres Tipográficos Nacionales, 1933.
NOBOA, GUILLERMO. *Pueblo y Soldados de Mi Patria.* Quito: Editorial El Comercio, 1942.
NÚÑEZ DEL ARCO, RAMÓN. *Los Hombres de Agosto.* Quito: Litografía e Imprenta Romero, 1940.
OCHOA ORTIZ, FRANCISCO. *Ley Orgánica del Poder Judicial.* Guayaquil: Editorial Jouvín, 1932.
ORELLANA, J. GONZALO. *Resumen Histórico del Ecuador.* Quito: Editorial Fr. Jodoco Ricke, 1948.
OSSORIO, ANGEL. *Nociones de Derecho Político.* Buenos Aires: Editorial Atlántida, S. A., 1943.
PAREDES, ANGEL M. *Naturaleza del Poder Público y del Sometimiento del Hombre a las Autoridades del País.* Quito: Imprenta de la Universidad Central, 1929.
———. *Problemas Etnológicos Indoamericanos.* Quito: Casa de la Cultura Ecuatoriana, 1947.
———. *Sociología General Aplicada a las Condiciones de América.* Quito: Nestor Romero Díaz, 1924.
PARTIDO LIBERAL-RADICAL ECUATORIANO. *Estatutos, Principios Doctrinarios, y Programa de Acción del Partido Liberal-Radical Ecuatoriano.* Quito: Junta Provincial Liberal-Radical de Pichincha, 1940.
PATTEE, RICHARD. *Gabriel García Moreno y el Ecuador de su Tiempo.* México: Editorial Jus, 1944.
PAZ, CLOTARIO E. *Larrea Alba, Nuestras Izquierdas.* Guayaquil: Tribunal Libre, 1938.
PAZ Y MIÑO, GENERAL LUIS TELMO. *Atlas Histórico-geográfico de los Límites del Ecuador.* Quito: Imprenta Nacional, 1936.
———. *La Distribución Geográfica de la Población del Ecuador.* Quito: Imprenta de la Universidad Central, 1934.
———. *La Población del Ecuador.* Quito: Talleres Gráficos de Educación, 1942.
PÉREZ, AQUILES R. *Geografía del Ecuador.* Quito: Editorial Gutenberg, 1940.
PÉREZ GUERRERO, ALFREDO. *Ecuador.* Quito: Casa de la Cultura Ecuatoriana, 1948.
PIÑO Y ROCA, J. GABRIEL. *Leyendas y Tradiciones y Páginas de la Historia de Guayaquil.* Guayaquil: Editorial Jouvín, 1930.
PIZARRO, PEDRO. *Relación del Descubrimiento y Conquista del Perú.* Lima: Imprenta San Martín, 1917. 4 vols.
POZO D., OLMEDO. *El Drama de Una Generación.* Quito: Editorial El Comercio, 1945.
PRIETO A., JORGE. *Bases de Reconstrucción Nacional.* Guayaquil: Reed y Reed, 1945.
Programa y Estatutos del Partido Conservador Ecuatoriano. Quito: Editorial Espejo, 1946.
QUEVEDO, ANTONIO. *Ensayos Sociológicos y Políticos.* Quito: Editorial Chimborazo, 1924.
QUEVEDO, BELISARIO. *Historia Patria.* Quito: Talleres Gráficos Nacionales, 1942.
———. *Sociología Política y Moral.* Quito: Editorial Bolívar, 1930.

QUIJANO, MANUEL J. *La Emancipación de la Iglesia Neograndina.* Popayán: Imprenta del Gobierno, 1872.

RESTREPO, JOSÉ MANUEL. *Historia de la Evolución de la República de Colombia en la América Meridional.* Bogotá: Talleres Gráficos Luz, 1942.

REYES, OSCAR EFRÉN. *Breve Historia General del Ecuador.* Quito: Talleres Gráficos de Educación, 1942. 2 vols.

———. *El Reino de Quito.* Quito: Talleres Gráficos de Educación, 1941.

———. *Los Incas Políticos.* Quito: Imprenta Nacional, 1936.

RIOFRIO VILLAGÓMEZ, EDUARDO. *Gobierno y Finanzas Municipales.* Quito: Imprenta Municipal, 1945.

RUBIO ORBE, GONZALO. *Nuestros Indios.* Quito: Imprenta de la Universidad Central, 1947.

———. *Rumiñahi, Ati II.* Quito: Talleres Gráficos de Educación, 1944.

RUMAZO, ALFONSO. *Gobernantes del Ecuador.* Quito: Editorial Bolívar, 1933.

———. *El Ecuador en la América Prehispánica.* Quito: Editorial Bolívar, 1933.

RUMAZO GONZÁLEZ, JOSÉ (ed.). *Libro Primero de Cabildos de Quito.* Quito: Candido Briz Sánchez, 1934. 2 vols.

——— (ed.). *Libro Segundo de Cabildos de Quito.* Quito: Archivo Municipal, 1934.

SAAD, PEDRO ANTONIO. *El Ecuador y la Guerra.* Guayaquil: Emporio Gráfico, 1943.

SÁENZ, MOISÉS. *Sobre el Indio Ecuatoriano.* México: Secretaría de Educación Pública, 1933.

SAMANIEGO, JUAN JOSÉ. *Bioestadística en el Cosmos Ecuatoriano.* Quito: Talleres Gráficos de Educación, 1943.

SÁNCHEZ ANDRADE, JAIME. *Un Año de Tiranía.* Quito: Imprenta Ecuador, 1934.

SILVA, RAFAEL EUCLIDES. *Biogénesis de Santiago de Guayaquil.* Guayaquil: Imprenta de la Universidad de Guayaquil, 1947.

SUÁREZ, PABLO ARTURO. *Contribución al Estudio de las Realidades Entre las Clases Obreras y Campesinas.* Quito: Tipografía Fernández, 1934.

TERÁN GÓMEZ, LUIS. *Los Partidos Políticos y su Acción Democrática.* La Paz: Editorial La Paz, 1942.

TOBAR DONOSO, JULIO. *Desarrollo Constitucional de la República del Ecuador.* Quito: Editorial Ecuatoriana, 1936.

TORO NAVAS, TARQUINO. *Ronda de Ciudades.* Ambato: Tipografía A. M. Garcés, 1937.

XIII CONGRESO DEL PARTIDO SOCIALISTA ECUATORIANO. *Estatutos del Partido Socialista Ecuatoriano.* Quito: Imprenta La Tierra, 1946.

UHLE, MAX. *Estado Actual de la Prehistoria Ecuatoriana.* Quito: Talleres Gráficos Nacionales, 1929.

VALLANILLA LANZ, LAUREANO. *Cesarismo Democrático.* Caracas: Empresa El Cojo, 1919.

VAQUERO DÁVILA, JESÚS. *Aspectos Sociológicos de la Nacionalidad Ecuatoriana.* Quito: Manuel Piedra M., 1930.

———. *Génesis de la Nacionalidad Ecuatoriana.* Quito: Imprenta de la Universidad Central, 1941.

VELASCO, PADRE JUAN DE. *Historia del Reino de Quito.* Quito: Agustín Yerovi, 1841. 3 vols.

VELASCO IBARRA, JOSÉ MARÍA. *Conciencia o Barbarie.* Buenos Aires: Editorial Claridad, 1938.

———. *Experiencias Jurídicas Hispanoamericanas.* Buenos Aires: Editorial Americalee, 1943.

———. *Un Momento de Transición Política.* Quito: Talleres Tipográficos Nacionales, 1935.

VIDAL VERGARA, CARLOS. *Los Derechos Individuales en las Constituciones Modernas.* Santiago: Editorial Nascimiento, 1936.

WOLF, TEODORO. *Geografía y Geología del Ecuador.* Leipzig: F. A. Brockhaus, 1892.

YÉPEZ, MANUEL A. *Clave de la Legislación Ecuatoriana.* Quito: Imprenta Nacional, 1922.

ZALDUMBIDE SILVA, MANUEL MARÍA. *Bolívar y su Descendencia.* Quito: Talleres Gráficos de Educación, 1940.

ZEVALLOS REYRE, FRANCISCO. *Lecciones de Derecho Constitucional.* Guayaquil: Imprenta de la Universidad de Guayaquil, 1947.

ZUÑIGA, NEPTALÍ. *Fenómenos de la Realidad Ecuatoriana.* Quito: Talleres Gráficos de Educación, 1940.

UNPUBLISHED MANUSCRIPTS

BUITRÓN, ANÍBAL, and COLLIER, JOHN. "Taita Imbabura." Quito, 1948; published as *The Awakening Valley.* Chicago: University of Chicago Press, 1950.

PÁEZ, FEDERICO. "Sud América." Chicago, 1947.

ARTICLES IN ENGLISH

BECKER, CARL. "Progress." *Encyclopaedia of the Social Sciences* (New York: The Macmillan Company, 1937), Vol. XII, pp. 495–499.

BOAS, FRANZ. "Race." *Encyclopaedia of the Social Sciences* (New York: The Macmillan Company, 1937), Vol. VII, pp. 25–36.

COOPER, JOHN M. "Areal and Temporal Aspects of Aboriginal South American Culture." *Primitive Man,* Vol. XV (January and April, 1942), pp. 1–38.

FITZGIBBON, RUSSELL H. "Glossary of Latin-American Constitutional Terms." *The Hispanic American Historical Review,* Vol. XXVII, No. 3 (August, 1947), pp. 574–590.

HINTZE, HEDWIG. "Regionalism." *Encyclopaedia of the Social Sciences* (New York: The Macmillan Company, 1937), Vol. VII, pp. 208–218.

KROEBER, A. L. "Caste." *Encyclopaedia of the Social Sciences* (New York: The Macmillan Company, 1937), Vol. III, pp. 254–257.

MCBAIN, HOWARD LEE. "Constitutions." *Encyclopaedia of the Social Sciences* (New York: The Macmillan Company, 1937), Vol. IV, pp. 259–262.

MEUSEL, ALFRED. "Revolution and Counter-Revolution." *Encyclopaedia of the Social Sciences* (New York: The Macmillan Company, 1937), Vol. VII, pp. 367–376.

MUMBERT, PAUL. "Class." *Encyclopaedia of the Social Sciences* (New York: The Macmillan Company, 1937), Vol. III, pp. 531–536.

MURRA, JOHN. "Historic Tribes of Ecuador." Bureau of American Ethnology, *The Andean Civilizations* (Washington: Government Printing Office, 1946), pp. 785–789.

RADIN, MAX. "Status." *Encyclopaedia of the Social Sciences* (New York: The Macmillan Company, 1937), Vol. VII, pp. 373–378.

REDFIELD, ROBERT. "What We Do Know About Race." *Scientific Monthly,* Vol. LVII (1943), pp. 193–201.

SPENCER, HENRY R. "Coup d'Etat." *Encyclopaedia of the Social Sciences* (New York: The Macmillan Company, 1937), Vol. IV, pp. 508–510.

Articles in Spanish

Anon. "Documentos para la Historia de las Islas Galápagos." *Boletín del Centro de Investigaciones Históricas*, Vol. VI, Nos. 8–11 (Guayaquil, 1941), pp. 175–181.

Bermeo, Antonio. "Relaciones de la Iglesia y el Estado Ecuatoriano." *Boletín del Centro de Investigaciones Históricas*, Vol. VII, Nos. 12–17 (Guayaquil, 1947), pp. 298–322.

Buitrón, Aníbal. "Vida y Pasión del Campesino Ecuatoriano." *América Indígena*, Vol. VIII, No. 2 (April, 1948), pp. 113–130.

———, and Buitrón, Barbara. "Indios, Blancos, y Mestizos en Otavalo, Ecuador." *Acta Americana*, Vol. III, No. 3 (July–September, 1945), pp. 187–193.

Camacho, Efraín. "Don Vicente Rocafuerte." *Boletín del Centro de Investigaciones Históricas*, Vol. IV, Nos. 4–6 (Guayaquil, 1936), pp. 10–63.

Huerta, Pedro José. "Relatos Sobre Historia Guayaquileña." *Boletín del Centro de Investigaciones Históricas*, Vol. VII, Nos. 12–17 (Guayaquil, 1947), pp. 193–260.

León Barandiarán, Augusto D. "¿Cual Fué el Nombre Católico de Atahualpa?" *Boletín del Centro de Investigaciones Históricas*, Vol. V, No. 7 (Guayaquil, 1937), pp. 84–86.

Parks, Lois F., and Nuermberger, Gustave A. "El Saneamiento de Guayaquil." *Boletín del Centro de Investigaciones Históricas*, Vol. VII, Nos. 12–17 (Guayaquil, 1947), pp. 159–177.

Rolando, Carlos A. "Anuario Administrativo de la República del Ecuador." *Boletín del Centro de Investigaciones Históricas*, Vol. VII, Nos. 12–17 (Guayaquil, 1947), pp. 260–297.

———. "Los Presidentes del Ecuador." *Boletín del Centro de Investigaciones Históricas*, Vol. IV, Nos. 4–6 (Guayaquil, 1946), pp. 234–246.

Silva, Rafael Euclides. "El Dorado Amazónico." *Boletín del Centro de Investigaciones Históricas*, Vol. VI, Nos. 8–11 (Guayaquil, 1941), pp. 30–80.

Villagómez, Elegrio. "Algunos Datos Sobre la Evolución Financiera y Económica en el Ecuador." *Boletín Mensual del Banco Central del Ecuador*, Vol. XVI, Nos. 189–190 (April and May, 1943), pp. 21–41.

Newspapers

El Comercio, Quito. May 30, 1944, to September 1, 1948.
El Debate, Quito. April 1, 1948, to September 1, 1948.
El Día, Quito. April 1, 1948, to September 1, 1948.
El Telégrafo, Guayaquil. May 29, 1944, to September 1, 1948.
El Universo, Guayaquil. April 1, 1948, to September 1, 1948.
La Patria, Quito. April 1, 1948, to September 1, 1948.
La Prensa, Guayaquil. April 1, 1948, to September 1, 1948.
La Tierra, Quito. April 1, 1948, to September 1, 1948.
Ultimas Noticias, Quito. April 1, 1948, to September 1, 1948.

Press Services

Associated Press Dispatches, June 1, 1944, to February 15, 1946.
United Press Dispatches, June 1, 1944, to February 15, 1946.

INDEX

Administrative Organization of the Republic of Ecuador, Law of, 148, 150
Agriculture: in the Sierra region, 17, 20; sentimental agrarianism of Indian, 17, 42, 176; electoral college for, 106
Albornoz, Miguel Angel, 44–45
Andes Mountains, 1, 14, 21
Antonio Páez, José, 8
Antonio Saad, Pedro, 108
Archivo y Biblioteca del Poder Legislativo, 39
Argüella, Jorge, 132
Army: budget, 36; instrument of power to caudillo, 36, 39, 101; emphasis on militarism, 36; privileges under Constitution of 1945, 37; not loyal to Velasco Ibarra, 51; under ministry of national defense, 95
Arosema, Carlos Julio: reduces army budget, 36; "constitutional president," 36, 38, 54, 57, 87; uncoöperative, 57; inaugural address, 57; and June, 1948, election, 76, 80, 82; cabinet meetings, 97
Arroyo del Río, Carlos Alberto: overthrow of, 13, 42, 43–44, 46; last Radical Liberal president, 13, 67; in campaign for 1944 election, 44–45 *passim*, and comment on, 64
Atahualpa, "father of Ecuadoran nationality," 5, 6, 11

Barredo Hidalgo, Fernando, 85
Benalcázar, Sebastián de, 6, 41, 161
Berlanga, Fray Tomás de, 27
Bolívar, Simón, 7, 33–34
Boloña Rodríguez, Enrique, 167
Bonifaz, Neptalí, 29–30, 173
Brujo, 40
Budget: national, 2, 102; army, 36; congress enacts, 102, 113; president may divert funds, 102; provincial, 149; municipal, 158
Buitrón and Collier, quoted on Indians, 155

Cabildo, Spanish, 159, 160
Cabinet: fluidity, 32, 99; responsibility to congress under Constitution of 1945, 51; administers duties of executive function, 94; appointed by president and partly responsible to him, 94, 97; number of ministries, 94; development, 96, 99; meetings, 96–97; political significance, 99. *See also* Ministers
Cantonal courts, 126–127; civil and commercial suits, 126
Cantons: Conservative party directorates in, 62–63; Radical Liberal juntas, 66; political chief, 126, 153; as government unit, 142, 143; rural, 152–153; and Indians, 152–153; urban, 153, and municipalities, 156–157
Cara or Shyri Indians, 4, 17, 161
Cárdenas de Bustamante, Hipatia, 173
Cardoza-Suárez case, 131 ff.
Carrera Calvo, Aurelio, 166
Caudillismo: principle of succession, 34, 39, 101, 172; intra-class struggle, 35, 172; relationship with militarism, 36; uncertainty of, 36–37; and written constitution, 37–38, 72, 170
Caudillo, 34 ff.; from "white" group, 35, 42; characteristics, 35–36; and divine right, 35; must control army, 36, 101
Censure, power of: legislative power, 102, 103; more effective than impeachment, 103; by congress in joint session, 113
Chamber of deputies: membership, 109–110, 111; proportional representation, 110; officers, 111; powers, 111; political composition, 112. *See also* Deputies
Cholos (mestizos), 14, 172, 173; cultural type, 16, 177; role of, in Sierra region, 16; future of, 16, 177; liquidated Indians, 156, 177; share in "national life," 177
Church, Roman Catholic: period of dominance, 8; privileged position in Constitution of 1830, 9; appointment of high officials, 9 n. 6; union of Church and State under García Moreno, 12; power reduced in Radical Liberal period, 13, 23, 24; freedom of worship under 1939 charter, 13; regains influence since 1944, 13; influence on Sierra Indians, 17, 18, 20; in Sierra region, 18, 28–29; in Coast region, 23; instrument of power, 37, 39, 170; constitu-

[189]

Church, Roman Catholic (cont.)
tional protection, 37; Conservative party political spokesman for, 63; García Moreno greatest hero of, 63; no participation by officials in government under 1937 agreement, 100 n. 1

Citizenship: only for practicing Catholics in García Moreno era, 12, 37; for montuvios, 22–23; nationals, 73; exercise of political rights, 73; senate may restore, 109

Class structure: in Sierra region, 16 ff.; position of Indians, 19; in Coast region, 22–23; basis in division of labor, 20, 32; a basis of legislative infirmity, 100. *See also* Cholos; Indians; "Whites"

Clerk, Jacob Heremite, 164

Coast region: boundaries, 1; struggle for power between Sierra region and, 14, 28, 29; geography, 21; climate, 21; population, 21; senators, 21, 24, 108; deputies, 21, 24, 110; class system, 22; landownership, 22, 23; elections, 23, 24; liberalism, 23; revolutions originate in, 23, 24, 30–31; Radical Liberal party of, 24, 59, 65; commercial economy, 28. *See also* Guayaquil

Communist party: of Coast region, 24; in March 1944 coalition, 43, 48, 68; refrains from participating in Velasco Ibarra administration, 52; 1946 manifesto against Ibarra, 53; refrains from 1946 elections, 53; a "third" party, 60–61, 68; three members of 1948 congress, 69; coöperate with Socialists, 69; foreign policy, 69; insist U. S. relinquish Galápagos Islands bases, 69; oppose "Yankee imperialism," 69; opposition party, 70; in 1947 Guayaquil election, 167

Concentration of Rightists, 163

Congress: bicameral, meets every four years under Charter of Slavery, 9; weak, under García Moreno, 12; Coast and Sierra regions control, 29; political parties in, 61, 65; president convokes sessions, 89; president's power of veto, 89; has vote of censure, 97; members, 100; personalismo and, 101; constitution prohibits dissolution, 101; sessions, 104–105; powers in joint session, 112–113, 116, 117; powers in separate sessions, 114–115, 116–117; measures introduced, 116–118; standing committees, 117; questions of constitutionality, 137. *See also* Chamber of deputies; Senate

Conservative party: party of Sierra region, 21, 59, 63, 171; 1948 election in Coast region, 24; proposes 1946 constituent assembly, 53; in 1946 election, 53–54; "Constitutionalists" support Suárez Veintimilla for presidency, 55; before 1895, 60, 61, 63; strength since 1944, 61, 64; in 1948 congress, 61; structural organization, 61–63; political spokesman for Church, 63; strength since 1949, 64; leadership, 64; joins Ecuadoran Democratic Alliance, 64; 1945 municipal victories, 64, at Quito, 64, 162–163; 1948 candidates, 78; Concentration of Rightists, 163

Constituent assembly of 1944–1945: Communists and Socialists dominate, 51, 69; confirms Velasco Ibarra as president, 51; Constitution of 1945, 51; marks break between Velasco Ibarra and leftist groups, 52; greetings to Soviet Union, 52; "adhesion to socialism," 52; adjourns, 52–53 of 1946: Conservatives propose, 53; Velasco Ibarra calls, 53; Radical Liberals and leftists abstain from, 53–54; confirms Velasco Ibarra in presidency, 54; Constitution of 1946 promulgated, 54

Constitution of 1945: departure from separation of powers, 8; checks on executive, 51–52; suspended, 53; 1906 charter substituted for, 53; unicameral legislature, 106; heavy representation to labor, 107

Constitution of 1946: equality of all Ecuadorans including Indians before the law, 18; literacy qualification for voting, 19; nationalism proviso, 28; on landownership, 37; Church under, 37; vice-presidency restored, 54, 92; provision for elections, 72; presidential system, 83; with Constitution of 1945 in coördination of functions, 85, 172; executive and judicial subordinate to legislative function, 85–86,

100, 172; council of state, 86; functional representation, 106
"Constitutional presidents," 38, 57, 52, 101
"Constitutionalists," 55, 56
Constitutions: fifteen written, 8 ff. and n. 5, 32, 39–40, 170; of 1830, 8–9; "Charter of Slavery," 9; 1906, democratic, 13; and political process, 37; Church and, 37; "real" and "written," 38–39, 171; seven basic elements in real, 39, 56; characteristics of written, 39; title, 39; authority to amend, 103, 112; practice to replace, 103; classes of, 170–171; and caudillismo, 170; separation of powers, 172
Council of state: purpose, 86, 87; membership, 86–87, 109; powers, 87; record, 87; shares interpretation of law, 136, 138; opinions must be ratified, 138
Cuenca: department of Ecuador under 1830 constitution, 8; council of, 157; political autonomy, 160
Cueva Tamariz, Carlos, 79–82 *passim*
Culture, speech determines, 15. *See also* Education

Dampier, William, quoted on Galápagos Islands, 27–28, 164
David, Edward, 164
Defense powers, 113; emergency power of president, 114
Deputies: from Sierra region, 14, 110; from Coast region, 21, 24, 110; from Oriente region, 26, 110, 111; from Galápagos Islands, 110, 111. *See also* Chamber of deputies
Divorce, a political issue, 135. *See also* Cardoza-Suárez case

Echeverría, J. A., 174
Ecuador, name, 8
Ecuadoran Democratic Alliance: leftist coalition, 43, 45, 51, 68; responsible for 1944 revolution, 45, 51, 68; power of government delivered to, 46; six-point program, 46; 1944 election victory, 51; majority in 1944–1945 constituent assembly, 51; dissolution, 52; Conservatives in, briefly, 64
Ecuadoran Nationalist Revolutionary Association (A.R.N.E.), 61, 70, 163

Ecuadoran Nationalist Revolutionary Union (U.N.R.E.), 61, 70, 163
Education ("culture"): white monopoly, 20, 23, 175; universities, 95; ministry of, 95
Electoral colleges, 106
Elections: lack of integrity, 71–72, 75; provided for in "written" constitutions, 72; under Constitution of 1946, 72; supreme electoral tribunal, 72, 112; provincial electoral tribunal, 72–73, 74–75; parish registration board, 73; local boards, 73; citizens vote, 73–74; list of candidates, 74; ballots, 75; mesas, 75; proportional representation, 75; election of 1948, 76 ff. *See also* Suffrage
Elicio Flor, Manuel, 78–82 *passim*, 135, 136
Eloy Alfaro, Colón: Franklin quoted on, 12; leads revolution of 1895, 13; a military caudillo, 35; ambassador to United States, 44; hero of Radical Liberals, 67
Enriquez Gallo, Alberto, 79–82 *passim*
Executive function in government: strong under García Moreno's first constitution, 12; subordinate to legislative, 85; budget, 86. *See also* Presidency
Export trade, 2

Ferrero, Guglielmo, quoted on monarchy and democracy, 174
Flores, Juan José: Bolívar's military representative, 8; heads secessionist movement from Gran Colombia, 8; 1830–1845 era of, 8; first president, 8; police concept of government, 8; privileged position of Church in first constitution, 9, and in "Charter of Slavery," 9; bicameral congress, 9; financial chaos, 9; opposition to, 9; revolution of March 6, 1845, 9; exile, 9; a military caudillo, 35
Foreign policy: within province of president, 89; conducted through ministry of foreign relations, 95; economic collaboration with South American countries, 95
"Four Days' War," 30
"Four Presidents, Month of," 54, 64

Franklin, Albert B.: quoted on García Moreno, 12; on political lieutenants, 154
Frontier disputes, 7
Functional senators: national, 106; regional, 106

Gaceta Judicial, 95, 130–131
Galápagos Islands, 2, 14, 26–28; visitors, 27, 28; Melville's description, 27; animal life, 27; elections, 28; government and administration, 28, 95; U. S. naval and air bases, 28; no provincial status, 107; deputies, 110; senators, 108; no courts, 121; legal cases, 126
García, Aurelio, quoted on 1945 and 1946 constitutions, 85
García Moreno, Gabriel, 9; era of, 12–13; two constitutions, 12, 37; reformation of Church, 12, 37; only Catholics citizens, 12, 37; nonmilitary caudillo with Church as instrument of power, 13, 35, 36; assassinated, 13; greatest hero of Conservatives, 63
Geography, 1 ff.; division into three regions, 1, 14; seventeen continental provinces, 142
Gil Gilbert, Enrique, 111
Gilbert, Abel A., 77–78, 167
Girón, Sergio Enrique, quoted on 1944 revolution, 46
González Suárez, Federico, quoted on Quito, 6
Government, national: authoritarianism, 39; "democracy in Greek sense," 39, 48–49, 169, 173; power over provinces and subdivisions, 143, 144; unitary system, 144–146, 160–161
Governor, provincial: qualifications, 146; factors in appointment, 146–147; agent of national government, 147, 149; duties, 147–150; powers, 150–151
Gran Colombia, 7–8, 95
Guayaquil: a department under Constitution of 1830, 8; major port and commercial center, 21, 30, 115, 164, 166; municipal council, 31, 157–158; 1944 revolution, 42–43, 45; proclamation, 45; mayoralty, 151; urban canton, 158, 160; "capital" of Coast region, 161; headquarters of Radical Liberals, 161; population estimate, 164; history, 164; appearance, 164; newspapers, 164; health, 164–165; 1947 election, 166–168
Guayas, 80, 110–111, 151
Guerrero Martinez, Alberto, 168
Guerrero Valenzuela, Rafael, 167, 168
Guevara Moreno, Carlos, 53
Guzman, L. A., 173

Hall, Francisco, 9
Huayna Capac, and family, 4–5
Hurtado Flor, Carlos Enrique, 166

Impeachment, 108–109, 111–112
Inca Empire: conquest of Quito, 4, 5, 7; Emperor Huayna Capac, 4–5; divine-right monarchy, 32
Independence days, 159
Independent Popular Movement (M.P. I.), 163
Indians: criterion of race, 15; in Sierra region, 16–18, 19, 40; complete separation from "whites," 16–17; cut off from "national life," 16, 40, 42, 56, 68, 154, 173, 177; sentimental agrarianism, 17, 42, 152–153, 176; submissiveness, 17–18, 32, 34, 38, 176; Church influence, 17, 18, 20; culture pattern, 17, 25–26, 38, 40, 41; Constitution of 1946 recognizes equality before the law, 18; under Spain's Laws of the Indies, 19; relationship to state, 19; illiteracy, 19; none in Coast region, 22; in Oriente region, 25; Socialists only party to recognize, 28; brujo, 40; two functional representatives in Socialist congress, 68; government of, 141–142, 153, 172–173; political lieutenant as governor for, 154–156; parish council and, 154–155; future of, 177
Indigenistas, 19, 68
Indo-American society: divine-right monarchy, 32; tradition of submissiveness, 32
Interregnum: constitutions provide for, 37–38; under "constitutional president," 38, 170
Investments, U. S., 2

Jácome Moscoso, Rodrigo, Derecho Constitucional Ecuatoriano, 130

Jaramillo Alvarado, Pío: quoted on Sierra Indians, 19; mayor of Quito, 64; quoted on separation of powers, 84; on weak congressional supremacy, 102

Jijón y Caamaño, Jacinto, 64, 162

Jivaros, 25–26

Judiciary: subordinate to legislative function, 85, 172; elected, 112; judicial powers of congress, 115; budget, 120; four levels of tribunals, 121–127; cases heard in three instances, 122, 127–128; judicial practices, 127, 134–140; codes, 127; classes of litigation, 128; appeals, 128, 129; written opinions, 129; literature on constitutional law, 130; naming cases, 131; interpretation of laws, 136 ff.; theoretical distinction between Roman and common law, 172; similarities to U. S. judiciary, 172

Kingman, Nicolás, 111

Labor: electoral college for coastal, 106; functional senators for, 107; Constitution of 1945 favors, 107; relatively unorganized, 107

Landownership: in Sierra region, 17; in Coast region, 23; in Constitution of 1946; instrument of power, 39; reform and, 174–175

Laws of the Indies, Spain's Indians under, 19

Legislative commission: prepares bills, 115, 116; joint session ratifies, 115; membership, 115–116

Legislative function: 1945 and 1946 constitutions place above executive and judicial functions, 85–86; 100, 102; president convokes, 89; cabinet sometimes responsible to, 97; "whites" control, 100–101; rubber stamp for executive, 100; caudillismo and, 101; loose party organization in, 101; budget, 102; power of censure, 102, 103; amends constitution, 102, 103; rules on unconstitutionality, 102, 103

Lemos Rayo, Faustino, 13

Luis Tamayo, José, 32

Maldonado Tamayo, Luis, 56

Mancheno, Carlos: leads "one-shot revolution," 55; president, 55; revolt against, 56; resigns, 56; quoted on sessions of congress, 105

May 13, 1830 ("last day of despotism and first day of same thing"), 8, 34, 169

May 28–29, 1944, 13, 42–43

Mendoza, Ildefonso, 30

Mendoza Avilés, Rafael, 166

Mestizos. See *Cholos*

Militarism: opposition to, 11; relationship with caudillismo, 36; emphasis on, 36. See also Army

Ministers, cabinet: appointed, 94; responsible to president, 94, 97; duties, 94; ministries, 94–96; qualifications, 97–98; regionalism and, 98. See also Cabinet

Monarchy: tradition of, in Spanish culture, 32–34, 38, 39; basis in two systems, 32, 34, 38, 39, 56; hereditary principle lost, 56, 169; called a republic, 56, 169 ff. See also Government

Monetary system, 114–115

Monopolies, government, 96

Montuvios: in Coast region, 22–23; and rural parishes, 154

Municipalities: revenue, 144; qualifications for cantons, 156–157; created, 157; council, 157–158; economic conditions, 158; plaza, 158; mayor, 158; Spanish cabildos, 159, 160; autonomy, 159–160; political position, 160–161, 173

Music, five-tone minor scale, 36

Narváez, Aurelio Mosquera, 69, 77

Nast, Thomas, 164–165

National, a, 73

National Civic Democratic Movement (M.C.D.N.): in Coast region, 24; "ad hoc" party, 61, 70; purpose, 70, 162–163; candidates for 1947, 71; for 1948, 71, 77, 78; future significance, 71; strength, 80; 1947 Quito election, 162–163; Guayaquil election, 166, 167, 168

"National life," 16, 42, 56, 68, 154, 169, 170, 173, 177

Nationalism: rejects government by foreigners, 9; antimilitarism, 11; period of, 1845–1859, 8

Negroes, in Coast region, 22, 23
New Castille, Viceroyalty of, 7
New Granada, Viceroyalty of, 7
Newspapers: *El Comercio* (Quito), 42–43, 54, 80, 107, 145; *El Quiteño Libro* (Quito), 9; *El Telégrafo* (Guayaquil), 107, 167; *El Universo* (Guayaquil), 80; of Quito, 162; of Guayaquil, 164
Ninth Infantry Battalion, in anti-Mancheno revolt, 56
1944, period since, 13 ff.

Ochoa Ortiz, Francisco, *Ley Orgánica del Poder Judicial*, 130
"One-shot revolution" of August 23, 1947: led by Mancheno, 55; removes Velasco Ibarra, 55
Orellana, Francisco de, 164
Oriente region, 1, 25 ff.; description, 25, 26; population, 25; senators, 108, deputies, 110, 111; no courts, 121, 125, 126; unitary organization and, 145; governors, 150; provincial council, 151; rural cantons, 152; rural parish, 154; future of, 176
Ormaza E., G., 174

Paredes, Angel M., 84
Parishes: Conservative organization in, 63; local units of government, 142; political lieutenants, 143, 154; urban, 153; functions, 153; rural, 154; parish councils, 154
Parró, Alberto Arco, quoted on Sierra social classes, 15
Pérez Guerrero, Alfredo, quoted on Sierra region, 21
Pérez Pallares, Alfonso, 163
Periods, six, in Ecuador's history, 8 ff.
Personalismo, 35, 59; relationship between president and congress, 101
Peru, Viceroyalty of, 7; boundary difficulty, 7
Pizarro, Francisco, 6, 156
Pizarro, Pedro, quoted on Atahualpa, 6
Plaza Lasso, Galo: quoted on Indians, 19; on cabinet, 31; ambassador to U. S., 76, 77; M.C.D.N. urges candidacy, 76–77; youth in U. S., 77; senator from Pichincha, 77; political philosophy, 77; election, 79–81; president, 82; cabinet meetings, 97; formula for appointing ministers, 99
Police force: rivalry with army, 36; under Constitution of 1945, 37
Political instability: period of 1875–1895, 13; regionalism and, 24, 29, 31, 32 ff.; on presidential level, 32; on cabinet level, 32; and caudillos, 36
Political lieutenant, in each parish, 126, 141, 143, 154
Political parties: influence declines after 1944, 13; basic function of, 59–60; three-fold background, 60; intra-class struggle, 60, 171; major parties, 60, 68; third parties, 60–61, 68–70; ad hoc parties, 61, 70–71; loose organization, 101
Ponce, Belisario, 135
Popular Alliance (Guayaquil), 167, 168
Popular Union, 70
Population estimates, 2–4; of Sierra region, 14, 15, 29; cholos, 16; of Coast region, 21, 29; Negroes, 23; of Oriente region, 25; "whites," 58; no census, 143 n. 2, 157; Pichincha and Guayas, 151
Presidency: Constitution of 1830 patterns, after U. S. system, 9; term, 9, 12, 32, 88; presidents, 10–12, 32; basis is separation of powers until 1945 and 1946 constitutions, 13, 85–86; election, 88; salary, 88; constitutional powers, 88–89; commercial and fiscal powers, 89; administrative matters, 89; power of veto, 89, 118–119; relation to legislative function, 89; judicial and emergency powers, 90; prohibitions on, 91, 113; no constitutional succession, 94
Prieto, Jorge A., estimate of percentage of "whites" in government, 58
Principle of chance, 121–122, 135, 136
Printing office, government, 95
Protocol of 1942, establishes basis for new frontier, 2
Provinces: senators, 107; number of, 142, 146; power of national government over, 142–143; relative autonomy, 143–144; governor, 146–151; provincial councils, 151
Provincial courts: judges, 125; criminal cases, 126; original jurisdiction, 126

Quechua, 15 and n. 1
Quito, city of: national capital, 14, 162; municipal council, 64, 157, 160; population, 161; dominates Sierra region, 161; Conservative stronghold, 161, 162; Census Day, 161–162; newspapers, 162; center of agricultural economy, 165
Quito, Kingdom of (Presidencia, Royal Audiencia), 1, 30; under Cara Indians, 4; Inca conquest, 4, 7; name changes, 6; southward orientation, 7; Royal Audiencia created, 7, 30; Department of the South within Gran Colombia, 7; secessionist movement, 7, 8, 161; divine-right monarchy, 18, 32, 158
Quitu Indians, 4, 32, 161

Radical Liberal party: 1895–1944 era of, 13, 60, 65; revolution of 1895, 13, 23, 24, 67; power of Church reduced by, 13, 23, 24; Constitution of 1929, 13; Arroyo del Río and, 13, 44, 67; party of Coast region, 24, 59, 65, 67, 171; 1946 joint manifesto against Velasco Ibarra, 53; refrains from 1946 elections, 53, 162; 1944 revolution removes from power, 64, 65, 67; weakness since 1944, 65, 67–68; structural organization, 65–66; juntas, 65–66; principles, 67; history of, 67; for separation of Church and State, 67; interest in development and trade, 67; landownership, 67; drift toward coalition with Socialists, 78; four factions, 78; refuses coalition, 78–79; nominates Trujillo, 79
Railways and highways, 2
Regionalism, 28–31, 39; part in politics, 28, 29, 59; in intra-class struggle for power, 35; function of vice-presidents to straddle, 92, 175; cabinets and, 98; functional representation and, 107; develops around cabildos, 159–160; attempts to meet, 175–176
Registro Oficial, 95, 118, 138
Religion. *See* Church
Republic of Ecuador: established, 8; three departments, 8; little difference from monarchy, 18, 34, 56; unitary state, 142 ff. *See also* Government

Revolution(s): of 1845, 9, 11; intra-class struggle, 41, 171; meaning of term in Ecuador, 41; affects only "white" group, 41–42; of 1944, 42–43, 51
Riobamba, 6, 56, 160
Robles, Francisco, 12
Rocafuerte, Vicente, 9
Ruminahui, "scorched earth" tactics, 6

Sáenz, Moisés, quoted on Indians, 17, 18, 155, 156, 176
Senate: upper chamber, 104; apportionment, 105, 108; functional representation, 107, 108; membership, 108, 109; officers, 108; standing committees, 108; powers, 108–109; political make-up, 109
Senators: from Sierra region, 14; from Coast region, 21, 24; from the Oriente, 26; functional, 105–106; qualifications, 105; term, 105; national, 106; regional, 106; provincial, 107–109; power relationship, 108
Separation of powers: presidential system rests on doctrine of, 13, 83; Constitutions of 1945 and 1946 alter, 13, 85
Sierra region: geography, 14; population, 14; class system, 14 ff.; "whites," 15–16, 20; cholo or mestizo group, 16, 20; Indians, 16–19; feudal economy, 17; Conservative party stronghold, 21, 59; Church in, 28–29; agricultural economy, 29; senators from, 108; deputies, 110
Social welfare: ministry of, 96; minister usually a Socialist, 98
Socialist party: stronghold in Coast region, 24; March 1944 coalition, 43, 48, 68; refrains from participating in Velasco Ibarra administration, 52; resignations, 52; 1946 joint manifesto against Velasco Ibarra, 53; refrains from 1946 election, 54; a "third party," 60–61; opposition party, 68; only party to recognize Indians, 68; bid for coalition, 79, and terms, 79; Popular Alliance, 167; 1947 election in Guayaquil, 167–168
Socialist Revolutionary Vanguard, 43, 61, 70

Sotomayor y Luna, Manuel: vice-president, 61, 64, 82, 93; 1948 Conservative candidate, 78, 93; 1948 election, 80, 81

Suárez Veintimilla, Mariano: Conservative leader, 53; petitions Velasco Ibarra for constituent assembly, 53; vice-president, 54, 64, 93; "Constitutionalists" support for president, 55; president for 15 days, 56, 87; in Velasco Ibarra cabinet, 64; quoted, 78, 104–105, 173–174

Succession, "caudillist process," 39

Suffrage: literacy qualification, 19, 29, 37; in Sierra region, 20, 29; for montuvios, 23; in Coast region, 23, 29; in the Oriente, 26; in Galápagos Islands, 28; for "citizens," 73; optional for women, 73–74; nuns, 74; compulsory for men citizens, 74; Church bloc, 74

Superior courts: judicial districts, 124; judges, 124; original or appellate jurisdiction, 124; constitutional duties, 125; appointive and administrative duties, 125, 128–129; share interpretation of laws, 136

Supreme court: regional distribution, 31; qualifications, 121; three chambers, 121; principle of chance, 121–122; types of cases, 122; jurisdiction, 122–123; liaison duty, 123; administrative duties, 123–124, 128–129; interpretation of laws, 123, 136; *Gaceta Judicial*, 130–131; Cardoza-Suárez case, 131 ff.

Terán Coronel, Rafael, 174

Trujillo, José Vicente: a Radical Liberal leader, 44, 79; foreign minister, 79, 98; Radical Liberal candidate, 79; withdraws, 79

Tsantsas (shrunken heads), 26

Unconstitutionality, concept of: power to rule on, 103, 114; concept of double, 137; procedural, 137–138; substantive, 138; statutes, 138–139

Utilities, public, 95

Veintimilla, Ignacio de, 67

Velasco Ibarra, José María: doctorate, 35; May 29, 1944, 42–43; "Great Absentee," 43, 45, 46–47; "National Personification," 47, 50, 52; president 1934–1935, 44, 46; accepts program of Ecuadoran Democratic Alliance, 46, 48; president 1944–1947, 46, 48; academic career, 47; political ideas, 47–49; public works program, 49; orator, 50; as a caudillo, 50–51; Constitution of 1945, 51–52; breaks with leftist elements, 52; suspends constitution, 53; joint manifesto against, 53; orders new election, 53; tied to Conservatives, 53–54; 1946 constituent assembly confirms as president, 54; removed from office, 55; destroyed politically, 87; few cabinet meetings, 97; quoted on laws, 139–140

Vera, Alfredo, 167

Vice-presidency: restored by Constitution of 1946, 54, 92; term, 92; qualifications, 92; functions, 92; political significance, 92–93

Weber, Max: quoted on caudillo, 35; on law, 140

"Whites": in Sierra region, 14–15, 20; social differentiation, 15; population, 15; descent, 15–16; education monopoly, 20; in Coast region, 22, 23, 35; caudillos from, 35, 42; "democracy in Greek sense," 35, 39, 49, 169, 173; intra-class struggle for power, 35, 39, 169–170, 174; suffrage limited to, 37; control government, 39, 58; are the "national life," 40; revolutions made by, 41; percentage of population, 58, 100, 142, 169; forced to vote, 74; all officials, 100; senators, 108; deputies, 111; instruments of power, 170, 174

Yumbos, 25

Zaldumbide, Gonzalo, 44

Zaparos, 25

Zevallos Reyre, Francisco, *Lecciones de Derecho Constitucional* cited, 84, 130; quoted on legislative function, 102

www.ingramcontent.com/pod-product-compliance
Lightning Source LLC
Chambersburg PA
CBHW021707230426
43668CB00008B/755